Spotify Teardown

Inside the Black Box of Streaming Music

Maria Eriksson, Rasmus Fleischer,
Anna Johansson, Pelle Snickars,
and Patrick Vonderau

The MIT Press
Cambridge, Massachusetts
London, England

This book was set in Stone Serif by Westchester Publishing Services. Printed and bound in the United States of America.

Library of Congress Cataloging-in-Publication Data
Names: Eriksson, Maria. | Fleischer, Rasmus | Johansson, Anna. |
    Snickars, Pelle, author. | Vonderau, Patrick, author.
Title: Spotify teardown : inside the black box of streaming music / Maria Eriksson,
    Rasmus Fleischer, Anna Johansson, Pelle Snickars, and Patrick Vonderau.
Description: Cambridge, MA : MIT Press, 2019. | Includes bibliographical
    references and index.
Identifiers: LCCN 2018011908 | ISBN 9780262038904 (pbk. : alk. paper)
Subjects: LCSH: Spotify. | Music and the Internet. | Sound recording industry.
Classification: LCC ML74.4.S64 S64 2018 | DDC 780.285/4678--dc23 LC record
    available at https://lccn.loc.gov/2018011908

10 9 8 7 6 5 4 3 2

Spotify Teardown

Contents

Acknowledgments

This book and the research on which it is based have benefited from much collaboration. Christopher Kullenberg joined us during the early stages of the project and contributed vitally to one of the chapters in this book. We are deeply indebted to system developer Roger Mähler and the resourceful staff at Humlab, Umeå University, especially Johan von Boer, Andreas Marklund, and Fredrik Palm. Their enthusiasm and inventiveness inspired the trajectory of our research and analysis from start to finish and helped to guide the course of our inquiry.

This book also has benefitted from the insights of an extraordinary community of interlocutors. Our thanks to all the professionals in the advertising, digital media, and IT industries who took the time to explain and reflect upon their work and practices and to Mollie Panzner (Ghostery/Evidon) for expert advice on mapping ad tech networks. We would like to thank Jennifer Holt and Lisa Parks for hosting us at the University of California, Santa Barbara, in November 2015, as well as Kristoffer Gansing for inviting us to present Songblocker to an unsuspecting crowd at Transmediale—Festival for Art and Digital Culture 2017 in Berlin. David Hesmondhalgh, Geert Lovink, Bernhard Rieder, Richard Rogers, Christian Sandvig and Mirko Tobias Schaefer provided invaluable advice on legal and ethical matters.

An extensive constellation of colleagues, peers, and friends sustained and enriched this project through its different iterations. In addition to the valuable feedback we gleaned from audiences at the diverse conferences, workshops, and lectures where we presented pieces of the work, we had the good fortune to receive input from Jean-Samuel Beuscart, Joshua Braun, John Thornton Caldwell, Abigail and Benjamin De Kosnik, Andrew Leyshon, Ramon Lobato, Denise Mann, Paul McDonald, Jeremy Wade Morris, Alisa Perren, and

Cornelius Puschmann. Somewhat closer to home, we also would like to thank C. F. Helgesson, Sofia Johansson, Hans Kjellberg, Ivy Kunze, Susanna af Leijonhufvud, Johan Lindquist, Anette Nykvist, Christian Rossipal, and Jonas Andersson Schwarz, as well as Francis Lee, Steve Woolgar, and the Algorithm Study Network for their curiosity, inspiration, and suggestions. We are especially grateful to Holger Schulze and Pit Schultz for discussing ideas in the earliest phase of the project and to Dan McHale for his generous hospitality during our stay in San Francisco.

We have been fortunate to have editorial assistance during the production of this book. In this respect, we owe much gratitude to Heather Macdougall and especially Joshua Boydstun. Gita Devi Manaktala, Doug Sery, and Noah J. Springer provided determined support from beginning to end. We are grateful to our anonymous readers, who offered helpful feedback. Our greatest thanks go to the Swedish Research Council/Vetenskapsrådet (Framework Grant scheme, D0113901) for generous funding of our project over the past four years and to the colleagues and administrators at Umeå University and Stockholm University for their enduring support.

Other versions of some of the materials and ideas presented in this book appeared in the following books and articles:

Eriksson, Maria. "Close Reading Big Data: The Echo Nest and the Production of (Rotten) Music Metadata." *First Monday* 21, no. 7 (2016), doi:10.5210/fm.v21i7.6303.

Eriksson, Maria. "Unpacking Online Streams." *APRJA* special issue on Research Values (forthcoming, 2018).

Eriksson, Maria, and Anna Johansson. "'Keep Smiling!': Time, Functionality and Intimacy in Spotify's Featured Playlists." *Cultural Analysis* 16, no. 1 (2018): 68–84.

Eriksson, Maria, and Anna Johansson. "Tracking Gendered Streams." *Culture Unbound* 9, no. 2 (2017): 163–183. doi:10.3384/cu.2000.1525.1792163.

Fleischer, Rasmus. "If the Song Has No Price, Is It Still a Commodity? Rethinking the Commodification of Digital Music." *Culture Unbound* 9, no. 2 (2017): 146–162. doi:10.3384/cu.2000.1525.1792146.

Fleischer, Rasmus. "Nätutopier och nätdystopier: Om 2000-talets sökande efter internets väsen" [Network utopias and dystopias: The search for the essence of the internet in the 2000s]. In *Samtider: Perspektiv på 2000-talets idéhistoria* [Contemporary times: Perspective on the history of ideas in the 2000s], edited by Anders Burman and Lena Lennerhed, 261–303. Gothenburg, Sweden: Bokförlaget Daidalos, 2017.

Fleischer, Rasmus. "Swedish Music Export: The Making of a Miracle." In *Made in Sweden: Studies in Popular Music*, edited by Alf Björnberg and Thomas Bossius, 153–162. New York: Routledge, 2017.

Fleischer, Rasmus. "Towards a Postdigital Sensibility: How to Get Moved by Too Much Music." *Culture Unbound* 7, no. 2 (2015): 255–269. doi:10.3384/cu.2000.1525.1572255.

Fleischer, Rasmus, and Pelle Snickars. "Discovering Spotify—A Thematic Introduction." *Culture Unbound* 9, no. 2 (2017): 130–145. doi:10.3384/cu.2000.1525.1792130.

Fleischer, Rasmus, and Pelle Snickars. *Den svenska enhörningen: Storyn om Spotify*. Stockholm: Mondial, 2018.

Mähler, Roger, and Patrick Vonderau. "Studying Ad Targeting with Digital Methods: The Case of Spotify." *Culture Unbound* 9, no. 2 (2017): 212–221. doi:10.3384/cu.2000.1525.1792212.

Snickars, Pelle. "More Music is Better Music." In *Business Innovation and Disruption in the Music Industry*, edited by Patrik Wikström and Robert DeFillippi, 191–210. Cheltenham, UK: Edgar Elgar, 2016.

Snickars, Pelle. "More of the Same—On Spotify Radio." *Culture Unbound* 9, no. 2 (2017): 184–211. doi:10.3384/cu.2000.1525.1792184.

Snickars, Pelle, and Roger Mähler. "SpotiBot—Turing Testing Spotify." *Digital Humanities Quarterly* 12, no. 2 (2018).

Vonderau, Patrick. "'Where Ideas Are Free': Scientific Knowledge in the Algorithm Economy." *Media Fields Journal*, no. 10 (2015). http://mediafieldsjournal.squarespace.com/where-ideas-are-free/.

Vonderau, Patrick. "The Politics of Content Aggregation." *Television & New Media* 16, no. 8 (2015): 717–733. doi:10.1177/1527476414554402.

Vonderau, Patrick. "The Video Bubble: Multichannel Networks and the Transformation of YouTube." *Convergence* 22, no. 4 (2016): 361–375. doi:10.1177/1354856516641882.

Vonderau, Patrick. "The Politics of Content Aggregation." *Television & New Media* 16, no. 8 (2015): 717–733. doi:10.1177/1527476414554402.

Vonderau, Patrick. "The Spotify Effect: Digital Distribution and Financial Growth." *Television & New Media*, November 21, 2017. doi:10.1177/1527476417741200.

Vonderau, Patrick. "Technology and Language, or, How to Apply Media Industries Research?" In *Applied Media Studies*, edited by Kirsten Ostherr, 127–140. New York: Routledge, 2018.

Vonderau, Patrick. "Access and Mistrust in Media Industries Research." In *Making Media: Production, Practices and Professions*, edited by Mark Deuze and Mirjam Prenger. Amsterdam: Amsterdam University Press, 2018 (in press).

Introduction

Spotify welcomes the growing interest in streaming media but is concerned about information it received regarding methods used by the group of researchers responsible for this project. This information suggests that the research group systematically violated Spotify's Terms of Use by attempting to artificially increase plays, among other actions, and to manipulate Spotify's services with the help of scripts or other automated processes. Spotify determines that the group of researchers was aware that such actions explicitly violate its Terms of Use and aimed to mask this violation by technical means. In light of the above you are hereby asked to confirm by 26th of May 2017, in written form, that you have received this note and that the group of researchers has ended such actions that are in violation of Spotify's Terms of Use, and that it does not intend to take up such actions again in the future. Note that in this context, violation against the Terms of Use may imply responsibility for possible damages resulting from this violation.

On May 19, 2017, legal counsel of the Swedish music streaming service Spotify contacted the authors of this book via email to inquire about the methods used in a then-ongoing research project, titled "Streaming Heritage: Following Files in Digital Music Distribution." During the autumn of 2013, this project had received over $1 million[1] in grant funding from the Swedish Research Council for investigating the challenges and consequences of streaming services, such as Spotify, for the heritage sector.[2] A guiding question for the project was how people's practices and approaches toward cultural forms such as songs, books, or films—practices including the production, expression, and exchange of those cultural forms—are transformed under the shift from commodity ownership to commodified experience.[3]

While research within this project soon went beyond the initial focus on cultural heritage, the project itself had been explicit and open about its critical approach from the very start. In fact, various forms of public activism were part of the project's interventionist research design, for which it had

received—in a fierce national competition—the second highest of the council's assessment grades. Blog posts, newspaper articles, and interviews on
both television and radio, not to mention the 2013 project application, had
outlined the project's strategy as one based on digital methods, including the
use of bots and the dissemination of self-produced sounds via Spotify.[4] The
project opted to study Spotify using the same tools that organize online information.[5] More importantly, Spotify's apparent lack of interest in data sharing
necessitated an approach that would go beyond interviews, direct observation, and other standard methods of media industries research.[6] While
the project team members met and engaged with several Spotify employees
over the years, listening to company spin and "industrial self-theorizing"
felt inadequate.[7] To follow a formal procedure of gatekeeper introduction or
even to seek official endorsement by Spotify would have limited and biased
this research.

Complementing front-end inquiries (such as interviewing) with experimental back-end studies of digital media infrastructure, metadata generation, and aggregation practices, the project instead aimed to initiate public
debate about the often subtly changing standards, values, and politics of
cultural dissemination online. Given this aim, the question is not why Spotify responded to this research in May 2017, but why had this not happened
earlier and why only by mailing a formal complaint. We will return to these
questions at the end of this book, which is based on the very research that
Spotify aimed to stop.

Back in 2013, Spotify was still widely seen as pioneering solutions to
issues of concern to the music industry. Its à la carte, on-demand music
streaming had arguably created a sustainable revenue model for artists. Spotify seemed to have stopped the downward spiral in earnings and income
that had plagued physically distributed music recordings since 2002, and it
had delimited informal practices of media circulation, effectively advancing
the fight against unauthorized (or pirate) forms of file sharing.[8] Despite the
Spotify hype of those years, however, critical questions also kept coming up.
What was the substance of the service that the company claimed to offer,
given that its founders themselves had little of value to offer? Spotify was
neither providing a cultural good nor offering valuable contacts in the field of
cultural production. Initially, the company could not afford licensing for the
music or the bandwidth to distribute it. With the launch of its first beta version in 2007, Spotify largely built both on the peer-to-peer (P2P) technology

already in wide use within Sweden's file-sharing community and on a vast, unauthorized music catalog that had been shared by members of this community.[9] How were artists to be remunerated? Spotify's business model never benefited all musicians in the same manner but rather appeared—and still appears—highly skewed toward major stars and record labels, establishing a winner-takes-all market familiar from the traditional media industries.[10] How then is this streaming market different from traditional media markets? And what distinguishes Spotify from a regular media company?

The history of our encounters with Spotify has developed along these questions. It began with a brief conversation with Spotify's then head of marketing, Sophia Bendz, in Stockholm in the fall of 2012. Asked if Spotify would not qualify as a regular media company—given its declared business interest of providing content to audiences while selling those audiences to advertisers—Bendz rushed to praise Spotify's achievements as a tech company. A follow-up meeting with a company executive in Spotify's headquarters (before we received the grant funding) led to mutual expressions of respect but little more. At this point, Spotify had already been made aware of our research interest in working with the company's data. Over the following years, we met individually with engineers, marketers, data professionals, and academics related to the company. But conversations often fell apart as soon as Spotify's tech identity was questioned. At the same time, the company's attempts to add television content made it obvious that Spotify increasingly operated like a traditional American media enterprise. Between 2013 and 2017, the company's equity rounds, market and debt capitalization, and changing board of directors tied its corporate strategies more and more to US-based financial interests. At the end of a decade-long process of financialization, Spotify is neither particularly Swedish nor solely about music.

In this respect, Spotify's transformation resembles Facebook's. "Digital content curators fit quite well within the established parameters of media organizations," Philip Napoli and Robyn Caplan observe in their aptly entitled article "Why Media Companies Insist They're Not Media Companies, Why They're Wrong, and Why It Matters."[11] Although Spotify, of course, *also* offers a technical solution for music distribution, the aggressive discursive framing of Spotify's operation as being primarily technological has tended to obscure its long-term entrepreneurial, financial, and culture-changing strategies. Such "politics of standards" often have regulatory consequences.[12] Since 2015, for instance, Spotify has implemented a

Figure 0.1
Spotify London subway advertisement in November 2016.
Photograph by the authors.

plan—and the technology—to generate data based on its music streaming that allow for the study of human behavior at scale. The company acts, in other words, not only as a music provider but also as a private data broker. It has openly promoted its massive collection of contextual data as a service to marketers and, in November 2016, even launched a global outdoor ad campaign in fourteen different countries, with ads jokingly showcasing aggregate data sets: "Dear 3,749 people who streamed 'It's the End of the World as We Know It' the day of the Brexit vote, hang in there."[13]

The ad implied that Spotify knows you at scale—it knows what you listened to and what it meant to you. But what is the commodity being sold here? And how does this service relate to the European Union's new General Data Protection Regulation and its provisions on profiling?[14]

At the time of writing (early 2018), Spotify's desktop interaction design looks very different from how it did in 2008 or 2012. Once, user interaction was organized around tracks, search options, and community-activating features, such as self-made playlists. Today, Spotify's interaction design reorganizes music consumption around behaviors, feelings, and moods, which are channeled through curated playlists and motivational messages that change several times a day. A large number of these playlists are created by third-party playlist services such as Filtr, Topsify, or Digster, owned by Sony, Warner, and Universal, respectively—the three major record labels that, in turn, own stakes in Spotify. In 2016, evidence emerged that Spotify had begun filling some of their mood-oriented playlists with fake artists, illustrating the company's interest to use playlists as a device for framing and measuring user behavior.[15]

The present situation—where music has become data, and data has become contextual material for user profiling at scale—invites us to pause and reflect about the way that songs, books, or films are now typically made accessible. Internet critics and journalists have documented that social media companies such as Facebook use tools to microtarget their users based on emotional states.[16] Similar claims have been made about Spotify by Stanford psychologist Michal Kosinski, who developed a model for behavioral prediction now used by Cambridge Analytica, a firm notorious for "psyops" electoral manipulation in support of Brexit and the Trump campaign.[17] As Kosinski and others argue in a paper entitled "The Song Is You: Preferences for Musical Attribute Dimensions Reflect Personality," industries should abandon the traditional order of knowledge that organizes music according to genre and style and, instead, strategically exploit the link between music choices and personality traits.[18]

Access and Interventionism

This book and the project on which it is based developed out of a concern with the tendencies of mainstream work either to overlook and suppress such difficult ethical, political, and ideological issues of digital media, or to prejudge and scandalize these issues. We observed an increasing divide between political and public debates about the social responsibilities of digital media companies, such as Facebook and Google, and the social research that aspired to cover the digital. Fields such as digital sociology foreground the computational dimension of social inquiry as well as social life, locating research largely in a "field of devices."[19] Yet political events and debates involve more heterogeneous constellations of actors and also underline a widely recognized "need to inform public debate about online business practice," as researchers and "journalists have long done in the offline world."[20] In responding to this need for greater transparency, we felt that the adoption of existing tool kits from media industries research or the digital humanities to be similarly insufficient. The obvious power of digital media companies to establish their own order of knowledge through sponsored and applied research or, as seen in our own case, through coercive legal practices suggested that using qualitative social science methods to "study up"—to research the powerful—would not yield satisfactory results in this case.[21] While media companies have always aimed to control research access and output, sociologist Noortje Marres rightly points to the "highly troubling relations of dependency" between today's platforms and researchers, especially where the latter simply "sign up to the terms of use stipulated by digital industries," which Marres identifies as a major ethical "problem of complicity with the organizations that serve as our sources of information."[22] Why make Spotify the object of studying up in the first place, given the company's soft brand image and origins in Sweden's illicit file-sharing community, a company that allegedly still remains so close to its users?

An established but still useful idea we adopted is to focus on the process that allowed Spotify to grow from micro- to macrosize, rather than on the powerful global organization itself. As Michel Callon and Bruno Latour have suggested, size alone is insufficient for substantially distinguishing between institutions or organizations on the one hand and individuals or groups on the other. "There are of course macro-actors and micro-actors," Callon and Latour explain, "but the difference between them is brought about by power relations and the constructions of networks that will elude analysis if we presume a priori that macro-actors are bigger than or superior to micro-actors."[23] Accordingly, the task is not for the researcher (microactor) to study the corporation (macroactor) but to trace the manifold transactions that allowed an initially opportunistic and semilegal project to turn into the allegedly ultimate solution for music listening. Again, at the beginning, Spotify founders Daniel Ek and Martin Lorentzon themselves had little of value to offer, apart from the advertising tech firms they had worked with. It was through a long chain of associations and by enlisting bodies, materials, discourses, techniques, feelings, and laws that this faceless Swedish group of engineers and digital advertising technologists became the voice of digital culture.

Following the process by which Spotify created lasting asymmetries between itself and us, in terms of capital as much as cultural power, throughout this book, we will come to open not only one but many of the *black boxes* of music streaming. In the terminology of science and technology studies (STS) from which this metaphor is imported, actors grow with the number of relations that can be put into black boxes, that is, be made invisible by their own success. A black box contains that which no longer needs to be reconsidered, those things whose contents have become a matter of indifference.[24] Think of streaming, for instance, as *the* solution to illicit downloading. Or consider the way that Spotify's infrastructure, including its reliance on P2P networks (until 2014) and user devices, has been black-boxed. Gideon Kunda, in his seminal study of a computer company, wondered about the way in which this company understood *culture* as "something to be engineered," in the sense of a "mechanism" of normative control extending well beyond the corporation itself.[25] Macroactors' power largely relies on their ability to keep such boxes firmly closed and to make us believe that it could not be otherwise.

This book traces, on various levels, the process of Spotify's becoming. It partly enters its black boxes technically, by employing digital methods such as bots, or small software scripts. Over the last decade, such digital methods have been developed and widely deployed to perform social science and humanist inquiries on big or midsize datasets.[26] Part of the research also relies on interviews, document analysis, archival work, and nonparticipant forms of observation. Overall, the research design has been strongly influenced by autoethnographic and self-reflexive forms of fieldwork, as they are common in social anthropology and ethnology.

A reason for this is the difficulty usually encountered when industries are subjected to studying up. Over the years, much discussion has surrounded the problem of access that besets social and cultural studies of media companies and the way they organize processes of content production and distribution. Informed consent, taken as an iron rule in clinical research, seldom applies fully in critical studies of digital industries, for which experts advise that researchers "move beyond overly simplistic ideas about informed consent."[27] In research on media organizations, researchers often embrace perceptions of difference rather than ideals of objectivity through immersion.[28] As organization scholar Barbara Czarniawska notes, "an observer can never know better than an actor; a stranger cannot say more about any culture than a native, but observers and strangers can see different things than actors and natives can." An idea of "symmetric field-work" that does not strive to be "nice to the natives" is both fairer and more adequate in an industry context, because it "allows one-self to be problema-tized in turn—at a certain cost to the researcher, of course."[29]

In drawing from these methodological insights and experiences, this book subscribes to an idea of interventionism that aims to change, or at least shed light on, an emerging order of knowledge. Such an intervention is not an activist call to arms but rather an effort to generate questions, by means of our own probing and partly performative research practice, about the conditions of transparency in digital culture. A famous model for this kind of approach is Harold Garfinkel's "breaching experiments," which aimed to break the mundane, routine, implicit, tacit, and taken-for-granted social rules in a given setting. Being interventions into the normal stream of daily life as participants experienced it, these experiments consisted of low-level disruptions of ordinary scenes (such as taking items from a stranger's basket in a grocery store) that aimed to make the familiar appear strange. Although they were a series of (public) demonstrations rather than formal experiments, these tests were productive in showing how the social order is maintained and how the trust arrangements that stabilize it can be ana-lyzed.[30] More specifically, we understand Garfinkel's demonstrations as a model for how the social order governing our access to the field could be turned against itself. What if instead of adopting the conventional interview routine, with its clearly demarcated roles of insider and outsider, we were to have an ethnographer observe each conversation in order to understand how corporate spin and the power relationships of studying up play out in our own research practice? What if we were to complement interviews, document analysis, and overt observation of the front end of Spotify with experimental, covert access to its back end in order to compare and verify the information given and to confront interlocutors with the results? How about making *following files* a research-guiding metaphor, in accordance with economic and social anthropology's interest in the social life and cultural biography of things, as if it were possible to follow the transformation of audio files into streamed experiences in the simple way a postman would follow the route of a parcel?[31] How about distributing sounds and music via Spotify in order to gain firsthand experience of its aggregators while also programming bots, or software scripts, that would listen to this music, thus short-circuiting the system? And how to design this project in such a way that it could unveil and challenge ethical standards of social research that take *overt* and *covert* as simple binaries, instead of acknowledging the "continuum of deception" that digital industries are themselves actively part of?[32]

The title of this book, *Spotify Teardown*, signals our intent to break from corporate protocols by taking up these questions. Borrowing the notion of teardown from reverse engineering processes, we aim to disassemble the way Spotify's product is commonly conceptualized. Our teardown, however, is meant in an imaginative rather than purely technical sense. We primarily mean to perform teardowns—publicly, through the interventions that this book documents and itself forms part of—as a form of creative engagement with our research object. In this sense, "interventionist methods" are also "inventive methods," that is, methods or means by which "the social world is not only investigated but may also be engaged." As Celia Lury and Nina Wakeford have pointed out, inventiveness is not intrinsic to methods but rather emerges in relation to the purposes to which they are put.[33] An actor is strong insofar as he or she is able to intervene. Thus, by examining the associations used by actors such as Spotify to grow to macrosize with "the same daring as the actors who make them," internet research may, we hope, recapture part of the strength it seems to have lost.[34]

Platforms and Companies

One reason why some research currently seems to lack determination in confronting the critical ethical, political, and ideological issues of digital media is that research is also regularly enlisted by macroactors. It is not accidental that Facebook, Google, Microsoft, Intel, and Spotify all invest in social research. Technology drives both the news and the academic agenda. Organizational environments, with their built-in instrumentality, also might predispose us to think about methods in empiricist terms, as an essentially technical affair to be taken up like a hammer from a toolbox. This book does not offer models, nor does it present findings that are easily operationalized. It follows

Eszter Hargittai and Christian Sandvig's call for a more "positive conceptualization of method as a creative act," revealing the "messy details" of what
we were doing, including failures and open questions.[35] The turn to method
also had the pragmatic function of opening an interdisciplinary space for
collaboration between social anthropology, media studies, economic history,
musicology, and ethnology—the disciplines that form our various organizational and intellectual homes.

This is not to say that the digital methods presented in this book could
not be reused or repurposed. Some of them were inspired by those developed by Richard Rogers and the Digital Methods Initiative in Amsterdam
and thus have already been "repurposed or built on top of the dominant
devices of the medium."[36] Here, Spotify's "system is the method," as Klaus
Bruhn Jensen puts it, insofar as usage of the service produces data that are
already "documented in and of the system" and, "with a little help from
network administrators and service providers," can be used as an empirical
base for research.[37] This is largely how we collaborated with a team of programmers at Humlab, Umeå University's digital humanities lab, while also
consistently building on more than one empirical base.

In highlighting the performative, playful, ad hoc character that governs
parts of this research, we do not mean to avoid laying bare the project's
conceptual premises. While this book, throughout its four main research
chapters and the interventions that punctuate its main narrative, visits different sites to answer different questions, its conceptualization started from an
engagement with a basic concern of what we were actually studying. Given
our critical take on Spotify and our call for more public debate around issues
of transparency, how were we to ascribe agency and to whom? As a research
group conducting experiments on Google's advertising privacy settings once
noted, "We like to assign blame where it is due. However, doing so is often
difficult."[38] In the case of our project, the difficulty largely related to the way
that Google, Facebook, and Spotify had previously been conceptualized: as
platforms. In what ways does the notion of a platform relate to that of a
corporate actor or firm, and is it productive for analyzing the relationship
between the two?

In December 2017, the European Court of Justice decided that Uber,
widely understood to be a platform that merely connected unlicensed private car drivers to passengers, was in fact operating like a conventional
taxi firm. Uber claimed that it had only acted as an intermediary offering

Figure 0.2
Spotify once described itself as a platform to manage one's music—but should
it still be seen as one? Advertisement for the "Discover Weekly" playlist in the
New York City subway in 2016. Photograph by the authors.

information rather than transportation services. The court found sufficient
evidence to the contrary and rejected this claim, with no possibility of appeal,
creating a regulatory precedent for "looking at what tech companies actually do, not how they do it," as one journalist put it. "For legal purposes, if
it quacks like a duck and waddles like a duck, it's a duck, not an alien robot
from outer space."[39] As we will elaborate in later chapters, Spotify, Facebook,
Twitter, and YouTube can indeed be regarded as media companies that sell
audiences to advertisers, implying legal responsibility for the content dissemi-
nated through their interfaces. At the same time, one also has to acknowledge
the differences between ducks. In the digital sphere, some of them come in
flocks, or systems, and develop a competitive dynamic rather different from
conventional ducks. Some live and die alone.[40]

The notion of *platform* has been declared a paradigm of internet research
by some,[41] but it has done very little to shed light on the differences between

digital companies and other varieties; to distinguish the manifold relations between services and providers, supply chain and partner networks, and algorithmically personalized catalogs and global strategies; and to develop a means to measure the relevance or irrelevance of all these actors. Organizationally, the center of any platform is hard to pin down. This, perhaps, is not surprising given that this concept was first launched by the digital industries themselves.

In the computer industry, the term *platform* has been used since the mid-1990s, when Microsoft began describing Windows as a platform. After circulating first within management and organization studies, the term entered media scholarship simultaneously with the rise of the notion of Web 2.0.[42] Partly in response to Netscape founder Marc Andreessen's description of Facebook and Amazon as platforms, Ian Bogost and Nick Montfort launched the notion of platform studies in 2007 at the Digital Arts and Cultures Conference. They further elaborated on the concept in their book *Racing the Beam: The Atari Video Computer System* (2009) and on their joint blog, http://platformstudies.org. A key impulse for Bogost and Montfort's work at the time was the existing gap in media studies regarding knowledge about computing systems. As they correctly observed, "new media scholars" needed "to learn more about the ways computer hardware and software are designed and programmed," in order to be able to "connect them to culture."[43] At present, there is no universal definition of *platform*,[44] nor is such a substantial definition necessary for analyzing the layers or phenomena that matter within a given context. There is, however, a tendency to understand the term as Andreessen did in 2007; that is, as the missing link between computing and business, an online marketplace that bridges the interests of industries and users.

In this current use, *platform* most often implies a techno-economic view of services such as Facebook or Spotify. In a computational sense, Spotify is a platform to build applications on. At the same time, a platform using the social web is also a business and therefore should be described in terms of business models and pricing structures, according to this view. Abstracting a conceptual model from Facebook, Apple, Amazon, and Google, for instance, Benjamin H. Bratton defines *platform* as a "standards-based technical-economic system," while José van Dijck sees it as a "techno-cultural construct" within some "socioeconomic structure."[45] Similarly, Anne Helmond adopts a "techno-economic outlook" on Facebook in order to examine how its "technical architecture" links to an "economic model."[46] Whatever the wording, an interplay between computation and economics is seen as foundational for platforms, usually mediated through the figure of the user, whose apparent unpredictability introduces ideas of generativity into platform theory. Put simply, in order to investigate platforms, platform scholars need to triangulate by relating user participation, computing technology, and economics in one way or another.

Information technology companies and some internet scholars keep the platform terminology because it comes with two major promises. The first is the promise of social web platforms as representing some sort of "ontological distinctiveness,"[47] as being new and technologically unprecedented. There was never anything like Spotify before the advent of the social web. The second promise is that platforms epitomize a new form of market, or what the economics literature has dubbed a multisided market. *Multisidedness* means that a market is not ordered hierarchically—as in a shop where a salesperson may coerce you into buying an unwanted pair of shoes—but rather contains strong network elements, or "positive indirect network externalities."[48] In this view, a platform is less like a market and more like a network that brings two or more different sides together, like a shopping mall that links shops to customers. There is, in any case, some kind of positive interdependence or externality between groups of actors that are served by an intermediary, the platform. Think of Spotify Free, for example, where the platform is said to positively affect supply and demand by providing more listeners with more music while decreasing fixed and marginal costs. Advertisers are meant to benefit from the presence of many consumers, while consumers benefit from the information provided by many advertisers.[49]

When it comes to the task of identifying Spotify's corporate responsibilities, strategies, organizing principles, and the markets it creates or folds into, this techno-economic notion of the platform has limited value. Strategically launched by the digital industries, it connotes egalitarian ideas of participation and sociality. It also implies that some businesses are intrinsically multisided: after all, in plain language, a platform is a "raised level surface," with several sides.[50] Corporate stakeholders appear as just another type of user in this setting, as if Facebook, Google, and Spotify were indeed community services that only "helped change," as noted in the case of Apple, the "economic and legal conditions for music production and distribution."[51] Furthermore, centering accounts of Spotify or Facebook on platforms downplays historical trajectories of market behavior that had multisidedness as a dominant feature long before the advent of digital infrastructures—think of television or newspapers.[52] The widespread idea of the social web as being an emergent phenomenon, rather than a strategically or centrally planned one, is contingent on the notion of the generative internet, that is, subscribing to some version of the theory that a network of adaptable machines without centralized control would result in open and socially beneficial innovation processes.[53] Yet, there is also evidence that suggests interaction over the internet to be both strategic and centralized, such as political economic analyses of Apple, Microsoft, Google, Amazon, and Facebook as global media corporations.[54]

Most importantly, however, the platform in its current use is a concept that offers a flat rendering of *digital* markets. Not all digital markets take on the character of a platform, and not all behavior on platforms is transactional. Explaining the web as organized around platforms often focuses attention on monopoly actors, such as Google or Facebook, and their competitors, rather than acknowledging how platforms relate to other actors. There is certainly value in studying even unsuccessful tech companies.[55] Markets also never appear in isolation but are always codependent on other markets. As Karine Nahon has argued, being inside the box of platforms means focusing too much on one kind of power and one perspective of the problem, instead of looking at the more complex ecosystems with different forms of power working at different levels.[56] Organizations need both an inside and an outside (and the inside/outside binary) to stabilize, and their study needs to cut across these different domains. Finally, the platform view tends to ignore so-called negative network externalities or side effects, like an enthusiastic freeway user attempting to ignore the risk of crowding.[57] It is precisely those negative externalities or unexpected consequences of the social web that today are most widely discussed: surveillance and private data brokerage, precarious creativity, platform capitalism, and the unregulated global proliferation of intermediaries.[58]

For these and many other reasons,[59] using the term *platform* comes with a great many caveats. Since it has been widely adopted, it will also be used in this book. Using the term, however, does not mean to stick to an essentialist idea of what platforms are as companies. To the contrary, we use the term here merely as a shorthand to evoke the "action nets" involved in making Spotify grow and prosper, that is, in accordance with the processual orientation of this research overall, the emphasis is on organizing rather than organizations. To think of Spotify and other digital macroactors as action nets means to grasp this quality of companies as temporary entanglements of unlike yet related actors.[60]

About This Book

While it is not the task of this book to review or remedy existing gaps in platform theorizing, we have to qualify and provide nuance to our use of the term—and our understanding of our research field—against this background of critique. In order to not render overdetermined the partly experimental or ethnographical work that follows, a few guiding signposts here may suffice. First, as already stated, an overall aim is to de-essentialize both the idea of the platform and that of the corporate organization, emphasizing instead the changing, interspersed, multidirectional character of Spotify. We strive to avoid an "ontologization of an epistemology," that is, the notion that in order to understand digital culture, there is no alternative to the platform view (and the digital methods devised for studying platforms).[61] Consequently, the book begins with the question "Where Is Spotify?," opting to approach a taken-for-granted object through the history of its venture capital funding rounds.

Second, despite a surge of research interest in digital intermediaries, as well as Spotify's self-definition as intermediary, we prefer to treat Spotify as a "mediator" in Latour's sense, that is, as an actor that transforms, translates, and modifies the meaning of the elements it is supposed to carry.[62] Chapter 2, "When Do Files Become Music?," paints a vivid picture of the many mediating actors and infrastructures involved in music streaming today. In a less technical wording, which resonates with the traditions of qualitative social and humanist inquiry to which our idea of access is indebted, one may call Spotify a producer. In chapter 3, "How Does Spotify Package Music?," the productive forms of refashioning files for various constituencies is laid out in detail. Chapter 4, "What Is the Value of Free?," sets out to explore the market dynamics of Spotify. In doing so, it also sheds light on the relation between markets, variously theorized in previous literature as intertype competition, platformization, or platform systems.[63]

Instead of presenting knowledge as a set of prepackaged findings reducible to any one single concept, this book deliberately delves into the extensive, irreducible fabric of contingencies that marks the lived realities of our own knowledge production. Borrowing from Allaine Cerwonka and Liisa H. Malkki, we are ready to "improvise theory"—to recreate the centrality of surprise encounters with the often-undisciplined realities of our various research fields.[64] While most of the mutual mentoring and productive misunderstandings among ourselves or between us and our informants— human and digital—have been edited out for reasons of readability, our book is still coauthored, interspersing research chapters with experimental interventions. The interventions are shorter texts that, in one way or another, interfere with Spotify and/or established research methods. They can be read independently, but they are also thematically linked to discussions in previous chapters.

Different approaches have informed and inspired the interventions in this book. Consequently, the interventions can be presented in two different ways. First, according to the methodological approaches they test and introduce: 1) following the controversies of a social media campaign; 2) establishing a record label for research purposes; 3) intercepting network traffic by way of packet sniffers; 4) conducting a reflexive analysis of methodological decision making; 5) building a digital application as part of an arts performance; and 6) engaging in web scraping of job listings. Second, the interventions could be presented according to the topics they concern: 1) the local political significance of tech corporations; 2) the power dynamics and financial logics of music distribution; 3) the infrastructural entanglements of streaming services; 4) the perils of collecting data; 5) online advertisement logics and the phenomenon of ad blockers; 6) and Spotify's recruitment history. Our section on methodological decision making (Intervention: Too Much Data) critically reflects on the process of working with experimental digital methods and discusses data-driven knowledge production in relation to qualitative research. In general, however, the interventionist chapters are meant to serve as experimental suggestions—and practical "how-tos"— for future research. They frequently ask more questions than they provide answers. At the same time, they also offer concrete examples of how alternative and inventive research can be done. Therefore, one way to think about our interventions is to read them as provocation pieces meant to inspire research, without taking on a prescriptive character.

Importantly, this book itself has turned into an intervention, due to Spotify's legal response quoted in the opening of this introduction. In the conclusion, we will follow up on how the narrative of this unplanned rapport between us and our object of study unfolded while we were in the very process of writing up the research. Back in May 2017, upon receiving Spotify's request for information, we immediately assured Spotify, in written form, about the motivation of our research and the fact that all activities that potentially could be understood as a violation of Spotify's terms of service had stopped. We never collected any private user data, nor did we reveal company secrets or damage the behavior or interests of subjects. Yet, bypassing our suggestion of a joint conversation about findings and methods, Spotify then moved on to contact the Swedish Research Council directly to suggest cutting the funding for the project. Given that such a move by a major platform appears to be unprecedented, we will dedicate some final reflections to the relationship between ethical and legal frameworks for research and to the ethics and legal frameworks that govern corporate behavior. While Spotify did not follow through with legal action, the questions raised in the process, and the public debate that accompanied it, are of interest for future research in this field.

Intervention: The Swedish Unicorn

In the spring of 2016, a campaign to support Spotify spread across social media in Sweden. On Twitter—and within Stockholm's hipster business circles—the campaign rapidly became known as #backaspotify, which roughly translates to "encourage Spotify" or "support Spotify." Curiously, the #backaspotify campaign was a local business action in support of a technology company known as a "unicorn" in the business press because of a market valuation exceeding $1 billion. Prior to the company IPO in April 2018, Spotify was the Swedish unicorn *par excellence*, and the #backaspotify campaign was a vivid example thereof. The campaign reached a climax when the Stockholm Chamber of Commerce, which had already supported the #backaspotify campaign in different ways, hosted a support rally for Spotify with a number of prominent speakers. A dedicated Facebook group promoted the event, and some three hundred people turned up. Maria Rankka, the CEO of the chamber—and, according to rumor, a personal friend of one of Spotify's cofounders—declared in an interview that "Spotify seemed ready to go from words to action."[1]

In hindsight, it is difficult to pinpoint in detail what the #backaspotify campaign was about. It all started with an open letter to the Swedish government from the cofounders of Spotify. A common thread in the discussions that followed was the promotion of a better national business climate, which is why the Chamber of Commerce took an active stance in the debate. Given that Sweden has a long social democratic tradition, it is highly unusual for political demonstrations to be mobilized in support of globally operating media corporations. Nevertheless, the #backaspotify campaign clearly had an ideological slant. The launch of the event at the Stockholm Chamber of Commerce demonstrated that #backaspotify was a

Figure 0.3
Former Swedish prime minister and foreign minister Carl Bildt speaks at the
#backaspotify event at the Stockholm Chamber of Commerce on April 22, 2016.
Image courtesy of the Stockholm Chamber of Commerce.

coordinated operation with the aim of improving the business climate for
Spotify and similar corporations.

In our project, we began to trace various lobbying activities related to
the #backaspotify campaign by closely following its traces in social media,
as well as in the trade and daily press. By virtue of the proliferation of digital data and metadata, new ways of studying the interactions of corporate
actors have been made available to researchers. Here, we were interested in
exploring Spotify's entanglement in political discourse on Twitter, a social
media service that occupies a particular spot in public debates. As Marcel
Broersma and Todd Graham have argued, Twitter functions as a "beat" in
the everyday work of journalists, as it is both the source of information and
a channel for distributing and re-mediating content.[2] This beat makes Twitter attractive for the dissemination of political messages. It also makes Twitter
suitable for the study of political mobilization. We propose approaching
Twitter through a quali-quantitative analytical framework that is sensitive
to the context of tweets and the medium specificity of Twitter itself.[3] This

implies using recorded digital fragments of political speech to map Spotify's location in a broader sphere of public debate.

At the end of April 2016, we retrieved all tweets related to #backaspotify via the Twitter application programming interface (API) and turned the campaign into a case study. Collaborating with a former project member—the programmer, hacker, and theorist of science Christopher Kullenberg (University of Gothenburg)—we used the Python module Tweepy and downloaded 1,791 tweets by requesting all Twitter messages containing the word *backaspotify* (which included the hashtag #backaspotify). While the campaign was short-lived and faded out within a few weeks during the late spring of 2016, a broader network analysis of the collected tweets reveals that the #backaspotify campaign is illustrative of Spotify's political significance in Sweden. The campaign also accentuates the soft power that lies dormant within streaming media corporations.[4]

For anyone living in Sweden today, Spotify cannot be ignored. According to the annual report *Swedes and the Internet*, almost 90 percent of the population under thirty-six now uses the service on a weekly basis.[5] Almost every day, Spotify-related news items are published in tabloids and trade magazines. During Spotify's IPO on the New York Stock Exchange in April 2018, a veritable Spotify craze was rampant in Swedish media, with live coverage on both radio and television. A major part of the tech scene revolves around the company and has done so for almost a decade. Thousands of Spotify playlists are featured on national public radio, and the Swedish government regularly boasts about the service. The former prime minister and foreign minister of Sweden, Carl Bildt, even introduced a new practice at state visits, offering visiting dignitaries a virtual gift: a Spotify Premium account preloaded with playlists of Swedish music. The Royal Court of Sweden, in turn, maintains a Spotify account for sharing playlists, and Prince Daniel has enlisted Spotify's cofounder Martin Lorentzon in a program for supporting young entrepreneurs.

It is sometimes argued that Stockholm has produced one of the highest numbers of unicorns per capita in the world—a claim that Swedish politicians are generally keen to pick up on. While Spotify was initially mentioned cautiously during Swedish Parliament debates on digital piracy, parliamentary minutes from the 2010s and onward strikingly reveal how the company gradually came to be seen as the epitome of Swedish high-tech innovation.[6]

In January 2017, for instance, German chancellor Angela Merkel visited Sweden, and prime minister Stefan Löfven gave a speech at the Royal Swedish Academy of Engineering Sciences: "Innovation is one of the things I personally find most fascinating and inspiring," he stated. "As the proud founding country of Skype and Spotify, with Stockholm being second only to Silicon Valley in terms of the number of startups per capita in the world, we will continue to foster a development where new ways of thinking and smart solutions are encouraged, from preschools to universities."[7]

If Spotify is vividly present in Swedish politics and entrepreneurial discourse, the company is also physically manifest within Stockholm's cityscape. Spotify's headquarters is located in the city center at Birger Jarlsgatan 61. The company is spread out on several floors of the building in a characteristic startup environment, complete with open spaces, colorful furniture, and foosball tables. The Stockholm office has been described as "insanely cool" and contains meeting rooms bearing the names of rock songs, such as "Teen Spirit," "Pretty Vacant," and "Paranoid."[8] Daniel Ek is usually a low-key person, hardly a prolific agitator who would use Spotify's political popularity in order to gain advantage. One exception, however, has been the issue of housing, which was also one of the rationales behind the #backaspotify campaign. Ek has often expressed concerns about the housing crisis facing Stockholm because Spotify employees' struggle to find places to live has allegedly been a recurring human resources problem. In the spring of 2015, for example, it was reported that Spotify had even started its own waiting list since apartments were scarce in Stockholm.[9] Given that Stockholm is built on islands, available space for building new apartments is limited, and the real estate market is one of the most overpriced in Europe.

Housing problems were also the main topic of the aforementioned open letter to the Swedish government that Spotify's cofounders, Daniel Ek and Martin Lorentzon, published in early April 2016 on the blog platform Medium. The Swedish-language post was titled "We must act or be overtaken!," indicating that the cofounders meant business:

> When we founded Spotify, our dream was to build a company in Sweden that could compete on the highest global level, thereby hopefully inspire others in our country to start a company and make it grow. For us it is crazy that Europe, with a larger population than the United States, does not have a single company in parity with Facebook, Google, Apple, Microsoft, Amazon, and other major US companies. We want to show that it can be done! Having said that, we Swedes

have to decide what kind of country we actually want to be. Are we a country that believes that growth will also come from fast-growing new companies, or do we think it's the traditional industry that will support growth?[10]

By juxtaposing the interests of high-tech startups with those of "traditional industry," the open letter articulated three political demands to the Swedish government: housing, taxes, and education—with a special priority given to the first issue. In their letter, the Spotify cofounders explicitly demanded better access to rental apartments in Stockholm to facilitate the recruitment of skilled employees. Rent regulations should be abolished, they argued, allowing for higher rents—and more available apartments—in the city center, as low-income tenants would be forced to move to suburban areas. Ek and Lorentzon also called for lower taxes on employee stock options. In addition, the Spotify cofounders proposed that computer programming should be integrated in the primary school curriculum to meet future demands of the information technology sector. If the Swedish government did not act fast enough in following their advice, there was a risk that "thousands of Spotify jobs" could be relocated "to the United States instead of Sweden."[11]

The open letter rapidly received widespread public attention in Sweden and consequently formed the starting point for the #backaspotify campaign; the hashtag started to be used the very same day the letter was published. Almost immediately, a number of Twitter users began linking to Ek and Lorentzon's post on Medium, with some also tweeting in English: "Spotify founders speak out against Swedish politicians: housing in Stockholm, lack of programmers, and stock option taxation. #backaspotify."[12] The Medium post was also quickly picked up by international journals, such as *Newsweek*, which stated that startups in Sweden were planning a number of "protests after the founders of Spotify threatened to move the world's largest music streaming service away from the country unless significant reforms were made."[13] This was an apparent misinterpretation of Ek and Lorentzon's Swedish letter, which mainly addressed the *future* location of *potential* new jobs. Another exaggeration was the reference to the "thousands of jobs" at Spotify; at this time, only about four hundred people were working at the crowded Stockholm headquarters.

In the context of this evolving debate, Maria Rankka, CEO of the Chamber of Commerce, stated in an interview that a possible relocation of the Spotify headquarters would be severely "negative for the image of Sweden."[14] *Forbes*, in turn, interpreted the headquarters relocation as a real threat and stated that Ek and Lorentzon had used their "powerful voices to complain about many issues facing the business community in Stockholm, from education to taxes, and especially…housing."[15] *Relocation—flytta* in Swedish—came to be one of the most common words used in the almost 1,800 tweets we retrieved, together with words such as *business, Sweden,* and *Spotify*. Since the original Medium post extensively elaborated on the housing shortage that faced future Spotify employees, people using the #backaspotify hashtag concluded that the dearth of apartments in the city might cause Spotify to leave Stockholm. Another likely reason that the theme of a housing shortage appeared so frequently was that a number of politicians from the liberal end of Sweden's political spectrum used Ek and Lorentzon's open letter to argue for neoliberal housing reforms. "We need Spotify more than Spotify needs us," Annie Lööf, leader of the Swedish Centre Party, famously wrote in one article.[16]

Political speech, however, is always enacted by a plurality of actors, and the tweets we had collected made it possible to study interactions and interlinkages within this political discourse. We looked closer at the most frequent speakers in the discussion and their profiles in order to situate the actors in their respective networks. While the most active #backaspotify discussion on Twitter lasted little more than a week, its emergence and disappearance renders visible a list of actors—detectable as Twitter users—in a network. Even if this specific and unstable actor network has now perished, a recorded database of the interactions (such as the one we collected from Twitter) can be used to reconstruct debates and map other, more stable political networks. It can also be used as a way to understand the broader political significance of Spotify, as well as its role as a political idea and arena.

One point of departure was to interrogate the profiles of the most frequent Twitter users in the #backaspotify discussion. Among these were users Fredrik Andersson (@Feffe2010), Diana Van (@MissDianaVan), Klas Vestergren (@kvestergren), and Andre Frisk (@Andrefrisk)—who, to our surprise, all worked at Miltton Labs, a firm that promises to deliver "cutting-edge digital public affairs, and develop proprietary digital tools…inspired by how Spotify turned the music industry on its head."[17] Another notorious tweeter during the #backaspotify campaign was Gustaf Reinfeldt (@Gustaf-Reinfeldt). Not only is he the son of Fredrik Reinfeldt, former Swedish prime minister and the leader of the liberal-conservative Moderate Party, he was

Figure 0.4
An extended but graphically simplified network of some of the most frequent
tweeters during the #backaspotify campaign.

also hired by Miltton Labs just as the #backaspotify campaign was coming
to an end. As figure 0.4 demonstrates, several of the most frequent pro-
Spotify tweeters were associated with, or worked for, right-wing political
parties, in particular the youth branches of the liberal-conservative Moderate Party and the center-right liberal Centre Party.

The dynamics of online discussions, however, are more illuminating than
the participants themselves. Participation in online discussions can reveal
interesting patterns of interaction between the actors that encircle the #back-
aspotify discussion on Twitter. So-called in-degree networks, for example, measure the number of incoming links. When retweets are included as in-degree
factors, they can be used to determine popularity or influence in a similar
manner as citations are used in scientific literature or web pages are ranked
in search engines. This method helped us identify actors in the #backaspo-
tify campaign who were, whether intentionally or unintentionally, principal
interlocutors. For example, Annie Lööf's tweet (figure 0.5), which included a
picture of herself, received 137 tweets, including retweets.[18] Still, she actively
tweeted only five times during the campaign.

Figure 0.5
"Sweden needs fast-growing companies more than they need Sweden.
#backaspotify"—Tweet from Annie Lööf, leader of the Swedish Centre Party,
on April 15, 2016. Image courtesy of the Centre Party.

In a similar manner, Linda Nordlund, an editorial columnist at the daily newspaper *Svenska Dagbladet* and previously the leader of the youth branch of the Liberals, achieved a very high in-degree status when her following tweet was retweeted sixty-five times: "Wait time for rental apartment: Berlin – 0 w[eeks], NYC – 0 w[eeks], Brussels – 0 w[eeks], Stockholm (county) – 208 weeks. Guess why businesses are moving? #backaspotify."[19] However, not all in-degrees were the result of a successful interaction. The official Twitter account of the Swedish Social Democrats (@socialdemokrat) did not tweet about #backaspotify at all but received many critical tweets from the conservative party's youth section (@mufswe), which basically argued that social democratic politics were undermining business in Sweden.

Social media services such as Twitter encourage this type of tongue-in-cheek dialogue. Among other aspects of the #backaspotify campaign was a playlist that the Stockholm Chamber of Commerce circulated on Spotify, entitled "#backaspotify." It featured pop songs that in various ways alluded to the idea of Spotify abandoning Sweden: first on the list was "Should I Stay or Should I Go" by the Clash. A few #backaspotify memes also circulated. The youth wings of the three center-right parties in Sweden produced meme-style images in support of Spotify. One slogan read, "Backa bakåt or #backaspotify" (Go backward or support Spotify), with backwardness illustrated by a cassette tape. Another meme (figure 0.6) pictured the current Swedish prime minister, Stefan Löfven, holding an old-fashioned cassette tape in his hand, asking himself, "Vad är problemet?" (What's the problem?).[20]

By advocating a more liberal business climate, the #backaspotify campaign clearly had an ideological purpose. Swedish right-wing parties simply saw the opportunity to align themselves with a globally successful company,

Figure 0.6
#backaspotify and the local production of memes: "Vad är problemet?" (What's the problem?), the Swedish prime minister and Social Democrat, Stefan Löfven, asks in a twitter meme from @Rodgronrora.

using Spotify to try to gain approval for entrepreneurial political ideas. Since the Stockholm Chamber of Commerce is the leading business organization in Sweden's capital region, its active role during the campaign was not surprising. But our network analysis of retrieved tweets from #backaspotify also reveals a number of distinct links to persons and organizations on the right wing of the political spectrum.

Surprisingly, Spotify itself did not take part in the #backaspotify campaign in any visible way. After publishing their open letter, Ek and Lorentzon remained silent. One concrete blowback against Spotify nevertheless arose when it became publicly known that the company—despite its complaints about Stockholm's housing deficiencies—had turned down an offer from Järfälla municipality to rent twenty-four newly built apartments for its employees.[21] Järfälla is a well-connected suburb, and the commute to Spotify's headquarters would have been only twenty-five minutes long, which is considerably shorter than the average commute for residents in the Stockholm area. That Spotify declined to accept these apartments led to a discussion about the role of urbanity in attracting skilled employees in a global labor market. Supporters of the #backaspotify campaign defended Spotify's decision. It would be "embarrassing" for Spotify to offer employees housing in a suburb such as Järfälla, tweeted a representative of the Confederation of Swedish Enterprises.[22] And the most influential of Sweden's editorial pages, *Dagens Nyheter*, wrote, "An international company, with employees who choose between living in New York, San Francisco, and Stockholm, cannot direct people to a suburban bed. Especially for the young, the city is an attraction and an employee benefit in itself."[23]

As our intervention demonstrates, the #backaspotify campaign sheds light on the political significance of Spotify in Sweden. It shows that the company can be linked to elite lobbying efforts and political strategies that go way beyond the music industry or even the tech sector. Within such a discourse, Spotify appears as a national icon, a disruptive entrepreneurial hero, and a pioneering industry actor with preeminent importance for the future of the Swedish economy. Through the Twitter campaign, Spotify was also deeply drawn into party politics, as manifested by the participation and utterances of politicians from centrist and right-wing parties. What mobilized political discourse over the course of the #backaspotify campaign were mainly the conditions of entrepreneurship. This shows how Spotify is not simply a tech company but an actor around which larger political claims may be formed. By intervening in—and carefully unpacking—the actions that occurred around the #backaspotify campaign, an image of Spotify as a locus for political tension arises. Notably, music was hardly mentioned at all in these discussions. Apart from the occasional reference to pictures of cassette tapes it remains somewhat ironic that Spotify was nevertheless always framed and portrayed as the future of music distribution.

1   Where Is Spotify?

Daniel Ek, Spotify's cofounder and CEO, has been called the most powerful person in the music business,[1] as well as one of "the most influential minds in tech."[2] In 2017, he made it on *Time* magazine's list of the world's "100 most influential people" for having "helped transform the way people listen to music and the way artists interact with fans."[3] Based on what the press reports about Spotify, it would seem that Daniel Ek rules an empire and is destined to implement a personal and unique vision of technology and music. While Spotify certainly is shaping the way music is attended to, the habitual attribution of agency and power to this company and its CEO raises more questions than it answers. What kind of autonomy does Spotify possess as a corporate enterprise? What makes Spotify a Swedish success story, given the financial losses the company has sustained each year of its existence? Who owns and rules over music streaming?

Spotify's story is often told as a narrative of how the rise of streaming caused the decline of piracy, thus saving the music industry from crisis: "From the very beginning, our vision was to offer a legal music service, as good or better than the pirate sites, giving users access to all music in the world, for free." That was how Ek put it in 2009.[4] Today, he would omit the last two words. As this chapter will demonstrate, however, history did not follow a linear path guided by entrepreneurial vision. Rather, we argue that Spotify is a shape-shifting service developed by a company that constantly adjusted, if not entirely changed, its main strategies and goals. Accordingly, the emergence of music streaming as a cultural practice can be historicized in more than one way. While Spotify will appear as a key actor in any historical narrative, the company has played more than one role—and not always successfully.

The Precarity of Spotify

The first thing to note is that the company is not owned by its founders. After founding the company in 2006, Daniel Ek and Martin Lorentzon lost their majority share by 2009. Since then—at least until its IPO in April 2018—Spotify has been principally owned by a number of venture capital firms based in different parts of the world. Their primary interest is not to make Spotify profitable but to make it valuable. Venture capital bets on return on investments at the time of an "exit," that is, when Spotify is either acquired by a larger corporation or introduced at the stock exchange. Meanwhile, more and more venture capital is needed to cover the recurring losses and keep up the growth. So, while the executives must submit to the owners, the current owners must submit to the expectations attributed to an imagined future or the capital may be lost.[5]

However, ownership does not equal control. Spotify's very existence remains dependent on the willingness of the so-called Big Three—the global record companies Universal, Sony, and Warner—to renew music licensing deals. In essence, these must not demand more royalties than Spotify is able to pay. The Big Three form an oligopoly that can act as a cartel when dealing with any music streaming service. Importantly, Spotify and its competitors all depend on the same product: a distribution license for what consumers accept to be "all music." This product can be bought from only one source: the recorded music cartel led by the Big Three. With a few exceptions, Spotify and its competitors offer the same catalog of music. In what sense, then, could Spotify possess a "unique selling proposition"? Would it be possible for the Big Three to start their own music streaming service and let Spotify vanish, after having squeezed it on venture capital? The answer to these questions depends on whether one considers Spotify to be simply an intermediary or rather the producer of a new commodity—a personalized music experience.

Yet Spotify is dependent on more than venture capital and music licenses. To deliver its product to consumers, the service also necessitates a larger infrastructure, as we will discuss in greater depth in the next chapter. At the one end, there need to be data centers to send out music files and fetch back user data. At the other end, consumers need to have appropriate playback devices; ideally, Spotify would have its software preinstalled in everything from smartphones to cars. In between these two ends, there must be enough available bandwidth for music to keep streaming without interruption. To guarantee a favorable infrastructure, Spotify has closed numerous deals with data center operators, hardware manufacturers, and telecom carriers.

None of this is unique for a music streaming service. The dependence on venture capital and infrastructure operators is a characteristic feature of most technology startups that intend to become platforms. As we have argued in the introduction, current platform discourse tends to overstate the power that is *in* a platform, downplaying the variety of positions these companies may take on markets. Spotify's current dominance in music streaming does not simply mirror the market dominance enjoyed by other platforms, such as Facebook. The latter is designed to facilitate forms of exchange between users, not to distribute copyrighted works. The opposite goes for Spotify, which makes its survival more dependent on licenses. Copyright also works differently in different media. In music, copyright protects the musical work of songwriters and lyricists and allows for these rights to be monopolized by collecting societies. But there is also a separate right to the sound recording, which usually belongs to a record company. This legal construction was historically motivated by the high costs of recording sound. While that circumstance has changed, the record industry cemented a very strong market position thanks to these "related rights."[6]

Ever since the tape recorder was introduced, the development of consumer electronics has tended to gradually undermine the enforceability of these rights. This process accelerated in the digital realm with the proliferation of file-sharing networks such as The Pirate Bay, also based in Sweden. The record industry was thrown into a crisis—to which Spotify could present itself as a solution. Spotify's early history is therefore entangled with (Swedish) politics, and this chapter will demonstrate the service's ambivalent relationship to music piracy.

Spotify, in other words, relies not only on investors, rights holders, and network operators but also on policymakers. Music piracy must not be too rampant, collecting societies too powerful, or privacy protections too strict if Spotify is to succeed in a country. Rather than being an autonomous actor with the power to shape the future of the music business, Spotify exists at the intersection of industries such as music, advertising, technology, and finance.

Accordingly, the history of Spotify is not just a story of success but also a story of precarity. To keep afloat, and to attract new venture capital that can cover its losses before an acquisition or IPO, Spotify has to sustain the hype around its service, framing it as a lifestyle for users and an economic opportunity for artists. Spotify also has to maintain the image of a company that is always expanding, looking forward, and headed on the straight path toward a future monopoly position. In each country, Spotify has had to adapt to different patterns of music use and make deals with different partners. All these interactions have contributed to how Spotify has changed its interface, away from the centrality of the search box and toward the promise of "the right music for every moment."

The question has often been asked whether Spotify has a sustainable business model or not. We do not aim to answer that question here. The question itself seems inadequate, as no business can sustain itself on a market. Rather, it must be sustained by others, as the following historical narrative of Spotify will demonstrate.

How to Historicize Spotify?

What is Spotify? First, it is the name of a company. Second, it is the name of the music service provided by that same company. Third, it is quite common to invoke Spotify as a metaphor to describe or evoke broader transformations of the media industries and the internet, as when trade journals describe other tech startups as a "Spotify for *x*." Such metaphorical invocations of the service convey an image of what the internet is or might be, provide clues to design intentions, and carry normative connotations.[7] In addition, the company, the music service, and the metaphor have all changed over time. A decade is a short measure of time in business history but not when it comes to digital media.[8] To provide a rationale and context for the methods and research presented throughout this book, it is necessary to historicize the present and past futures of Spotify. This counters a trend of presentist and functionalist accounts that emphasize seemingly emergent or unforeseeable developments.[9]

Periodization is unavoidable in any historiography or social negotiation of which continuities the present will recognize in its past. Anyone who conveys a historical account—be it a historian, a journalist, or a marketer—has to periodize in one way or another and, thus, to engage in a "politics of time."[10] The story of Spotify has often been told in the press and in academic publications, with different degrees of detail. It has also been conveyed by Spotify itself.

"Spotify—The Story" is the title of a one-minute video uploaded by the company for the public launch of its service in 2008. In this video, music streaming is presented as the culmination of a media history that developed toward the maximization of individual choice. The voiceover relates:

> In a world where everyone loves music. First came vinyl, the cassette tape, the compact disc, the MP3 player. Which brings us to the present day. Introducing Spotify, a world of music. You search, you find. … Whatever you want, whenever you want. Instant, simple, and free.[11]

In this succession of audio technologies, the absence of radio is striking, as we will discuss later. Spotify's periodization of media history is also entirely technological, which parallels most accounts of the company's rise to fame. These stories usually highlight the same breaks in time: "from physical to digital; downloads to streaming; ownership to access."[12] *Streaming* appears here as the name of a new paradigm in history. But what about the transformations *within* streaming and with regard to the changing expectations of what a streaming service should provide? In order to answer these and other questions, we will have to introduce an alternative principle of dividing time that is based not on technology, nor on the ups and downs of the music industry, but on *financialization* as a structuring principle of media history.[13] The main question asked in this chapter is how Spotify has managed to receive new funding for running its operations at ever larger losses for over a decade.

This chapter brings together media history and business history, integrating the global (technology and finance) with the local (politics and culture). As a media history, it picks up where most research on digital music has ended. In particular, it takes its cue from Jonathan Sterne's *MP3: The Meaning of a Format* and Jeremy Wade Morris's *Selling Digital Music, Formatting Culture*, both of which situate the affordances of software in a context of commodification.[14] As a business history, this chapter responds to the challenge of studying digital companies that are entangled in both public and private spheres but are unwilling to grant access to their archives. While eager to finance applied research to promote and develop its own service, Spotify has rejected any request to make historical documentation accessible.

What does exist abundantly, however, is hype about Spotify: speculations, rumors, and promises widely circulated by the press, by Spotify's own marketing affiliates, and in social media. In writing the history of Spotify, a major issue concerns how to approach this abundance of materials. Rather than discarding hype as noise to be filtered out, we understand media industry realities as always constructed, which requires that one pay attention to an industry's own outward self-representation and dismiss the belief in an authentic reality "inside the box."[15] This interest in hype as a source of historiography resonates with Gideon Kunda's observation that a high-tech company's "engineering culture" is not to be understood as something substantial but as a "mechanism of control" that works normatively both on its employees and its future customers.[16] Yet hype is more than just the outward construction of a company's culture; it also relates to the ways in which human agency is structured by time. Hype is a phase usually characterized by an upsurge in public attention and high-rising expectations about possible innovation. Hype comes first, modeling the future out of the present. Thus, it is interesting to see how plans and goals related to Spotify were constructed from its existing culture in a process of modeling and what came *after* each period of hype.[17]

In adopting a framework of *following the hype*, or a history based on widely accessible sources, this chapter mirrors this book's overall rationale of *following files*. It works through vast source materials in order both to develop an empirical narrative of change and to look for what Richard Barbrook has called "the beta version of a science fiction dream."[18]

The main part of the material used here stems from online archives. Keeping in mind that Spotify exists at the intersection of industries, we have chosen to consult trade journals from the diverse fields of technology (e.g., *Wired*, *TechCrunch*), music (e.g., *Billboard*, *Music Week*), and advertising (e.g., *Advertising Age*, *Marketing Week*), as well as some general news outlets. In addition, we have found Swedish press archives to be indispensable, particularly for tracing the earlier parts of Spotify's history.[19] Besides the press, there are a number of relevant web sources that are not accessible by search engine but rather require more complex forms of retrieval, such as scouring old job listings, excavating deleted blog entries, and mining historical Twitter accounts.[20]

It is much more difficult to study the software itself and how it worked in previous versions. The source code is not made public, and key functions are not executed on the local machine but are dependent on interaction with central servers. To historicize the software interface, then, we have largely had to rely on screenshots and scattered user reports. During the time period that our research project has been running, however, we have done real-time documentation of the software. As we hinted at earlier, none of these sources will give substantial insight into the inner workings of Spotify—information that business historians traditionally consider the most valuable. The external relations of Spotify are more discernable, while key documents are usually guarded by nondisclosure agreements, including the deals made between Spotify and the record industry.

The following narrative is structured chronologically in accordance with the funding rounds that have allowed Spotify to persist in making losses. While media historiography has largely abandoned such linearized narrative accounts, the format of corporate storytelling adopted here mirrors the significance of "narrative infrastructure" in industrial organization and product development processes. Narrative accounts are frequently produced to create coherence in multiactor, multilevel processes and to reduce complexity and uncertainty.[21] In line with the interventionist design of this book, we turn this practice against itself by showing how the narratives developed around Spotify resonate with its financial history. Spotify would not be valued at several billion dollars—and would not have had its losses repeatedly covered by venture capital—if there were not a story connecting its open-ended past to a certain and positive future.

Spotify's dependence on financial speculation thus provides the reason for this methodological choice to follow the hype. The first financing round (Series A) of about $20 million coincided with Spotify's public launch in 2008. Subsequently, larger amounts of capital have been injected, typically at an interval of twelve to eighteen months. For each round, the existing stockholders have seen their share of equity being diluted, so that the balance of ownership has been displaced in a new direction but always away from the founders, who were also the original investors. A limited amount of financial information is easily available on websites such as Crunchbase: the identity of the investors in a round, the total size of their investment, and the resulting valuation of Spotify. But in each deal, there are also secret conditions that entitle Spotify to act in a certain way. These are harder to discern. In recent years, Spotify has taken in billions of dollars in the form of convertible debt, at terms that create a strong incentive to rush toward a stock market launch. By following the hype and mapping it over an investment timeline, we aim to underline how Spotify's investors have influenced its development.

How to Count?

There are many numbers that document Spotify's growth and are often used to compare the company to its competitors, but it would be a mistake to take these numbers for hard facts. Not only is the financial valuation of the company highly speculative, as it tends to be biased by deals that guarantee some investors a more favorable "exit," but there are also good reasons to remain skeptical about other numbers invoked in the comparison between music streaming services. While Spotify currently claims to offer access to thirty million "songs" (as of January 2018), it is difficult to differentiate duplicates and nonmusical sounds from actual songs (as our discussion of "zombie music" will assert in chapter 2). User statistics circulated in the press may refer to the number of registered accounts or to those accounts that have been active within a given day, week, month, or year. What counts as activity here is not clearly defined; does the user have to play a song or just open the app? Furthermore, an account is not the same as an individual user. One individual may use several accounts, and one account may be shared within a household of several individuals. Therefore, more than just a grain of salt is needed when reading user statistics. In short, there is no way of knowing if 150 million alleged users (as of 2017) does really represent 150 million individuals. Counting the number of paying subscribers is a bit less problematic. But even here, the figure may well be boosted by giving discounts or by bundling the subscription price together with a mobile service, for instance.

Even more problematic are widespread claims about how much money Spotify generates for artists. First of all, these aggregate numbers show neither the distribution between record companies, songwriters, and performing artists nor between the superstars and the rest. Few industry insiders, however, dispute the claim that the Big Three have used their influence over Spotify to secure better royalty deals than their smaller competitors. They also get free advertising space and special access to user data. In addition, the Big Three are part owners of Spotify, since they have managed to get shares in return for licenses. All of this makes it difficult to discuss the issue of fair remuneration for artists.

Each year, statistics for the "global music market" are published by the International Federation of the Phonographic Industry (IFPI). These numbers are routinely used by journalists and academics as evidence of the increasing significance of streaming. "It makes up the majority of digital revenue, which, in turn, now accounts for 50% of total recorded music revenues," the most recent IFPI report states.[22] Such industry statistics have to be treated with skepticism. Aggregates such as "digital revenue" are defined in an arbitrary way, given the fact that virtually all recorded music today is digital, at least for parts of its journey from artist to listener. Even a vinyl record is almost always produced from a digital master track; that being said, even a digital stream must become analog when it makes its final journey from the loudspeaker to the listener's ears. In the widely cited IFPI statistics, digital revenue includes royalties from Spotify, but not from "broadcasters," although the latter category also includes pure internet services. Record industry statistics thus maintain an obsolete distinction between retail and broadcasting, with Spotify categorized as a retailer.[23] Industry statistics are just as arbitrary in their attribution of costs and revenues to national territories; the recurring claim that Sweden would be "the world's third-largest music exporter," for example, is presumably a misleading statement.[24] We should similarly be skeptical of the report that Spotify is now profitable in certain national markets, including Sweden.[25] While revenues from subscriptions and advertisements may come from national subsidiaries, Spotify is a company to which many costs—such as infrastructure and tech development—are of a global nature. It is therefore difficult to judge its profitability within a given country.

Spotify has also been associated with problems of quantification at a macroeconomic level. The company has become a prime example among prominent economists who claim that digital services are not adequately captured by established ways of estimating economic growth, inflation, and productivity.[26] These depend on the measurement of prices over time, but how is one to compare the price of music in 2015 to that in 2005? Is it meaningful to calculate a hypothetical "price per track listened to" when the listener is just paying a monthly fee? Should the price of using Spotify be compared to the price of buying records or to the (nonexistent) price of listening to the radio? If the supply of music in Spotify's catalog increases, should this be counted as an increase in the quality of the service?

It could also be argued that the very abundance of music is a problem, one which first must be solved by some kind of curation. If that is the case, how can we calculate the hypothetical value of a music recommendation system? Economists Erik Brynjolfsson and Andrew McAfee have therefore pointed to Spotify as an example of how national accounts fail.[27] But it would be just as easy to make the opposite argument: intensified surveillance and advertising means consumers are paying a price for their data and their attention that should be made visible in national accounts. Even more traditional calculation techniques, which focus on transactions where actual money is changing hands, run into difficulty locating the financial flows around Spotify. Recent government inquiries from Sweden and the UK have singled out Spotify as epitomizing the problem of measuring an economy built on digital services.[28]

The Technopolitical Context

Founded in 2006, Spotify emerged from a particular era in internet history. Mobile connectivity, for instance, was not the norm at the time but still the exception. Digital culture was not yet a *streaming culture* premised on constant connectivity but rather a *storage culture* dependent on ever-larger, ever-cheaper hard drives. In 2006, algorithmic culture was largely unheard of; rather, a culture of data storage and everyday archivism prevailed. Apple's music player, the iPod, may serve as a case in point: launched in 2001 with a storage capacity of 5 GB, the iPod's storage rapidly increased and peaked in 2007, when Apple produced a 160 GB model (approximately twenty thousand songs).[29]

Following the burst of the first dot-com bubble, the early 2000s were also a time when venture capital was at low ebb. This is not to say that innovation slowed down. Rather, it changed character, becoming less commercial and more decentralized. Three of the most characteristic innovations of the time, however, took off without the support of investors or any company in control and were based on open standards: the blog, the wiki, and the Bit-Torrent protocol. After some years of incubation, these forms of networking soon came to represent the future of the internet—a future that was already known in tech circles as Web 2.0.[30] By 2005, the term was well established. That same year, a political controversy over file sharing and copyright also erupted around The Pirate Bay, the world's largest BitTorrent search engine. These different digital contexts resulted in the formation of a new political party in Sweden, the Pirate Party, which made it into the European Parliament during the party's Swedish heyday (2006–2010) and subsequently spread to several other countries.

The file-sharing boom and the political dispute over copyright enforcement were both exceptionally intense in Sweden.[31] They gave extra momentum to anyone proposing that the media industries should disrupt themselves and switch to "new business models," which tended to rely on ideas put forward by *Wired* editor and business guru Chris Anderson, author of the *The Long Tail* (2006) and *Free!* (2009).[32] We would argue that it is far from certain that Spotify would have survived if not for its opportunistic, rather than innovative, strategy and the inconsistent ways in which the company positioned itself in regard to file sharing: sometimes presenting itself as the continuation of the ongoing illicit disruption, while at other times insisting on a binary opposition between illegality and legality. In retrospect, Spotify's early Swedish history appears in perfect sync with the legal proceedings against The Pirate Bay, which began with a police raid in May 2006—just weeks after Spotify was founded.

Finding the Files to Distribute

Neither of Spotify's two founders, Daniel Ek (born in 1983) and Martin Lorentzon (born in 1969), had experience working with music, neither in the music industry nor even as subcultural enthusiasts. While it is often reported that Ek played the guitar as a child, there is hardly any evidence that music defined his social life as he grew up.

The early history of Spotify—at least as it has hitherto been told—has thus been made more musical than it probably was. In interviews, Ek has explained that he started Spotify for two reasons: to save the music industry from piracy and to help friends with "really bad taste in music" to "discover better music."[33] Spotify's actual history is less straightforward. Swedish sources reveal a haphazard search for business opportunities that just happened to involve music. Indeed, given Spotify's later development, it is telling that both Ek and Lorentzon had a background in the business of advertising technology. Lorentzon had made a fortune with the company TradeDoubler, which he and Felix Hagnö founded in 1999. TradeDoubler survived the first dot-com crash and soon expanded to become one of Europe's leading affiliate marketing networks, going public in late 2005.[34] A few months later, in March 2006, TradeDoubler acquired a small startup called Advertigo, which developed a technology for so-called contextual advertising, from founder Daniel Ek.[35] This is how Lorentzon and Ek met: two Swedish multimillionaires—thirty-seven and twenty-three years old, respectively—both experiencing the boredom that may come with financial independence, as they would later explain. The two decided to start a business together.[36] It began to take form during the summer of 2006. That July, the new company was named Spotify—a name without any particular meaning.

Spotify was initially structured as a group of several firms that used a plurality of jurisdictions for owning different assets. Apart from Spotify AB, which is registered as a software company, there is Spotify Sweden AB, which has the official purpose of selling advertising connected to "services for digital distribution of music, film, TV programs, audiobooks, games, and similar content." In addition, for each country where the service has been launched, new subsidiaries have also been launched. They are all, however, owned by a holding company, Spotify Technology SA, which is registered at a post-office box in Luxembourg. This post-office box is the same one that Lorentzon uses for another holding company, which in turn owns another company registered to a post-office box in Cyprus, in which Lorentzon has placed the financial riches that he made with TradeDoubler and through which he now owns his shares in Spotify: a classic structure for tax avoidance.[37] Ek also owns a Cypriot-registered investment company, D. G. E. Investments,[38] and Cyprus is furthermore the virtual home of two subsidiaries that were already registered in 2006: Spotify Technology Sales Ltd. and Spotify Technology Holding Ltd.,[39] the latter being the original registrant of Spotify's patents and trademarks.

Spotify opened its first office at Riddargatan 20 in central Stockholm, where software development begun in August 2006. The software was initially for distributing data over the internet from a central server to a large number of recipients using a peer-to-peer (P2P) network, so as to unburden the central server. In other words, the core idea was to minimize the cost of digital distribution by using extra bandwidth available among the server's users. The kind of data to be distributed was, for Spotify, a secondary consideration at this point. "The media may here represent any kind of digital content, such as music, video, digital films or images," explained the US patent application that Spotify filed in 2007.[40] Speaking with the business press, the founders presented Spotify as a general "media distribution platform," indicating that the ultimate aim was to use it for video distribution. However, video demanded much more bandwidth than sound. "We begin with music streaming this spring," Lorentzon therefore explained.[41] Visitors to Spotify's first website were consequently met with the following presentation: "Spotify gives you the music you want, when you want it. Your choice is just a search box or a friendly recommendation away. You'll be amazed by the speed and control you have with Spotify."[42] To try out the technology, Spotify loaded its servers with the music files most easily available, namely those already stored on its employees' private computers. A large portion of these files were downloaded through file-sharing services such as The Pirate Bay.[43] Rights holders had not granted the company the licenses required to distribute the files online. Thus, Spotify began as a de facto pirate service.

The Beta Period (2007–2008)

On May 1, 2007, Spotify released its initial beta version to a small circle of acquaintances. Among them were some of Sweden's leading technology bloggers. This immediately resulted in a number of enthusiastic blog posts, and the comment fields were flooded with requests for invitations. Being invited to use Spotify became a sign of exclusivity, and Spotify controlled the growth of the circle by rationing the number of invites that existing users could pass on. If one were to look at the early user demographic, it would probably be rather affluent and dominated by men between twenty-five to forty years of age who lived in Stockholm's city center and worked in technology or media. Many of these early users saw themselves as passionate fans of new pop music, but their enthusiasm for digital technology was probably even stronger.

One of the first beta testers was Eric Wahlforss, a part-time musician and entrepreneur who would shortly go on to found SoundCloud, another music streaming service (which, years later, Spotify would consider acquiring). Wahlforss immediately recognized Spotify as "a preview of the future." It may be noted, however, that his enthusiastic blog post about Spotify had little, if anything, to do with music: "The thing that wows me the most is that the app is faster than iTunes on my local machine. Repeat, faster than iTunes. And now we're talking fancy peer-to-peer architectures, special audio codecs, custom databases, etc., etc....If this thing scales it will be bigger than Skype. Big, big ups to the Spotify team."[44] Spotify's first interface did indeed look very similar to iTunes: the user could search for music and add tracks to personal playlists. In addition, it also offered a radio-like mode of listening in which the user was asked to select one of eighteen predefined music genres (and one or several decades). Compared to today's personalized radio stations, this seems primitive indeed, but in fact, this was how Spotify Radio worked until late 2011.

During its beta period, Spotify consolidated a kind of on-demand doctrine as a service centered on the search box, giving access to "whatever you want." The user was effectively conceived of as a sovereign individual,

Figure 1.1
During the autumn of 2009, Spotify launched its first mobile music app
for the Apple iPhone.

who already knew exactly what he or she wanted to listen to and did not
need help with music recommendations. This doctrine was reinforced by
the sample of beta testers.

The hype intensified in early 2008, with a focus on two claims. First,
the new service would "make music free" by relying entirely on advertising
for revenue. Second, that the move "from ownership to access" was indeed
happening and that the personal archiving of MP3s would soon become an
outdated practice. If commentators saw anything lacking in the beta version,

it was that it did not yet live up to the promises of a Web 2.0 service, given that users still could not easily upload their self-made music. This, however, was a feature that many expected to see implemented soon.[45]

Period A (2008–2009)

The first public version of Spotify was launched in October 2008. But what exactly did it mean to "launch" a music service that was already up and running, serving thousands of users each day? Maybe it is better to say that Spotify was legalized. For a year and a half, Spotify's beta had, in effect, been run as a pirate service, distributing music to invited users without any license to do so. As previously stated, in many cases, the music originated from The Pirate Bay and other file-sharing networks, but this changed when Spotify started to sign deals with record companies and collecting societies, moving itself into legal territory.

For many of the existing users at the time, what happened in October 2008 was that parts of their playlists suddenly became unavailable. Spotify had to remove unlicensed music from its service, and in early 2009, even more music disappeared at the request of record companies that enforced country-specific listening restrictions. In addition, only users with a special invite could access Spotify Free; this did not change with the official launch. The only real addition was a paid version of the service, Spotify Premium. Being legal, the company could now also begin to really sell advertising, which gradually became ever-more present for users of Spotify Free.

Spotify's launch, in other words, was not the launch of a new service but the launch of new efforts to monetize an existing service. Spotify began expanding into new territories, with different versions of the service being offered in different countries. An October 7, 2008, press release from Spotify announced that the service was being launched in eight European countries: Finland, France, Germany, Italy, Norway, Spain, Sweden, and the United Kingdom.[46] Around the same time, Spotify also opened offices in London, Berlin, and Madrid.[47] Soon, however, the company encountered problems in Germany and Italy—partly because of local copyright collecting societies— and initially had to retreat from these markets. The official story now told by Spotify is that the service was not launched in Germany until March 2012 or in Italy until February 2013. The publicity around these later launches did not mention that these were really second attempts.[48]

Spotify's initial European launch—just like the US launch three years later—marked the conjunction of two interdependent business deals. One deal granted Spotify access to music licenses, while another gave it the money to pay for those licenses. With over $20 million in venture capital, Spotify could now run its operations for a year before a fresh funding round. The leading investor in the first round was the Swedish firm Northzone, which received an 11.9 percent stake in Spotify as well as a seat on the board. Later, information leaked that the biggest record companies had signed a deal that guaranteed not just a certain level of royalties but also equity in Spotify, amounting to a cumulative 17.3 percent share, a proportion which has since diminished with each new funding round. The fact that major record companies own shares in Spotify has complicated every discussion about fair compensation for artists, songwriters, and independent record labels. The dilution of shares in this round did not alter the basic balance of ownership. Throughout Period A, the absolute majority of shares was still held by Spotify's two cofounders, Ek and Lorentzon.

These initial conjunctions of various deals—later known as "the launch"— indeed confirm Spotify's place at the intersection of different industries: music and technology, advertising and finance. The timing is also notable: Spotify's launch happened to coincide with a global financial meltdown. It occurred only weeks after the bankruptcy of Lehman Brothers, precisely at the time when business magazines were busy producing front pages about the possible end of capitalism. The financial crisis was followed by the so-called Great Recession, with immediate consequences for media industries. However, it was not until the second half of 2009—Period B, in this context—that this economic downturn had a visible impact on Spotify.

In strategic terms, Period A was characterized by a focus on mobility. Spotify still had no mobile application, but in early 2009, it recruited many new developers to begin creating an app for the iPhone. Whether this app would then be accepted by Apple was still not certain.

During the same period, Spotify's center of gravity was shifting away from Sweden. Not only did the number of British users soon surpass the Swedish, a newly opened London office became Spotify's new company headquarters, even though tech development was still based in Stockholm. Accordingly, during 2009 and 2010, the international press consistently presented Spotify as a British company. Patent registries confirm this. From these, one can learn that Spotify's first patent—registered by the Cypriot subsidiary in July 2007—was transferred in October 2008 to Spotify Ltd. (UK), only to be

Figure 1.2
A screenshot of the Spotify Premium interface in 2011.

transferred again in June 2011, this time to Spotify AB (Sweden).[49] Hence, for almost three years—Periods A, B, and C, in our periodization—Spotify was a British and not a Swedish company, despite often being portrayed as a Swedish success story.

Spotify as a Metaphor

During 2008, the year of its launch, Spotify was widely hyped in the Swedish press. The company was frequently described as a revolutionary service offering immediate access to every conceivable kind of music. In exchange for just a few advertising jingles, all this music remained available for free. From early 2009 onward, many commentators also began to tout Spotify as a model for transforming the digital distribution of cultural goods in general. This idea was first promoted by Bredbandsbolaget, a major Swedish internet service provider (ISP), which had already struck a deal to offer each customer an invite to Spotify Free. Interviewed in January 2009, the CEO of Bredbandsbolaget proposed that there should also be "a Spotify for movies," which would arguably be "the most effective way to combat illegal file sharing."[50] At the time, there was no company plan to offer such a service in Sweden, but the vision caught on in the public conversation, mainly because it was politically appealing at that time.

The first half of 2009 came to mark the climax of the disputes over copyright enforcement in Sweden. The criminal case against the founders of the Pirate Bay search engine, which had been in preparation for several years, finally went before the district court of Stockholm in February 2009. With these court hearings still ongoing, the Swedish parliament voted in favor of implementing an EU directive that would open new possibilities for copyright holders to sue individuals suspected of illicit file sharing.[51] Later that spring, the court announced that the four defendants connected to The Pirate Bay had been found guilty of abetting copyright infringement, and each one was sentenced to one year in prison and ordered to pay a total of €3 million in damages.[52]

Press coverage of these events was largely "unfavorable to the positions taken by rights-holders," the US embassy noted in a confidential cable later made public by WikiLeaks. For the Swedish government, the "political sensitivities" pervading issues of copyright were at this time "very delicate," according to the embassy cable.[53] Leading politicians were clearly uncomfortable in taking sides, and when pressed, many tried to avoid the question by simply referring to Spotify as *the* solution. The US embassy explicitly mentioned the risk that strong media attention to the file-sharing issue might give "the Pirate Party a boost in the EU Parliamentary elections in June 2009." This is exactly what happened: after receiving 7 percent of the Swedish vote, the Pirate Party entered the European Parliament. While political developments in a country such as Sweden might come across as marginal, they form an important part of Spotify's early history. Were it not for the political conflict over file sharing, Spotify's trademark would clearly not have received so much attention in the Swedish mass media.

In July 2009, news broke that Sweden would suddenly get its "Spotify for movies."[54] The discussion that followed illustrates the metaphorical meaning of *Spotify* at that time. In collaboration with Bredbandsbolaget, Voddler launched a beta version of its film service, with the backing of 100 million kronor of venture capital investment (approximately $10 million). The timing coincided with the annual Almedalen Week, during which virtually all of Sweden's politicians, lobbyists, and political reporters convene on the island of Gotland for seminars and free drinks. Only a few weeks had passed since the electoral success of the Pirate Party, making file sharing one of the hottest issues debated during the week. Consequently, the major Swedish tabloid *Expressen* published an editorial hailing the Spotify/Voddler model not only as "the way out from the file-sharing quagmire" but as potentially even pointing toward "the way out of the financial crisis."[55]

By its premiere date, Voddler had hoped to offer free streaming of Hollywood blockbusters. It was an aspiration that would turn out to be unrealistic given the movie industry's territorial licensing and distribution practices. The allegedly universal model exemplified by Spotify and Voddler was characterized by the combination of three features: streaming on demand, P2P networking, and offering content at no cost to the consumer. Of these three aspects, the latter two pointed to a continuity from file-sharing networks such as The Pirate Bay to new streaming services such as Spotify and Voddler. The solution to mass pirating was supposedly found in the file-sharing experience: adding advertisements and using the resulting revenue to pay copyright holders.

Period B (late 2009)

In October 2009, Daniel Ek appeared uncharacteristically humble. Offering "a few thoughts on the past year," Ek's post on Spotify's blog read as an exercise in self-criticism:

> I care more than most about figuring out a revenue model that doesn't devalue music … Someone asked me a while back, during a fireside chat, what was the biggest mistake I've made so far with Spotify? I can't recall my answer, but I've since thought more about the question. I would say that the biggest mistake that I've made is that Spotify, unlike any of the other businesses I've been a part of, depends on our partners (artists, composers, labels etc.) and I haven't always acted with this fact at the forefront of my mind.[56]

Ek's statement should certainly not be read as a personal blog post directed at a general audience. Rather, its publication appears to be part of an ongoing negotiation over music licenses, indicating that at least parts of the record industry were still suspicious of Spotify. Ek's public demonstration of remorse over past arrogance was hence a tactical move, probably well grounded in discussions with investors who had just agreed to provide Spotity with a second round of capital to stay afloat.

Until late 2009, Spotify had been regarded primarily as a free music service, based on the founders' vision that advertising can make music "free but legal." This vision died over the course of 2009. The reason for this—and for Ek's newfound humility—can be found in the global financial crisis. The Great Recession of 2009 effectuated a steep downturn in the total market for advertising. In this context, it became difficult for Spotify to convince investors and license holders of advertising support as a main source of income. As is well known, newspapers were hardest hit, which may well explain why journalists at the time quickly adopted a more skeptical stance toward the concept of *free*—in contrast to the uncritical reception that Chris Anderson's ideas had enjoyed before the recession.

The financial crisis also affected the availability of venture capital. During 2009, it was reported that digital music services had a harder time attracting investors. But the downturn was only temporary. Central banks responded to the financial crisis by lowering interest rates and launching programs of quantitative easing, effectively forcing investors to chase greater risk. In brief, risk was sought in two main areas: among internet services and in emerging economies outside the West, especially Brazil, Russia, India, and China—the so-called BRIC countries. In mid-2009, the Russian investment fund Digital Sky Technologies (DST) made a $200 million investment in Facebook, marking the beginning of a new boom in the valuation of tech startups associated with social media.

How did Spotify fit into this new business climate? A growing number of commentators began to criticize Spotify's idea of free music. Meanwhile, a new consensus regarding the advantages of subscription was forming within the media industries. In the United States, subscription-based television services, for example, fared remarkably well through the recession. For a giant such as Time Warner, growth in subscription revenues more than compensated for shrinking ad revenues during this period. Subscription services appeared to be recession-proof.[57] The record industry took notice and began to promote the subscription model as the way forward. "We're bullish on subscriptions," a Warner Music executive explained in late 2009.[58]

As we have previously discussed, storytelling about Spotify is an integral part of Spotify itself. The narrative includes claims about continuity, as well as changes, in business models. "Spotify's business model is, and has been since launch, more about the mix of subscription and ad supported," Daniel

Ek blogged in October 2009.[59] This may be true if one understands *launch* as referring to the business deals made a year before. But as we have argued, it is not an accurate description of Spotify's original business model. The idea of selling subscriptions was rather forced upon Spotify by the holders of music licenses, and the economic crisis exerted an even stronger pressure in that direction. It was expedient at this time, however, for Spotify to modify its own history—and to distance itself from the pirate heritage. In the same blog post, Ek also promised that Spotify would not only offer music streaming but would also sell individual downloads on a pay-per-song basis.[60] This marked a break with the earlier claim that streaming was *the* future of music and affirmed the continuity between iTunes and Spotify as purveyors of "legal music." Download sales were integrated into the Spotify client, at least temporarily, which was certainly not Spotify's own idea but rather a demand from the record industry.[61]

In hindsight, it is striking how reluctant Daniel Ek was to affirm the idea of building his company on subscriptions. Instead, he repeated the claim that Spotify would become profitable by combining a multitude of revenue sources: "The new business model in music is a mix between ad-supported music, downloads, subscriptions, merchandising and ticketing."[62] There were indeed far-reaching plans to make Spotify a marketplace for concert tickets, band T-shirts, and other merchandise.[63]

A clever way to introduce a new subscription business is to bundle the monthly bill together with another one that the customer is already paying. This was the reasoning behind Spotify's strategy of seeking deals with telecom operators. The aim was to package the music service together with mobile services. The consumer would not really notice the payment, and the service would hence "feel like free." Consequently, Spotify made two such major deals: with Telia in Sweden and with Three in the United Kingdom.[64] At the same time, in October 2009, Spotify also began to buy advertising. Previously, marketing had relied on word of mouth, fueled by the sharing of invites to the free service. Now a television ad appeared on Swedish channel TV5. To one of Spotify's earliest employees, lead designer Rasmus Andersson, this signaled a change in the spirit of the company: "Yeah, it's true that we've become a Big Company™. Scary, a bit sad but mostly exciting."[65] If nothing else this indicated a tension within company culture, at precisely the time when the original founders were about to become minority owners in their own company.

Period C (2010–2011)

The year 2010 and the first half of 2011 were a frustrating time for Spotify, as it waited for an opportunity to launch its service in the United States. The company was not exactly at a standstill, as it continued to expand its European user base. Revenue—now mostly from subscriptions—did multiply from 2009 to 2010, but all earnings were swallowed by additional costs, which grew at an even faster pace.[66] Industry analysts agreed that Spotify needed to scale. Everything was set for its US launch, but the Big Three record companies were reluctant to allow free on-demand streaming in the American market. Warner Music, in particular, refused to grant Spotify the necessary permit. "Free streaming services are clearly not net positive for the industry," Warner's CEO declared in early 2010.[67] Conversely, the possibility of launching in the United States without the free tier was not an option for Spotify. The stalemate was not resolved until after Warner Music was acquired by a Russian businessman in 2011.

Calling 2010 a lost year in the history of Spotify would be an exaggeration, but this period does stand out for its slow expansion and relatively low level of press coverage. Indeed, the amount of money invested in Spotify's Series C funding round was also small: just $16 million,[68] compared to the two preceding rounds of $22 million and $50 million. The new money was in fact less significant than the identity of the investor: Sean Parker, the cofounder of Napster. As Parker took a place on Spotify's board of directors, this seemed to emphasize a certain continuity in which Spotify represented the fulfillment of the very same disruption that Napster had started.[69] More importantly, however, Parker had also been the founding president of Facebook and still played an informal but important role in its leadership. He was in a good position to forge a partnership between Spotify and Facebook, which would result in far-reaching attempts to integrate the two services. By early 2010, just after Parker joined, it was already possible to observe a Facebookian influence on Spotify's strategies, well documented in patents registered by Facebook engineers at that time.[70]

The marketing jargon at the time focused on *social*, *sharing*, and *platform*. In the language of Period C, Spotify would no longer be just an *app* that gives you *access* to music but a *platform* where you *manage* your music. The user interface also developed, probably more than in the two preceding periods. First, it became social, in Facebook's particular sense of the word. Users could now build a personal profile within the app, add friends, and then drag-and-drop to share music. The profiles were connected to Facebook accounts, to help users find more friends, as well as to facilitate company extraction of data among users.[71] If the push toward subscriptions largely relied on deals with other subscription-based businesses (telecoms), the efforts to become a platform was likewise premised on integration with an existing platform (Facebook).

Chapter 2 will chart these different data integration strategies in more detail. Suffice it to say that, at this time, Spotify also announced its first partnership with an audio hardware manufacturer.[72] Another new feature was that the client could now index and play music files stored on local computers. Thus, users could listen to music that was not present in Spotify's catalog if they had downloaded the files from other sources (legally or illegally). Indexing of the local hard drive was not just an option, it happened automatically. After installing Spotify on a computer, a program would go through the entire hard drive looking for stored audio files, which were then reported back to Spotify's servers. This did not spark a major debate over privacy, and we simply cannot know what happened to all the data that Spotify collected regarding personal MP3 archives. There remains the possibility that it was shared with record companies as part of a licensing deal.

Less effort during this period was put toward developing ways to discover new music. A "related artists" function was added to the client but still no personalized recommendations.[73] Industry observers did not consider this a flaw but praised Spotify for being fast, clean, and simple.[74] "Competitors tend to boast about the size of their catalog and their tools that help users make sense of their massive amount of music," *Billboard* stated in late 2010. "In contrast, Spotify assumes what people want most is a fast and easy-to-use product. ... Without a doubt, Spotify is the best subscription service on the market today."[75] Comments like this demonstrate how, at this time, personalized recommendations were still not regarded as an essential feature of music streaming services.

In May 2011, new restrictions were imposed on Spotify's free service. Users who did not pay for a subscription could now only listen for ten hours per month and only five times for each track. This resulted in some negative word of mouth and led commentators to finally declare the idea of ad-supported music to be dead. This was not an initiative by Spotify Sweden, however, but one dictated by the major record companies, who would not let Spotify launch in the United States before seeing hard evidence of a rise in paying users. Yet Spotify soon made a move in the opposite direction, opening up its mobile version to users of Spotify Free.[76]

The experiment seems to have satisfied two of the Big Three record companies, and only Warner Music blocked the road to America. As it happened, Warner Music was also up for sale and was acquired by the Russian businessman Len Blavatnik. Another bidder was Sean Parker from Spotify's board of directors. According to Parker, he only left the bidding process after getting a guarantee from Blavatnik that, under his ownership, Warner Music would let Spotify launch in the United States without giving up its free version.[77] According to a leaked contract, Spotify also had to accept paying hundreds of millions of dollars in royalty advances to the Big Three and provide free advertising space to Sony Music before the roadblock was finally lifted.[78]

Period D (2011–2012)

In the middle of the summer of 2011—on July 14, to be precise—Spotify launched its service in the United States. The launch had been made public the previous evening via press release, only a couple of hours after Spotify had signed the licensing deal with Warner Music. The launch, however, was not widely advertised. As usual, Spotify relied on word of mouth, and the key to get the hype going was the offer of free access to music streaming (i.e., the same offer that somewhat paradoxically had delayed the US launch for years). To try out Spotify, Americans had to either pay for a Spotify Premium subscription or get an invite for a Spotify Free account. Each user received a limited number of invites to pass on to their friends. This way, Spotify created a powerful marketing machine based on the free efforts of its own users. The limitation on invites not only ensured that network capacity would not be overloaded but also contributed to hype that associated Spotify with the lifestyle of those circles that were first to receive invites—primarily young, hip New Yorkers. This was largely a repetition of the marketing pattern that had proven successful during the Swedish beta period of 2007 and 2008 (except for the political element in the Swedish hype). Two months later, registration for Spotify Free opened to anyone with a Facebook account.[79]

The reception of Spotify in the US press was enthusiastic. In describing the service, reporters emphasized free access as Spotify's "unique selling point." Many accounts also stressed that the service ran with extraordinary speed; a song started playing almost instantly after it was clicked, partly thanks to the P2P network used by Spotify to distribute data. Social features, such as playlist sharing, were also mentioned but not the radio-like features, and Spotify was hardly ever described as a service helping users to discover new music.[80]

When Spotify launched in the United States, the company received $100 million in fresh venture capital, more money than in the three preceding funding rounds combined. Taken together, the three investor firms gained approximately 10 percent of Spotify's shares, and the company was now valued at $1 billion. The investment deal had already been signed in early 2011, on the condition that it would not be triggered until Spotify reached a licensing deal with the Big Three to allow a US launch.[81]

With this influx of money, Spotify could run for a year and a half before the next funding round. Apparently, a main condition of the investment deal was that Spotify would expand its operations in Western Europe. Later in 2011, Spotify launched in Denmark, Belgium, Austria, and Switzerland, followed in early 2012 by a relaunch in Germany and then in Australia and New Zealand. This pattern of expansion confirmed the Western geography of Spotify; not until 2013 would the service be available in parts of Eastern Europe, Latin America, and Southeast Asia.

Apart from international expansion, this period in Spotify's history was also characterized by a specific direction of service development. Data-driven personalization was still not widespread, and the developing arm at Spotify still treated neither discovery nor algorithms as defining concepts. Rather, their priority in 2011 was to transform Spotify from a music service into a platform that was integrated with other platforms, most notably Facebook. If the "platformization" of Spotify and the alliance between Spotify and Facebook had been established by Sean Parker in the preceding period, it was now confirmed by the fact that Series D investment was led by the Russian firm DST, which had made a large investment in Facebook two years earlier, in the middle of the economic recession.[82] This move by DST in 2009 had marked the beginning of a new gold rush in tech startups, this time with *social media* as the main marketing term and driven by trillions of dollars released by the Federal Reserve to stimulate the economy.[83]

Arguably, to become social was never more important for Spotify than in 2011 and 2012. But the attempt was not without complications. At the F8 conference in September 2011, Facebook CEO Mark Zuckerberg presented a number of new features, many of which related to the new concept of "frictionless sharing." This was another step in Facebook's ongoing redefinition of what it means to be social online. First, *social* had been associated with the active dissemination of words and images. Then the thumbs-up Like button had been introduced in 2009, reducing sociality to one click. Now Facebook was set to abolish even that and automatize the sharing of activities between friends without the need for any active choice. Instead of choosing to share a particular song, users who opted to add a music app to Facebook's platform would now share *all* songs they listened to. The prime example presented by Zuckerberg was Spotify, and he even invited Daniel Ek to the stage for a brief guest appearance.[84]

The integration of music services was clearly visible for users of Facebook. At the left-hand side of the interface now appeared a Music Dashboard, including statistics for which songs were trending among friends. On the right-hand side, the news ticker showed in real time what friends were listening to and what app they used for listening—giving Spotify's trademark valuable exposure. And in the central home feed, Facebook would occasionally provide updates.[85] "Music is one of the most social things there is," Ek explained on Spotify's blog. It is "inherently social."[86] In other words, music is not intimate and has nothing to do with privacy. Not every Spotify user agreed—which we will discuss in more detail in chapter 2. The integration had gone too far and was partially rolled back.

In late 2011, Spotify also launched its "app platform," inviting external developers to create new features to be offered within the client. Some of the apps provided news or lyrics, others specialized in playlist recommendations or ticket sales. With this move, Spotify also created a symbiotic relation with a number of "media partners," including *Rolling Stone*, *Pitchfork*, and the *Guardian*. They would feature links to Spotify from their music-related articles, and it would not be far-fetched to imagine that these media partnerships also affected the news reporting about Spotify.[87] Finally, in this period, Spotify also developed a new radio function to replace one based on music genres dating back to the beta period. But there was still no personalization of Spotify Radio; the listener first had to select an artist to be given the option of listening to a "Related Artists" station.

The Reinvention of Radio

Spotify's launch in the United States meant that it began competing with a number of music streaming services that were not available in Europe. The year after its US launch also happened to be a year when these services began to compete in a new way. One reason for this was the increased hype around Pandora Internet Radio, as it began trading on the New York Stock Exchange in June 2011, exactly one month before Spotify launched its service in America. This raised the question of whether Pandora and Spotify were direct competitors or wholly different services.

While both were indeed music streaming services, Pandora differed from Spotify by not being an on-demand service.[88] The user could not select individual tracks or build playlists but was instead supposed to lean back and enjoy a personalized radio station. Pandora also was far ahead of Spotify when it came to data analysis and was widely recognized as the best music recommendation service. Until this point, Spotify had not prioritized the "lean back" experience. This may be partly related to the fact that Europeans do not spend as much time in the car as Americans do. The main explanation, however, relates to copyright policy. In the United States, a streaming service without on-demand functionality may be classified as radio and therefore does not need to strike licensing deals with each record company. It would simply pay a certain royalty to a collecting society, SoundExchange. The result was that Pandora had to pay much less than Spotify for every minute of music streaming and hence could stick to an advertising-based business model. It also meant that Pandora could not expand beyond those few nations with a similar copyright system.

Pandora asserted that Spotify was not a competitor but "largely complementary"—and circulated a statement attributed to Daniel Ek that supported this view: "Daniel Ek says he thinks Spotify is the future of the record store, and that Pandora is the future of radio."[89] Interestingly, this was an attempt to enlist media history in a commercial effort to fence off a future market for media services. Yet this historical divide was already in the process of collapsing, resulting in intensified competition. It also mirrored a shift in the relationship between the tech giants that took place around 2011. If corporations like Google, Apple, Facebook, and Amazon had previously focused on wholly different products—sometimes even partnering with one another—they now expanded their field of operations so that they were pitted against one another as direct competitors.[90]

In the field of music streaming, services such as Slacker and Rara were already trying to combine the two models—radio and on-demand—within one interface. During the spring of 2012, a new service named Songza created a lot of hype for "falling right into that sweet spot between Spotify and Pandora." Songza had no viable business model, and a few years later, the service would be discontinued after Google acquired the company. But its approach to music recommendation would have an enormous influence on Spotify's subsequent trajectory. Songza did not ask the user to search for a favorite song or artist, or even to choose between genres. Instead, the guiding concepts were *activity* and *mood* (a tactic we will discuss in detail in chapter 3). Depending on the personal profile, the time of day, and the day of the week, Songza would give the user a choice between six different activities, each represented by an icon. For example, on a Wednesday morning, Songza could offer a choice between work, exercise, or staying in bed and then provide a soundtrack for this activity. Possible choices for a late Friday night could include "Making Out," "Getting High," or "Bedtime."

Figure 1.3

Activities could also be filtered by the selection of a predefined mood, such as "Aggressive" or "Introspective." The resulting playlists would be put together by Songza's own music experts. This focus on human curation was, at the time, seen as a unique selling point for Songza in its competition with Pandora and Spotify, which had both put efforts into developing algorithmic systems for music recommendation.[91]

During 2012, a new consensus emerged among music industry commentators: streaming services would henceforth compete with the best music recommendation features. Not long before, Spotify had been praised for being clean and simple. Now it was criticized by some for being "just a huge database of songs" and not assisting its users in choosing the right music.[92] *Billboard* wrote about "the resurgence of radio" and pointed to the multitude of startups involved in reinventing this old format by trying to

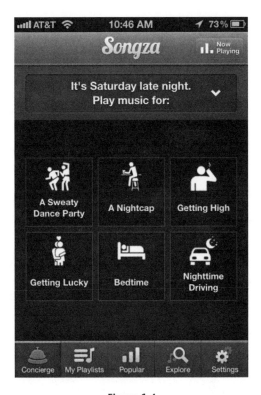

Figure 1.4
An influence on Spotify's later mood boards, Songza's mobile interface offered "activities" at different times of the week. Screenshots from 2012.

make it either personalized, mood-based, or local—and sometimes even by mixing music with news and weather reports. According to *Billboard*, this was all because of "the fact that people love to simply lean back and listen." Hence, Spotify's "lean forward" approach suddenly began to appear as a weakness rather than a strength.[93]

Period E (2013)

At the end of 2012, Daniel Ek made several statements indicating that Spotify would now adjust its ambitions for what a music service should deliver to its users. In 2012, the focus had been on growth in numbers, but 2013 would be the year for Spotify to address a very different issue: "The abundance of choice. How do you make sense out of 20 million songs?"[94] Until this point, Spotify had followed the on-demand doctrine, which tended to ignore the question of meaning making. The user was treated as a sovereign individual who already knew precisely what music he or she preferred to hear. Spotify's task was simply to respond to a request from the user, providing "whatever you want, whenever you want it." The individualism of this approach had been somewhat moderated by the "social turn" of Spotify, yet in effect, *social* was a term defined by a few dominant services and platforms, in particular Facebook.

For most of 2012, when Ek was asked about how Spotify would address the abundance of choice, he would hint at a social solution. According to the doctrine of social music discovery, friends would successfully help one another navigate the abundance of music, provided that the service allowed for frictionless sharing. But what if your friends had bad taste? Toward the end of the year, Ek shifted tactics and recognized the need for authority: "Here's what our users are telling us: Spotify is great when you know what music you want to listen to, but not so great when you don't.... The biggest unsolved question for most users is, how can you help me figure out what I'm going to listen to? And for artists, it's, how am I going to be heard?"[95]

Spotify's first solution was presented in December 2012, when it introduced a new, personalized recommendation function that would provide each user with "the most relevant content," as well as the ability to "follow" musical suggestions by "artists, trendsetters, editors and experts."[96] This was a step away from the symmetrical sociality of Facebook (where friendship is a two-way relation) toward the asymmetrical following system that characterizes Twitter (where a small number of users tend to become hugely influential).[97] "Now you can get music recommendations from only your most trusted musical influences," Spotify wrote in a press release.[98] In other words: friends cannot always be trusted to recommend the best music for you. Curating millions of songs was a task too large to be left to users.

The introduction of new discovery functions, however, was far from an innovative move. On the contrary, Spotify was rather late to follow this trend in the music streaming market. But when it finally did recognize that there were limits to the on-demand doctrine, Spotify changed its business strategy. The company gradually reoriented itself toward the aim of providing not only access to music but also recommendations for music that users would not have requested themselves. This meant that Spotify began to transform itself from being a simple *distributor* of music to the *producer* of a unique service. At the time, the nature of this service was still not clearly defined, but it began to take shape through a series of acquisitions that were made possible by the hundreds of millions of dollars that investors were willing to throw at Spotify. This time, the funding round was led by Goldman Sachs and also included the Coca-Cola Company, which had entered a marketing partnership with Spotify.

The first company acquired by Spotify, in May 2013, was Tunigo. For two years, this service had provided Spotify users with playlists based not only on genres but also on specific activities or moods, curated by a small team of music experts—clearly inspired by Songza. Tunigo had already been the object of much hype on Spotify's official blog and was one of the original apps when Spotify launched its app platform. After the acquisition, Tunigo's features were integrated into the Spotify client. In a larger perspective, this marked an incipient retreat from the platform strategy; significantly, the app platform that Spotify had launched in late 2011 would be dismantled in 2014. Tunigo had about twenty employees who would form the core of a new unit within Spotify. They would be joined by a growing number of "music editors" recruited to create local playlists for each country where Spotify was available.[99] This *curatorial turn* took some time to implement but can clearly be traced through Spotify's job listings, which were preserved by the Internet Archive. A snapshot from January 2013, for example, lists seventy-seven jobs, of which the vast majority were in tech development.

None of these jobs involved music curation.[100] In fact, it was not until 2014 that Spotify began recruiting people in different countries for positions such as "Music Editor/Playlist Curator":

> At Spotify, our vision is to provide the perfect music for every moment. ... We're growing our world-class music curation and editorial team and are looking for a multi-talented self starter, go-getter with limitless ambition and an undeniable hunger for progress and passion for music. This role calls for someone who can identify and execute the best music playlist listening experiences for a multitude of moods, moments, and genres, has a passion for performance-oriented analytics, and has her/his ears to the ground in the music community.[101]

Part of this job would also be to try out "playlist hypotheses, i.e. the perfect running playlist or music for a date night or a dinner with friends."[102] Running, dating, dining—these were indeed typical "moments" for Spotify, and by deploying such terms, it followed Instagram, Twitter, Tinder, and other popular apps.[103] Spotify even appropriated Tunigo's slogan: "Music for every moment." Indeed, it came to suggest something quite different from its previous slogan: "Music whenever you want it, wherever you are."

The early Spotify saw its task as providing access to music, filling the life of consumers with more music, as if they felt a need to remedy a general lack of music. But around 2013, Spotify's curatorial turn reconceived its product based on a different image of the consumer. Now the selling point was to provide not more music but *better* music. This meant, however, that Spotify needed to somehow define musical quality, something that it had so far avoided doing. The service had to steer a way between pure relativism (i.e., each individual has her own standard for what is good music) and pure absolutism (i.e., certain pieces of music are inherently better than others). This polarity was transcended by the idea that musical quality is dependent on context. This is a utilitarian approach in which music is understood as functional for certain activities, as we will demonstrate in chapter 3.

Period F (2013–2015)

The amount of venture capital invested in Spotify in each funding round continued to increase, not linearly but exponentially. In November 2013, a venture capital firm that had been active in Silicon Valley since 1995, Technology Crossover Ventures (TCV), made its biggest investment ever: $250 million. Proportional to the equity, the deal was read as a valuation of Spotify at over \$4 billion.[104] The high numbers could be interpreted as a bet on world domination for a company that, paradoxically, was not even close to being profitable. This tremendous elevation also made it improbable that Spotify could be acquired by a firm other than Facebook, Apple, or Google. Conversely, from then on Spotify would often be rumored as a possible acquirer of other music services, such as Pandora or SoundCloud.

As the sole investor in this massive funding round, TCV likely had some influence over Spotify's strategic priorities for 2014, which followed a distinct pattern. Spotify did expand to a few large countries: the Philippines, Brazil, and Canada. It also started a subsidiary in Russia and probably invested a lot of money in launching its service there—only to withdraw again because of Russia's economic crisis and its new, repressive internet legislation.[105] Above all, however, Period F was characterized by consolidation and centralization of the service. A truly significant change, enacted in Spring 2014, was Spotify's dismantling of its P2P network, which until then had guaranteed its supply of bandwidth.[106] From the very beginning, Spotify had provided users with a remarkably fast service and avoided paying market price for the bandwidth by harnessing the resources of those same users. It was a technology that Spotify had patented and that made the service different from other music streaming platforms. Now, with hundreds of millions of dollars, Spotify could finally maintain its own servers for the distribution of music.

The shutdown of one of the internet's largest P2P networks, which was then replaced by central servers, must be considered a major infrastructural event. Yet it was hardly recognized by ordinary Spotify users and was not even communicated on the company's blog probably because the move toward centralization did not fit the company's preferred image.[107] Not only was the P2P network silently dismantled but so was the app platform. This was a platform Spotify had once described as "the next big step in musical enjoyment,"[108] yet it took less than two years for Spotify to stop accepting new apps.[109] Some of the most popular app features were copied or acquired, as in the case of Tunigo.

During the spring of 2014, Spotify made its second acquisition: the music analysis firm Echo Nest. The Echo Nest was known for powering the algorithmic recommendations in Spotify, as well as in several of Spotify's competitors. The acquisition may be read as yet another move toward centralizing the infrastructure of streamed music. While it was said that the Echo Nest would continue to serve all of its existing customers, Spotify's acquisition was obviously considered a move to fend off competition. In fact, after just one week, Spotify's competitor Rdio abandoned the Echo Nest and had to find another supplier of music intelligence.[110]

Spotify seemingly preferred to challenge other streaming services in the arena of personalized recommendations. But later in 2014, another kind of competition arose. Taylor Swift, the superstar singer-songwriter, made a public statement and withdrew all her music from Spotify. In a later op-ed for the *Wall Street Journal*, she complained that Spotify's free service was undermining the value of music and expressed the opinion that an album should have a price.[111] Her move was explicitly anti Spotify, since rival services such as Rdio were still allowed to stream her albums (other than the most recent one). "Swiftgate," as this incident soon became known, marked the beginning of a new kind of competition over the exclusivity of content that would intensify in the coming years.

Period G (2015–2016)

After much anticipation, Apple finally launched its own music streaming service, Apple Music, in June 2015. Late to join the streaming market, Apple's obvious advantage was the control of a line of hardware, as well as its App Store. Furthermore, Apple could afford to accept even larger losses than Spotify—and for a longer time. Spotify's response was to try setting different terms for competition. The tone was set a month before Apple Music's launch, at an event in New York City in May 2015—an event that we will describe in detail in chapter 4. If there was one common factor in the new features presented there, it was Spotify's attempt to become much more than a mere distributor of music.

A typical example was the premiere of Spotify Running, a new feature that used the smartphone's sensors to detect the pace of a runner and play music at the same speed. Spotify also started cooperating with electronic music producers to create special compositions that could change or be rearranged according to the pace of running. This amounted to the establishment of a new musical format, beyond recorded music in the usual sense. Without a doubt, this feature was an attempt by Spotify to move beyond the realm of distribution toward becoming a *producer* of unique musical experiences. "Music is moving away from genres," Ek said at the May 2015 event. Spotify sought to compete with Apple Music by providing more sophisticated curation of playlists, tailored for "the moment." Beyond mere personalization, the algorithms would also take into account spatial data (where you are), temporal data (the day of the week, the season of the year), and maybe even the weather. If the assumption had previously been that musical taste is a property of the individual, now Spotify seemed to implicitly accept the view that it is rather "an aggregate of the supra- and the subpersonal."[112] The new recipe for delivering the best recommendations followed from two key acquisitions, first Tunigo (expert curation) and then the Echo Nest (algorithmic curation).

At the event in May, Spotify also declared its intention to go beyond music and offer other types of media, such as videos and podcasts. Videos were to be presented by a number of selected media partners, which included a cadre of major American television networks. To deliver all those features, and to compete with Apple in general, would not be cheap, so early in the summer of 2015, Spotify took in half a billion dollars in a Series G funding round led by Swedish telecommunication giant TeliaSonera. This was more money than in all previous rounds combined, and the investment resulted in Spotify's valuation more than doubling, from $4 billion to $8.5 billion.[113] As soon as the money was secured, Spotify acquired yet another music intelligence company, Seed Scientific—with Apple Music as one of its customers. It was clear that Spotify hoped to succeed by building a service on the most advanced algorithmic recommendation systems and to fend off its rival from music intelligence suppliers.

Apple responded by presenting its music service as a warmer and more "human" alternative, compared to the allegedly all-too-algorithmic Spotify. While Apple Music emphasized its radio station Beats 1, where human DJs play mostly mainstream pop, this positioning of man against machine should be taken with a grain of salt. Within industrial capitalism, all commodity production infers the combination of labor power and machinery; this holds equally for the production of curation as a commodity.[114] The question is mostly one of the proportion between human and algorithmic curation. Spotify has continued to hire music editors with expert knowledge in local culture, even as it invests in technology for "music intelligence."

In the summer of 2015, these efforts resulted in the introduction of "Discover Weekly," a playlist of personalized music recommendations delivered every Monday to each user of Spotify. This was a highly successful addition to the service and an important lever for success in the music industry.

A year later, it was reported that a significant proportion of Spotify's users—no longer "trapped behind a search box"—were regularly listening to "Discover Weekly" and also adding its tracks to personal playlists. "Discover Weekly" would be followed by more weekly playlist offerings: "Fresh Finds" and "Release Radar."[115]

For users of Spotify, the discovery of new music thus became scheduled for specific weekdays, which is reminiscent of traditional radio. It was first remediated by Songza, then copied by Tunigo, and subsequently integrated into the heart of the "new" Spotify. However, not every bid was successful. Spotify's attempt to integrate video was a failure, especially considering the great amount of money it had invested in efforts to enlist major media partners, who only provided content for a short while. Moreover, competing with Apple obviously requires enormous resources. In the beginning of 2016, Spotify therefore began to accept funding in the form of convertible debt. This meant that instead of receiving shares in Spotify, investors were given the promise that they could buy shares at a certain discount in the future, at a time when Spotify was expected to finally make its stock market launch. If the launch was to be delayed—in this case, beyond 2017—the interest rate would rise incrementally.

Toward an IPO

As a particular form of credit, convertible debt—which many consider quite risky—has created a very strong incentive for Spotify to transform itself into a publicly traded company. And no small amount of debt was taken in 2016, as $1.5 billion is roughly equal to the total amount invested in the company before that year. As of early 2018, Spotify had spent much of its money on a virtual shopping spree, acquiring ever-more technology companies with very different focuses. All these acquisitions give indications of Spotify's future trajectory, but it is still too early to integrate these in the broader company history of Spotify. For now, we can say only that Spotify was finally introduced at the New York Stock Exchange on April 3, 2018, as this book was going through its last round of edits.

This chapter has charted the business and media history of Spotify in some detail. While it is probably the first academic account of this sort, it is not the only possible one. Other scholars might choose to write Spotify's history from the perspective of the music industry or with a focus on individual executives within the company, for example. Here, we have instead structured the narrative in a way that highlights Spotify's dependence on venture capital and rights holders, which makes it surprisingly precarious. Rather than being an autonomous innovator with a divine power to shape the future of music, we have shown how Spotify has often been rather late to follow trends set by others. Several times, the service has proudly introduced new features, only to dismantle them shortly thereafter. The core business model has also changed several times: first it was not specifically about music, then it was about free and ad-supported music, and then the free service was reconceived as a way to market the subscription service. For many years, Spotify's interface was based on the idea of a user always possessing perfect knowledge of her own musical preferences, but then the curatorial turn occurred and personalized music recommendations gradually became the central feature.

Rather than positing the analog against the digital, or seeking to characterize some innate characteristics of streaming, we have highlighted a turning point in the development of Spotify and other streaming services, where music discovery becomes the main theme of competition. As noted early in this chapter, at the time of its launch in 2008, Spotify inscribed itself in a particular media history, making itself appear as the successor to the record store. A few years later, however, music streaming services began to rediscover the heritage of radio, and Spotify followed this trend. Yet we find that this shift is not reflected in much scholarship, where "music streaming" appears as a stable technological condition. The business history of Spotify, to which this chapter contributes, shows how the service first conceived of itself as a technology company working with digital distribution while not being particularly about music. More recently, Spotify has attempted to move beyond a distribution-oriented company profile by transforming into a producer of unique music-related experiences. This shift has coincided with a curatorial turn, in which the best music is the music that is best suited for a given context. This curatorial turn includes a localization of music recommendations, which are produced by music curators employed at Spotify's national offices. Finally, we must note that Spotify, after years of international expansion, is still a rather Western service—significantly more so than competitors such as Deezer or Apple Music. Spotify is still not available anywhere in the Middle East or Africa (except in Israel and South Africa, where it launched in 2018), nor in Russia, India, Korea, or mainland China.

Intervention: Record Label Setup

In October 2014, the album *Election Music* by Heinz Duthel was uploaded to services such as Spotify, iTunes, and Google Play. The album consisted of one electronic tune that had been modified thirteen times according to the voting results in different municipalities in the 2014 Swedish government election. The tempo had been adjusted on each track according to the number of voters in specific voting districts, so that a high number of registered voters corresponded to a fast beat, and a low number of voters corresponded to a slow beat. Specific instruments in the tunes had also been paired with particular political parties, making it possible to "listen to" local voting results and compare tracks with one another. Hence, album listeners could, for example, detect the slow pace (and thus the low number of voters) on the track "Rinkeby," a low-income suburb on the outskirts of Stockholm. Listeners could also discover how this track differed from the much faster rhythm on the track "Hörken," a small rural county in midwestern Sweden with many registered voters. On "Hörken," the prominent sound of a siren also indicated the local success of the extreme right-wing party Sverigedemokraterna (Swedish Democrats), which hit historic records in the 2014 election.

As readers may know, Heinz Duthel had already made a name for himself in 2008, when he appeared as the author of over two hundred books, many of which are still available for purchase on Amazon or through Apple's iBooks store. Duthel's collected works include biographies of Adolf Hitler, Angela Merkel, Pablo Picasso, Muhammed Ali, Joseph Stalin, and Charles Darwin, as well as writings on topics such as anarchism, the internet drug trade, cosmic intelligence, dementia, the philosophy of mathematics, alternative medicine, dialectical materialism, conspiracy theories, the Great Depression, and Thai

Figure 1.5
Self-produced "music" for research purposes: in 2014, the authors of this book
released the album *Election Music* under the *nom de plume* Heinz Duthel.

massage.[1] One of Duthel's publications in particular caused a debate in 2010,
when it turned out that Amazon was still marketing and selling his e-book
entitled *WikiLeaks Documents Expose US Foreign Policy Conspiracies: All Cables
with Tags from 1 to 5000*, even though Amazon had just expelled WikiLeaks
from its servers in protest of its release of classified government documents.[2]
Much like the rest of Duthel's releases, this book was essentially a reprint
of content scraped from the web and thus the product of algorithmically
aided bot-authorship. Heinz Duthel is most likely a software agent designed
to mass produce literature—albeit a bot writer with a particular taste for classical historical figures, foreign politics, and new age spirituality.[3]

The person behind the album *Election Music*, however, was not "Heinz
the bot." Instead, the release was part of an intervention that aimed to
study the back end of streaming services by launching a record label—and
self-produced "music"—for research purposes. The Heinz Duthel album was
originally conceived as a starting point for spamming Spotify with obscure
sound materials. In the Duthel case, the music concerned the odd sound-
scapes of Swedish election results. In other cases, we have played with the
idea of extracting audio advertisements from Spotify and then "feeding" the
same ads back into the Spotify system by uploading it in distorted versions.

Such efforts have been grounded in a desire to study the power dynamics of streamed music aggregation and distribution. Who or what decides what counts—or does not count—as music on Spotify? By which mechanisms are streamed sound materials filtered, selected, and handled?

One starting point for these record label interventions has been the recognition that digital corporations such as Spotify are not always open to inspection. Hence, to investigate how sounds are inserted into streamed distribution circuits, we produced and distributed our own music. We were thereby approaching and learning about the service in similar ways as aspiring musicians. Rooted in autoethnographic methods and building on the tradition of "breaching experiments" in ethnomethodology,[4] these interventions have helped us gain knowledge about the transformations and adjustments that sounds and/or music undergo in order to become "streamed music experiences." Similar to autoethnographic work, our record label experiments can be considered a type of "heuristic device, [and] a metaphorical learning tool" that lies in between practices of representing and performing experience.[5] Following Celia Lury and Nina Wakeford, our objective has been to use research methods that not only investigate the social world but engage in it; that not only report on events but act on them; that not only happen but make things happen; and that are not only the source of making but also unmaking, remaking, and picking apart.[6] By creating our own nonprofit record label, we were interested in critically describing the workings of Spotify's back end through our own personal experiences. This process has also allowed us to study unexpected file "behavior," aggregation platform strategies, processes of music (de)valuation, and the infrastructures that make these possible.

To date, our record label experiments have resulted in four different releases on major streaming services and online outlets for music. Apart from *Election Music*, we have released a self-titled EP of breakfast recordings by the pseudonymous Fru Kost (*frukost* means "breakfast" in Swedish), a recording from the Stockholm Metro Line 17 one morning in October 2014, and a full-length album by the Ethnologist entitled *The Silence of Scholarly Life*. In all of these releases, we have departed from the notion that fraud and trickery are inherent parts of digital technologies and have explored the boundaries and implications of this fact. Thus, our sounds have purposefully taken place alongside the spam and clones that currently populate services such as Spotify—for example, the music originating from the Birthday Song Crew, who have released about 1,400 different versions of the classic "Happy Birthday" song (including reggae, jazz, dancehall, and "hillbilly" variants).

Originally designed to coexist with such controversial cases of streamed music content (that is, content that challenges notions of what quality music is), our sound materials can be described as planned interferences with aesthetic conventions. With the exception of the album *Election Music*—an album that actually contains songs with a beat and melody—all of our sounds have deliberately foiled expectations about the kind of content that can be found on services such as Spotify. This has primarily been done in order expose some of the service's underlying norms and conventions. By attempting to release unappealing and mundane sound recordings, we have aimed to shed light on the rationalities of abundance that mark streaming services, as well as the logics by which sound recordings compete on growing digital archives for music. Does Spotify care about what type of content ends up in its archive? Or is the enterprise built on the notion of the more, the better?

Another aim of the record label endeavors has been to gain hands-on experience of the industrial processing of cultural data that takes place at the initial stages of streamed music's life journey. Our record label experiments have allowed us to monitor, in detail, how recorded sounds are aggregated, packaged, and shipped as cultural goods. This has involved close engagements with music aggregators, since most commercial streaming services do not accept direct music submissions from artists and instead rely on aggregators' ability to act as corporate middlemen who manage all direct contact between artists and streaming services.[7] While a service such as Spotify may appear as the primary host for streamed music, it only represents the tip of a much larger iceberg of actors who are involved in filling, organizing, and overseeing streamed music archives. So how did our record label experiments begin, and what did we learn about Spotify in the experimental process?

As it turns out, having music launched on Spotify is not always a straightforward process. After recording a series of sounds, our search for suitable aggregators who were willing to distribute them began on Spotify's website, which lists a series of recommended aggregators. Initially, we explored the deals offered by TuneCore, IndigoBoom, RouteNote, and CD Baby. Like most music aggregators, these companies either charge musicians an annual fee for distributing their sounds or distribute music against a certain percentage of future revenue. Even though we eventually managed to sign a deal with an aggregator for all of our releases, the process of doing so revealed the arbitrary methods by which music is approved for commercial streaming services. For instance, we found that our album *Fru Kost*—which contained a recording of breakfast sounds, such as the sound of coffee being poured—was rejected twice on our first attempt to have it released. Once, we were kindly and politely told that this was "not the kind of content" the aggregator was looking to sign up at the moment. Another time, our sounds were rejected with a blunt notification stating that the distributor in question "only distributes music." Whether a human or an automatic software system was behind this editorial decision remains unknown, yet the initial rejections that we received indicate that music aggregators are gatekeepers who perform the job of cleaning, sorting, and selecting which types of sounds end up on platforms such as Spotify. Thereby, they also play a crucial role in deciding what counts, or does not count, as music in today's digital landscape. Music aggregators such as Record Union—a service that ended up accepting our breakfast sounds against a $20 yearly fee—claim to "liberate music" and "democratize the access to global digital distribution." However, their very existence indicates that the Spotification of media has raised new and fuzzy barriers around digital music, as compared to earlier "open" Web 2.0 sites, such as Myspace. We also learned that what binds these aggregator companies together is not only their financial setup but also the strategies by which they prepare music and artists for entering digital marketplaces. One has to go through several standardized vetting processes before any songs or albums can be submitted. Our careful documentation of these procedures has been a key source of insight into how music streaming infrastructures operate today.

For one, we learned that signing up with an aggregator involves taking several steps to name and categorize sound content, steps that are central to the process of making digital music searchable and commodifiable. Before we could submit our sounds, the aggregator RouteNote asked us to choose between thirty-nine different genre specifications, which were organized in two steps: "first genre" and "second genre." These options included traditional genres, such as "Electronic" and "Instrumental," but also more curious genres, such as "Anime," "Indian," "Fitness & Workout," "Enka," and "Kayokyoku"—not to mention "German Pop" and "German Folk." Such genre attributions speak to the micropolitics of (self-)representation that artists are encouraged to participate in. (*Not* attributing a genre to our sounds wasn't an option.) This highlights that genres continue to matter, despite repeated modernist claims that genres have lost their importance in relation to the contemporary music scene.[8] Music metadata, such as genre specifications, fundamentally influence how streamed music moves and is displayed, not least because metadata underlie music recommendation algorithms and other automatized ways of bundling musical pieces together. Recorded music simply needs metadata and paratextual materials, or else it is extremely difficult to find or sell. Within the ecosystem of music streaming, aggregators perform the crucial role of prompting and collecting such music metadata, thus making music and artists "algorithm ready."[9]

Yet aggregators do not just collect metadata from individual artists when they sign a contract. They are also responsible for assembling pieces of metadata from other more obscure and centralized sources. Once our different sounds had been uploaded, for example, we were struck by the lack of descriptive and contextual data surrounding our music, such as who we were and where our music came from. Given the extensive amount of information we had provided to our aggregators, this seemed somewhat paradoxical. Even though our sounds were available on Spotify and other services, we were not in charge of our own artist pages. In fact, there was no possibility at all for us to directly intervene in how our music was being presented by textual and visual means. The process of adding artist biographies also proved to be tedious, since control over artist metadata is frequently outsourced in several steps. Indeed, music metadata now forms an industry in itself, as is shown by the multitude of companies that deal with such data.

For instance, we found out that Spotify gathers its artist biographies from AllMusic, a website that provides reviews, search functions, and recommendations concerning music. In turn, AllMusic extracts its artist biographies from TiVo (formerly Rovi and Macrovision). TiVo was in full ownership of AllMusic until 2013, when it sold off the consumer access side to All Media Network, while still controlling its content licenses.[10] TiVo now specializes in metadata provision, intellectual property management, and analytics provision within the culture industries. Since its inception in 1983, the company has been a major player in antipiracy debates over copyright protection. TiVo can be described as an "infomediary," that is, a company that monitors, collects, and controls information about cultural products in ways that affect how users find and experience them.[11] To adjust how our sound materials were presented on Spotify—and other streaming services—we would therefore need to get into direct contact with a global metadata corporation that is in control of large-scale music metadata archives and databases.

Nowadays, it is possible to submit artist biographies to TiVo via email. But in the fall of 2014, when we first tried to have our sounds released, TiVo only accepted physical copies of artist information that were sent to its headquarters in Santa Clara, California. According to the instructions then available, every submission was supposed to contain a press kit, including an artist biography, photographs of the musician(s), and physical copies of the music concerned. TiVo (or Rovi, as the company was called at the time) then promised to save and distribute all the information it had been provided, including the recorded music, for future purposes. On one occasion, we made an attempt to send such a press kit—including a recorded CD—to the office in Santa Clara, although the letter must have been rejected or lost along the way, since the biographical details were never updated on any streaming services. The difficulties in taking control of our artist biographies reveal how a small number of actors have secured a vital role in regulating narratives around streamed music. While Spotify may be the end point where such metadata is presented to the public, the same data is collected, stored, and managed by a number of other services.

From a slightly different angle, we have also used distributed sounds as a basis for investigating the financial logics and premises of streaming services. For example, the release of breakfast sounds by Fru Kost was used to critically assess the issue of limited payouts to artists. This was done by examining if it was possible to analyze Spotify's business model by

Figure 1.6
Swedish breakfast recordings were released under the pseudonym Fru Kost (*frukost* is "breakfast" in Swedish)—self-produced "music" for research purposes uploaded through the music aggregator Record Union. Notably, the popularity of the song "Katte" (coffee) was mainly due to our multiple preprogrammed bots.

automating fake Spotify listeners. The experiment resembled a Turing test, in which we asked ourselves what happens *when*—not *if*—streaming bots approximate human listener behavior in such a way that it becomes impossible to distinguish between a human and a machine. Does Spotify care if humans or machines are listening to its music? And in what ways are such differentiations nestled within streamed financial logics?

At Humlab, we therefore set up a so-called SpotiBot experiment, in which we programmed multiple bots to repeatedly play one of our self-distributed sounds: the song "Kaffe" (coffee) by Fru Kost.[12] Our record label releases thus became a testing ground for exploring Spotify's infrastructure for royalty payments. In detail, the bots that did the "listening" were scripted algorithms that exhibited human-like behavior. Using Web UI testing frameworks, the SpotiBot engine roughly consisted of three hundred bots that were put into action in approximately fifty parallel Spotify sessions. These bots were simultaneously put on a fixed repetition scheme that involved listening to a selected song and ran from one hundred to n times using different Spotify Free bot accounts. At the time, the registration of these accounts was easily automated since Spotify did not require any CAPTCHAs to be solved. As is well known, the original Turing test questioned whether a human could distinguish between a person and a machine.[13] In our case, Spotify's algorithms were instead implicitly challenged to make this distinction. Our bots interacted with the Spotify system, which tried to decide (via various unknown fraud detection tools) if communication was human or machine based.

One of the major controversies regarding the transition to music streaming services has centered on payouts to artists. With revenue (in USD) steadily increasing into the billions in 2017, music streaming is now the beating heart of the music business, yet many artists struggle with reduced royalties.[14] A heated discussion has focused on the issue of whether or not music streaming will be able to generate a sustainable income for musicians. Statistics on streamed royalty payouts vary and are difficult to find, since agreements and contracts are exclusive and proprietary. In addition, playlists have become increasingly important as a gateway regulating royalty; i.e. an artist who is not featured on a certain playlist gets zero revenue. Estimates, however, usually state that revenue per played track runs as low as $0.005 at Spotify.[15] Within the music industry, this has led to considerable debate. Most famously, Taylor Swift decided to remove her entire back catalog from Spotify in 2014, arguing principally that the ad-supported Spotify Free devalued her music (even if she later, during the summer of 2017 put all her music back again). As we discussed in chapter 1, confidential agreements and record label contracts with Spotify differ, but royalties are usually disbursed to artists (or more precisely, aggregators or record labels) once a song is registered as a play, which generally happens after thirty seconds—hence, the "thirty second royalty rule." Therefore, our hypothesis was that playing Fru Kost tracks repeatedly for twenty-five seconds would not be a problem, since such plays would not involve any financial transactions and would hence be of little interest to fraud detectors. If our bots would play a song for more than thirty seconds though, we suspected that Spotify would be more cautious about evaluating and securing the "humanness" of the registered users.

To our surprise, however, our SpotiBot engine was able to play Fru Kost tracks repeatedly for both twenty-five and thirty-five seconds. The bot "selenium57," for example, played Fru Kost's "Kaffe" 229 times; the "selenium_bot," as many as 1,141 times. That is, after thirty-five seconds of "Kaffe," the bots started playing the song again, and again, and again. It is important to note that the experiment did not run completely smoothly, and many of our bots did not "listen" to the exact amount of repeated plays they had been programmed to perform.[16] Yet the intervention did demonstrate that it was possible to automatically and repeatedly play tracks on Spotify via bots. The experiment further showed that no major difference existed between our bots playing an artist such as Fru Kost for twenty-five or thirty-five seconds. In Spotify's system, it seemed as though both listening sessions were simply treated as plays, since we could closely monitor our own royalty payments. While the experiment only generated a meager $6.28, each play was registered and archived properly via the aggregator Record Union. In other words, Spotify did not seem to care whether a computer or a human was listening to its music archive. Or at least, it appeared as though the company had not taken any serious steps to make sure that such a distinction could be made. Our Fru Kost experiment raises several ethical issues; we were, after all, contravening some of Spotify's user agreements. However, we never cashed the royalty check generated by our experiment. After the intervention, during the summer of 2016, Spotify also started using CAPTCHAs as well as reCAPTCHAs with image identification, allegedly to better protect its system. Repeating the same experiment after that change would have been considerably more difficult.

As a last comment, our record label experiments and interventions have also given us an awareness of the migratory lives of streamed music files—migrations into digital spheres that go beyond the reach of aggregator analytics tools. As it turns out, our sounds have rarely stayed in place and, instead, have taken on a kind of second life on the web. About a year after our first releases, some of our music had completely disappeared from the services where we first put them, simply because we forgot to renew our aggregator contracts. This is a problem that we suspect many artists deal with, and it illustrates how subscription logic for streaming platforms affects not only music consumption but also artistry.

Our album *The Silence of Scholarly Life* by the Ethnologist, for example, never really succeeded in attracting listeners, yet it had an interesting afterlife. During the year it was available on Spotify (2015), songs from the album were played a meager sixty times in total. Most of the streams occurred at the time of the album launch (and most likely because we played it ourselves). When the album was removed from Spotify due to an unrenewed subscription, however, it did not disappear completely. Instead, tracks from the album are still available for download on unauthorized websites. The site mp3red.me, for instance, at one point rated the track "The Dishes" as the best song on the album, claiming that "19 people think this track is stunning." And on the site Musixmatch, Portuguese lyrics were added to the nonvocal track "Lunch"—lyrics that upon closer inspection appear to originate from the song "Ela é tipo" by the Brazilian band Banda Swell. These types of unexpected appropriations reveal how the social lives of streamed music files stretch way beyond commercial platforms and are open to all kinds of reuses, rewirings, and recontextualizations. Through their entanglements with algorithms, global music metadata arrangements, and automatized web-scrapers, streamed music files get wrapped up in the whirlpools of data traffic that surround digital streams. The movements and appropriations of our sounds thereby testify to the fuzzy and porous boundaries of contemporary music streaming services.

2   When Do Files Become Music?

"Spotify paints it black." This message appeared on the Spotify company blog in January 2015, with the promise to bring phone users "the best-looking Spotify ever." The blog post claimed that, with the darker theme, playing your favorite music has "never looked so good." With its "refined interface," the new look "lets the content come forward and 'pop,' just like in a cinema when you dim the lights."[1]

Interfaces indeed pop forward—and, by doing so, hide their infrastructures. "When we purchase a device," anthropologist Lane DeNicola once noted in regard to the iPhone, "we are purchasing access to its 'surfaces,' a transient experience of use divorced from either internal mechanism or the particulars of production."[2] Transparent devices are highly intuitive, constituting an interface that rapidly disappears from our perception. The same holds true for a service such as Spotify, whose software and content are patented and copyrighted, whose standards and protocols are hidden, and whose graphical user interfaces are designed to make invisible the overcoming of any remaining barriers to downloading or file sharing, such as social interaction or technical skill.

This is not to say that listeners are unaware that experiencing music as software differs from listening to a CD or an LP. The "lean back" experience is less prominent. Online input is constantly needed. Active listeners are familiar with the prescriptive demands of the service and the ways that Spotify summons its users: "Know what you want to listen to? Just search and hit play. Go get the music. Check out, discover new tracks, and build the perfect collection." As Jeremy Wade Morris argues, music as software has introduced a new "technological relationship" to processes of search and discovery, listening and liking, exchanging or buying music. When streaming services code music and redefine it as a data-driven communicative form—with audio files and metadata being aggregated through various external intermediaries and with user-generated data being extracted from listening habits—the singularity of the music experience is transformed into what Morris has termed "a multimediated computing experience."[3]

Yet participating in multimediated computing experiences does not necessarily entail an awareness of the broader digital communication infrastructure of which Spotify is a part or of the sociopolitical environment in which this communication originated and to which it is addressed. In order to understand the logic and rationale of streaming services such as Spotify, we need to ask what exactly happens when data are turned into music and vice versa. The focus of this second chapter, therefore, is to find out what happens beneath the shiny black and green surface of Spotify's interfaces, or how music streaming is *infrastructured*. We speak of digital media infrastructure in a broad, inclusive sense of material and sociotechnical forms that allow for the possibility of exchange over space, and we understand *infrastructuring* as a process whereby this exchange is initiated, managed, and observed.[4] While the first chapter has followed the hype and mapped it over an investment timeline, the second chapter thus peels off a further layer, as it discusses Spotify's diversified data infrastructures and critically examines what happens prior to and during the computational experience of "listening" to files becoming music. After sketching out the contours of this process based on publicly accessible information gathered via trade journals and company blogs, among other sources, the chapter concludes with a first experimental case study.

Following the Data

Research on the cultural implications of software—whether in the form of software studies, digital humanities, platform studies, or media archaeology—has repeatedly stressed the need for in-depth investigations of how computing technologies work, combined with meticulous descriptions of technical specificities. Our analyses of Spotify relate to such an interest in the specifics of the computational base—that is, the mathematical structures underlying programs and interfaces—and in technically specific ways of understanding the operations of material technologies.[5] Yet what is at stake is not a complete understanding of all mathematical concepts and models

driving these programs. The claim that studying culture through data necessitates "a thorough training in programming so as to allow researchers...to
'look' into the 'black box' of the technology...misses the mark," as Mirko
Tobias Schäfer and Karin van Es have argued.[6] Rather, as we have previously
described, our aim is to understand Spotify's data infrastructures sufficiently
to approach the software with novel research questions, critical discussions,
and productive experiments.

As discussed in the introduction to this book, media environments today
are "increasingly essential to our daily lives (infrastructures)," yet they are
often "dominated by corporate entities (platforms)."[7] The relation between
these two concepts remains tricky, if not dialectical, with most scholars opting
for either platforms or infrastructures as a critical lens. Platform studies have
emphasized the dual nature of commercial platforms. YouTube, Facebook,
and Twitter support innovation and creativity but also regulate and curb participation, with the ultimate goal of producing profit for platform owners.[8] In
short, platform affordances simultaneously promote and constrain expression. Spotify, however, differs from other platforms. It is a service that caters
to record labels and artists by seeking to provide a regulated and commercialized streaming service with professional music, as opposed to an open
platform with user-generated content. Given these differences between
Spotify and SoundCloud or YouTube, the conceptual focus here will not be
on Spotify as a platform but rather on the infrastructuring of this service
and its environment: what technologies, data, and organizations have to
come together to make Spotify happen?

Spotify's proliferating data infrastructure includes more than meets the
eye. Its "event delivery system" is one of the foundational pieces of that
infrastructure. Most events that are produced within Spotify are directly
generated from millions of Spotify clients as a direct response to certain user
actions. All types of usage data can be defined as a set of structured events
that are caused at some point in time as a reaction to some predefined activity. Whenever a user performs an action in the Spotify client—say, listening
to a track or searching for an artist—a small piece of information (an event)
is sent to Spotify's servers. Event delivery, "the process of making sure that
all events get transported safely from clients all over the world" to the central processing system, is consequently a key requirement of Spotify's data
infrastructure.[9] But the latter is also dependent on actual music supplied
from outside the service. If one opens the "About Spotify" tab, for example,

it is strikingly apparent that music per se comes from elsewhere: "Content provided by" is followed by a series of logotypes for Universal Music Group, EMI, and Warner Music Group, among others.

As both Spotify researchers and listeners, we have repeatedly asked ourselves what types of data exchanges are mediated by the service and how these affect the ways in which music is distributed and consumed. The simple question of what a music or audio file is (or converts into) when being listened to has no simple answer, however. Data files become music on Spotify in various ways. Digital formats have made cultural commodities such as music "infinitely analyzable and quantifiable in ways that make them increasingly amenable to algorithmic exploitation."[10] Yet such numerical alterations at the back end remain invisible on the interface, or front end.

Sharing Data

Data exchange and interaction also occur constantly between Spotify and other companies, and it is these interactions that define what kind of service Spotify is. Spotify's cooperation with the music intelligence company Echo Nest can serve as a case in point, since it is a partnership that indicates how datafied music consumption came to alter the company. In chapter 1, we charted the development of Spotify in detail. Suffice it to say, the Echo Nest was important for instigating Spotify's data-driven music recommendation systems. Personalized music offerings were spearheaded by the American company Pandora Radio, however, which for a number of years was widely recognized as the best music recommendation service. Spotify's partnership with the Echo Nest initially concerned a similar radio function, and in a blog post in December 2011, it was announced that the company would now power Spotify Radio: "Thanks to Spotify's deal with The Echo Nest, users of the popular music service can now create streaming radio stations based on any artist or song on Spotify."[11] The cooperation developed, and in April 2012, Spotify began updating its desktop software with several new features, including a Pandora-like radio station. An online radio offering, it was proclaimed, "would advance Spotify's strategy of attracting users with free, ad-supported services who can be converted later into paying subscribers."[12] At the time, the Echo Nest did not exclusively power Spotify's radio recommendations. Since its application programming interface (API) was open, competitors such Rdio and Deezer were also using it. In March 2014,

Spotify acquired the Echo Nest, a deal that was said to strengthen its music discovery expertise and to "allow Spotify to leverage The Echo Nest's in-depth musical understanding and tools for curation to drive music discovery for millions of users around the globe."[13]

In recent years, Spotify has put a number of employees from the Echo Nest in charge of its most important discovery products. While Spotify's music discovery engine remains inaccessible to outside observers, Spotify itself also remains dependent on, if not conditioned by, actors outside of the service. As we have argued elsewhere, music distribution is increasingly driven by automated mechanisms that continuously capture, sort, and analyze large amounts of web-based data. Music metadata management and data ca(t)ching mechanisms powered by the Echo Nest have been key for the development of Spotify, with audio files constantly being linked and woven together with contextual information.

The partnership between Spotify and the Echo Nest thus suggests a more general observation regarding how files become music, as it makes it clear that audio files cannot be studied as isolated or autonomous entities. An audio file found and enjoyed via the internet is equally a product of different kinds of metadata. Metadata here need to be understood as a key element in setting the stage for what later becomes music listening, as they form a central part of contemporary algorithmic knowledge production. Consequently, metadata used by Spotify via the Echo Nest should not be perceived as an entity that sits discreetly in the background and assists those who actively search for it. Instead, metadata are constantly being marshaled to steer, direct, and reconceptualize both digital music artifacts and music recommendations.

On the one hand, these automatic systems for music information retrieval often reveal the diluted and flawed nature of online metadata. Confusion over names is a case in point. This is often not a major problem for popular artists, but for lesser-known musicians, poor metadata around name recognition can have devastating effects, leading to erroneous descriptions and recommendations. As noted elsewhere, our examination of the Echo Nest's API and its data collection revealed that data concerning Danish pop singer Dorthe Kollo was inaccurate. Some data even pertained to different Dorthes, as the Echo Nest had confused Dorthe Kollo with both Danish author Dorthe Nors and Danish singer Dorthe Gerlach.[14] Then again, the combination of the Echo Nest's "music intelligence" technology—even if its sophistication can occasionally be disputed—and Spotify's massive listening data trove has

Figure 2.1
Ad for Spotify's "Discover Weekly" in the New York subway in 2016.
Photograph by the authors.

paved the way for popular algorithm-generated and personalized suggestions, such as the "Discover Weekly" playlist.[15]

The fusion of Spotify and the Echo Nest in 2014 thus testifies to what
Anne Helmond has described as "platformization," or the "extension of
social media platforms into the rest of the web and their drive to make external web data 'platform ready.'"[16] As in the case of Spotify and the Echo Nest,
such extensions do not come naturally; they are strategically driven forward
and may sometimes fail. This also becomes obvious in regard to Spotify's
data integration with Facebook, an infrastructural tie-in that was highly visible across Spotify's interfaces. The partnership with Facebook and related
companies and actors is both instructive and explanatory, as it attests to the
gradual transformation of Spotify from a tech company that simply distributes content produced by others into a globally operating media firm. As
discussed in chapter 1, this cooperation is aimed at making the service more
"social." When Spotify merged its own login system with that of the social

networking giant, it also caused a spike in new users. "Spotify introduces music to your social life," Daniel Ek stated in a blog post in September 2011, referring to the F8 conference at which Facebook CEO Mark Zuckerberg announced their partnership. "Music is one of the most social things there is," Ek went on, arguing that integration with Facebook would "help everyone to discover more free music than ever before." Interestingly, piracy still loomed in the background, since Ek stated that "social discovery on Facebook means that we're bringing people back to paying for music again."[17]

Whereas chapter 1 described the historical context of this merger, what we want to accentuate here is that the social discovery of music testifies to the ways in which audio files, social media feeds, or updates are enmeshed in commercialized listening experiences. Through the widely adopted pub/sub system—a software architecture whereby publishers can transmit categorized messages to interested subscribers, without members of either group knowing the identities of or communicating directly with the others—Spotify has integrated social features to facilitate the sharing and following of music activities among users in real time.[18] At the same time as the Facebook deal, Spotify also decided to open its API to external developers, whose applications could retrieve data from the Spotify music catalog. For a while, basically any third-party developer could build HTML apps through the Spotify API, although they had to "go through a rigorous Spotify approval process before being released on the platform," as one report stated. The new potential for integration was championed as a "great achievement" but also raised some eyebrows: "Can Spotify shift its big-picture focus from sales and expansion to serving their … paying customers? No iPad app? Forced Facebook linking? … Has Spotify turned into AOL Music?"[19]

A number of popular music apps were developed, yet in October 2014, the so-called Spotify Apps API was discontinued. "As Spotify evolves and priorities change, we sometimes have to remove APIs from active development and shift focus to the relevant platforms," the developer blog explained.[20] Data integration came with a price and was hardly frictionless. Daniel Ek was proven to be mistaken since the "frictionless sharing" and "frictionless experience" with Facebook caused a considerable public debate. Critics agreed that intentional sharing had its advantages but soon noticed that the perception of an endless list of the music being played by Facebook friends risked turning into sheer noise. "Seeing a constant flow of songs in the news ticker is at best irrelevant and at worst annoying," as one critic put it.[21] In September 2011, less than a week after Ek's blog post and Zuckerberg's keynote at the F8 conference, Spotify found it necessary to issue a clarification and instruct users on how to control their settings: "It's entirely up to you what you decide to share and what you keep private. … To share the music you listen to with Facebook, make sure the box is checked. If you'd rather not share, just uncheck the box." Moreover, hinting at the awkward aspects of music sharing, the blog post was later updated to announce an additional feature: "Many of our users have told us that they like to share what they're listening to, but also want an easy way to hide their occasional guilty pleasures. So we've now added a new 'Private Session' mode to our latest update."[22]

Platformization thus had its disadvantages. The point we want to make here is that frictionless sharing with Facebook, engineered through aggregated information residing "outside" and then "pulled into" Spotify's data infrastructure, is of utmost importance to the ways in which the service wants to be used and understood. Linked data (as well as similar concepts around the semantic web) have been a trend in a number of public and commercial domains for more than a decade. Interoperability and machine-readable data have pushed organizations, and later commercial enterprises, to try to avoid the notion of data silos and, instead, to work toward data integration and interlinked content. Commercial streaming services, such as Spotify, Apple Music, Deezer, and Pandora, are no exception. They all integrate data and metadata to create attractive services that engage audiences. Hence, when files become music at Spotify, aggregation of data occurs on, at, and via many computational layers. As we argued in our introduction, reducing Spotify to a platform makes these exchanges invisible.

Moreover, old Spotify blog entries make it apparent that such data integration has been an essential commercial strategy for Spotify, with frequent and similar alliances and mergers occurring since the Facebook deal. In April 2013, for example, Spotify and Twitter, together with iTunes and Rdio, launched Twitter #music, a service that boasted it would change the way people found music online based on Twitter activity. Tweets, likes, and retweets were supposed to "detect and surface the most popular tracks and emerging artists."[23] At the same time, Spotify began to offer new tie-ins with the auto industry. A smaller deal with Ford came first, followed by one with Swedish car manufacturer Volvo and the launch of its Sensus Connected Touch, "a voice-activated music streaming service fully integrated with the car manufacturer's new touch-enabled dashboard."[24] Later, Spotify also collaborated with Uber, BMW (ConnectedDrive), and MINI. In March 2015, Spotify moved from cars to games, partnering with Sony and bringing music to its PlayStation console: "Listen while you play" was the slogan. And a year later, in September 2016, even love was added to the data integration list, when Spotify partnered with a well-known dating app: "Tinder, now with music by Spotify, not only gives you the capability to show your favorite artists and music preferences, but also to pick the Anthem that defines you … and maybe make a little music with someone new."[25]

These partnerships have been geared toward expanding the experience of using Spotify, securing the company a massive presence and visibility on different platforms and venues, and obtaining increasing amounts of both internal and external user-generated data and information. While data from listener activity and user profiles are essential for Spotify's data infrastructure in general and its music recommendation systems in particular, some data are never shared.

Spotify claims that all information the company has generated or gained access to in recent years "simply helps us to tailor improved experiences to our users, and build new and personalized products for the future." This quote, taken from an autumn 2015 blog post, is particularly interesting since it appears to be related to a number of new corporate alliances that had prompted (or forced) Spotify to update its "Terms and Conditions of Use and Privacy." Brand manager Candice Katz stated that the company wanted to be as "open and transparent as possible when it comes to how we describe our business, how we work with advertisers, what information we collect, and what we do with it." In corporate lingo, Katz assured that the privacy of "customers' data is—and will remain—Spotify's highest priority." Then again, her overview of the new policy made it all too apparent what was at stake:

> The *Information We Collect* section has been expanded to include new technical data such as additional cookies, device information, and network information. … We may ask for customer permission to collect information from new sources, such as address book, location, and sensor data from the mobile device to improve the customer experience and inform product decisions. We provide more clarity on how we share data with partners who help us with our marketing and advertising efforts for both Spotify and our brand partners.[26]

Spotify users were upset about these sweeping privacy changes, which gave the company greater access to personal data on users' smartphones, among other issues. The *Guardian* claimed that, from now on, Spotify would be able to collect sensor data, "about the speed of your movements, such as whether you are running, walking, or in transit." Some information would be shared with advertisers, "although Spotify did not spell out exactly what data it would pass on."[27] People took to Twitter and announced they were canceling their accounts: Swedish game developer Henrik Pettersson tweeted, "@Spotify account ended. I suggest you do the same. Privacy policies like that must die"; his colleague Markus "Notch" Persson (CEO of Mojang and the creator of Minecraft) retweeted this and stated, "I just cancelled mine too."[28] A heated exchange ensued on Twitter, in which Daniel Ek tried to persuade Persson, his business acquaintance, to change his mind. "People are quitting Spotify over its new privacy policy," *Business Insider* stated, and the Twitter conversation was picked up and quoted in a number of online media sources.[29]

The dispute led Ek to publish a blog post famously entitled "SORRY." He admitted that Spotify should have done "a better job" in communicating what the new privacy policies meant and how "information you choose to share will—and will not—be used." He then described the new types of information, "including photos, mobile device location, voice controls, and your contacts" that Spotify wanted to access. But "let me be crystal clear here," Ek asserted. "If you don't want to share this kind of information, you don't have to. We will ask for your express permission before accessing any of this data—and we will only use it for specific purposes that will allow you to customize your Spotify experience." Finally, Ek also confessed that Spotify did share data with partners "who help us with marketing and advertising efforts" but assured that all information was "de-identified—your personal information is not shared with them."[30]

Audio Files and Streaming Infrastructures

We have presented a brief contextualized discussion of Spotify's data infrastructure in order to demonstrate that it is constructed and assembled by more than just audio files. But what about the files themselves? A brief survey of data formats and streaming infrastructures here may suffice.

Spotify's audio streaming service uses the Ogg Vorbis format, not MP3, for music. Ogg Vorbis is an open-source lossy audio compression method that offers roughly the same sound quality as MP3 at a smaller file size, which is crucial for streaming. A streamed track is always played immediately after a small amount of audio data has been received—a technological fact that our subsequent intervention will analyze in detail. Music files are not permanently stored on the destination device. For music streaming to occur, the Spotify client and the server need to communicate, with the client storing a few seconds of sound in a buffer before starting to send it to the speakers. Consequently, low latency is key to the Spotify service. (Latency is a measure of the delay between requesting a song and hearing it; "low latency" means that when a user presses play, a track should start more or less instantly.) To achieve this, the Spotify web client fetches the first part of a song from its infrastructural back end and starts playing a track as soon as sufficient data has been buffered as to make stutter unlikely to occur. Therefore, "the main metric of the Spotify storage system is the fraction of requests that can be served with latency at most t for some small value of t, typically around 50 [milliseconds]."[31] There are different quality ratings for streaming: normal mobile quality (96 kilobits per second, or kbps), desktop and web player standard quality (160 kbps), and high quality (320 kbps), which is available only to Premium subscribers. It is also possible to make Spotify one's own "all-in-one music player." In addition to the more than thirty million tracks that Spotify offers from its catalog, "you can also use your Spotify app to play music files stored on your computer," as MP3, MP4, and M4P audio formats are also supported.[32]

As we have shown in chapter 1, the technical roots of the service are within file sharing and music piracy. Sharing files via Napster or the Pirate Bay, however, was never only about the actual exchange but always involved a networked sociability with actors and/or people. In a similar sense, music files on Spotify engage in a form of data sociality, resulting in assemblages of different digital assets (such as metadata) that usually include multiple formats. Spotify's tech stack includes hundreds of programs and services, from Amazon and Apache to Python and WordPress, engaging with one another. If the Spotify back-end architecture is heavily service-oriented (mostly written in Python or Java), audio files are also retrieved from remote and different locations, with streaming coded as a combination of server-based access to audio files (on Amazon S3) and peer-to-peer (P2P) technologies (prior to 2014). Spotify used to have at least four data centers around the world, including one in Stockholm and one in Ashburn, Virginia. The first characters of a server's hostname, such as "ash2-dnsresolver-a1337.ash2.spotify.net," indicate the data center's physical location (in this case, Ashburn).

In order to facilitate and sustain its infrastructure, Spotify ran one of the largest P2P networks on the internet for a number of years. According to Spotify, during that period, less than 10 percent of music playback came from its own servers, with roughly 35 percent coming from P2P networks and an astonishing 55 percent from the user's local cache. The exception was playout from smartphones, where all music was streamed directly from Spotify servers. At a presentation in 2011, Ricardo Vice Santos, then head of growth/new markets at Spotify, described streaming music in the following way: "Request first piece from Spotify servers | Meanwhile, search for peers with track | Download data in-order | When buffers are sufficient, switch to P2P | Towards end of a track, prefetch next one."[33] Spotify needed P2P to guarantee that all tracks could be played with the lowest latency possible. With a dedicated P2P system, a streamed song, played for the first time, would therefore be stored on a user's hard drive (cache). When playing the track again, the cached version was used instead of repeated downloads from the network, and the client would (via P2P) be able to use parts of a song from other users. When a client played a music track, data was thus obtained from a combination of three sources: "the client local cache (if the same track has been played recently), other Spotify clients through peer-to-peer technology, or the Spotify storage system in a backend site."[34] All of this happened in the background, however, and contributed to a smooth user experience.

Only in the spring of 2014 was it announced that Spotify would shut down its P2P servers. "We're now at a stage where we can power music delivery through our growing number of servers and ensure our users continue to receive a best-in-class service," the company stated.[35] In order to upgrade its infrastructure, Spotify started to buy or lease data center space, server hardware, and networking gear. In 2016, the infrastructural framework changed again. After a few years of operating its own data centers and running its "core infrastructure on [its] own private fleet of physical servers (aka machines) rather than leveraging a public cloud such as Amazon Web Services," it now announced it would start working with the Google Cloud Platform team to provide a new streaming infrastructure.[36] Spotify now determined storage, computing, and network services available from cloud providers to be sufficiently robust (and low cost). As Spotify declared, "Good infrastructure isn't just about keeping things up and running, it's about making all of our teams more efficient and more effective, and Google's data stack does that for us in spades."[37]

Aggregating Content

The brief survey we have provided demonstrates that turning files into music is a process that involves an exceedingly interrelated data stack and a complex streaming infrastructure of software services, metadata, and user-generated data. Spotify's data infrastructure is built on layers of interrelated services, streams, and exchanges. While postings on Facebook and elsewhere are important for Spotify's claims about making music more social—and while metadata flows (via the Echo Nest) are pivotal for blurring the boundaries between music and information about music—aggregation of actual content forms yet another important data layer of Spotify's online presence. In "Intervention: Record Label Setup," we described how our self-produced music helped us gain a number of insights into music aggregation procedures. In what follows, we will complement these insights with some considerations of how music aggregation and databases containing cultural content are conceptually structured in ways that enable certain forms of use and experience while disabling others. Spotify depends on aggregation practices. When files become music on Spotify, the aggregation of content is the first step.

Aggregation is a generic term for the internet's capacity to pull content from various sources and make it accessible at dedicated sites, such as Netflix, Wikipedia, and Spotify. While aggregation practices existed long before the internet—making cultural content available for free or a small fee is what libraries, circuses, and museums have done for centuries—online aggregation is often related to the internet's propensity to scale. Pulling together information into one single location is increasingly important online, and when it comes to music, it is aggregation—rather than the process of copying bits, called *streaming*—that shapes interfaces and listening experiences. Aggregation is not the source of the stream but a facilitating principle that unites the distinct data particles into a coherent whole.[38]

Music aggregators act as intermediaries that connect smaller rights owners to streaming services, while major conglomerates and labels usually entertain a direct business relationship with the service. In the case of Spotify, this is unsurprising, since the company is partly owned by Universal, EMI, and Warner. As intermediaries, aggregators intrude into, and fundamentally alter, existing distribution chains or information channels. According to Daniel Johansson, music aggregators can therefore be perceived as a new function within the music industrial system. Johansson estimated in 2013 that about forty music aggregators were operating in the market—a figure that may have risen substantially since then.[39] In many ways, however, today's digital distribution chain—label, aggregator, retailer—is reminiscent of the way in which recorded music on physical carriers used to be distributed: from a label to a record store via a distributor.

As a facilitating principle, aggregation stands for a techno-social trend that combines an ever-expanding scope of culture, knowledge, and commodities with completely new systems to sort, aggregate, and filter content. Aggregation is an example of what Jeremy Wade Morris calls *infomediaries*, "organizational entities that monitor, collect, process and repackage cultural and technical usage data into an informational infrastructure that shapes the presentation and representation of cultural goods." In Morris's view, the emergence of infomediaries marks a shift toward database and algorithmic technologies influencing not only "the organization of digital goods" but, more importantly, the curation of culture through "mining, repackaging and provision of data."[40]

Elsewhere, we have argued that as a business operation, music aggregation connects traditional institutional ideas of accumulation—think of the *library* and *catalog* metaphors used to explain online services—to the promise of new media.[41] What characterizes aggregation, however, is not so much the effects of aggregation per se but *the effects of the difference* between various aggregation practices, not least financially. Pricing mechanisms among music aggregators, for instance, vary substantially. There are also significant differences in pricing policies between aggregators working with record labels and those that target individual artists. Some charge a small amount per played track, others an initially fixed price or a fixed price per song or album upload, and still others a certain percentage of royalties.

In its current use, the term *aggregation* covers a broad spectrum of industry practices and technologies, yet exactly what the term denotes remains blurry and hard to delimit vis-à-vis distribution, programming, or syndication. As Patryk Galuszka has argued, aggregators "exist in several industries, but in the digital music market their role is largely unnoticed."[42] Few have heard of Awal, for instance, an aggregation service promoted by Spotify that promises to get one's music distributed "without upfront fees to over 200 different digital stores and services around the world." With offices in Atlanta, Berlin, London, Los Angeles, Miami, and Nashville, Awal in many ways lurks in the background of the contemporary music industry, offering

Figure 2.2
Aggregation as the facilitating principle behind streaming: online offers made by the music aggregation service Awal. Screenshot provided by authors.

a "simple digital distribution license" while charging 15 percent of revenues generated.[43]

An aggregator such as Awal bundles digital and intellectual property rights—both copyrights to sound recordings and artists'/performers' rights—and delivers content to digital music stores, either in the form of downloading (iTunes) or streaming (Spotify). Aggregators hence operate "on the business-to-business market, where one group of contractors are record labels or individual artists, and the other group are digital music stores."[44]

If one takes the community conversation about Spotify as an indicator, it usually takes about two weeks for a new tune to go through the aggregation process and reach the user. In order to ease and inform what aggregation means, Spotify has created an artist's guide "to walk you through setting up your artist profile, customizing your presence, and growing your fanbase on Spotify." The notion of "delivery" is the first category one encounters in this "Spotify for Artists" guide, which enthusiastically asserts that "getting your music on Spotify is easy." If an artist is already signed to a label or has started using an aggregation service, "they'll get your music on Spotify for you. If you don't, we have deals in place with a number of companies who can deliver your music to us and collect royalties for you." At the time of writing, Spotify lists six aggregation partners: TuneCore, CD Baby, EmuBands, Record Union, Spinnup, and Awal. They are described as aggregator services that handle "the licensing and distribution of your music," and administer royalties and monetary compensation "when your fans stream your music on Spotify." Spotify also stresses that these services do not work for free; usually there is "a small fee or percentage cut involved…so be sure to do a little homework before picking one."[45]

Looking at the offers from music aggregators, it becomes clear that, from their perspective, Spotify is one of the dominant players on the streaming market. Together with iTunes, Amazon, Apple Music, and Google Play, Spotify is heavily promoted by aggregators such as TuneCore, CD Baby, EmuBands, MondoTunes, and RouteNote. Spotify is also integrated with delivery platforms such as FUGA, Consolidated Independent, and the Merlin Network— all of which are also promoted on the "Spotify for Artists" site: "Deliveries via these platforms will speed up the time it takes to get your content on Spotify."[46]

One of these aggregators, TuneCore, boasts a "strong partnership with Spotify." TuneCore offers "Daily Spotify Trend Reports" as a way to keep track of "your success"—or failure, as in the case of our own recordings— and thus to be able to make timely business decisions. In addition, the "Spotify Verified Artist Accounts" allow TuneCore artists and labels "to easily build a community of followers and interact with fans directly from artist pages."[47] The TuneCore FAQ also explicitly tries to answer the tricky question of how much money can potentially be made through Spotify sales and its "paid streams." Spotify has deals with rights holders in all of the countries where the service is available, TuneCore asserts. "A royalty is based on how frequently your music gets played. Each stream earns you a share of Spotify's advertising revenue." The actual amount varies substantially and depends on "the ratio of advertising revenue and your percentage of the total number of streams on Spotify in a given month."[48]

For all types of streaming music, it should be stressed that aggregation in principle means that the distribution chain gets longer for smaller repertoire owners, as compared to major rights holders. It reduces revenues flowing back from streaming services, and in many cases, individual (and less popular) artists will find that making their tracks available through pricey aggregation services causes them to operate at a loss (since revenue per played track is almost insignificant). After all, Spotify monetizes usage, not units. On the Spotify Community Blog, there are consequently a number of complaints regarding aggregation and revenue, ranging from splitting royalties to aggregators refusing to remove music.[49] A Google search for "best music aggregator" will bring up a number of postings with similar pros and cons. Consider, for example, the following comments on a Reddit thread:

> I've been using CDBaby for over 10 years. It was the only option for a long time. One-time setup fee and they also handle rights management if you do the pro package. HUGE time saver.

> I use CDbaby too. A little more expensive to get started with, but I appreciate that I literally pay once and stuff is up forever.

> I think these days most services are good, the only thing that could tilt your choice is how you release your music. If you put out a new single every week CDBaby might get very expensive for you and maybe another one of the flat fee services would be better.

> tunecore is easily the best. most stores, most transparent, most information on their site, most high profile artists, etc.

> But tunecore makes you pay for every upload, which some people don't like. I for one don't make a lot per tracks, so I rather they took a percentage of my revenue like amadea music does.[50]

Music aggregators are thus a new group of intermediaries that have played a vital role in articulating the value of music over the past decade. Forming part of a wider techno-social ensemble that constitutes today's digital media infrastructures, music aggregators have also contributed to an experience of *devaluation* that these services were designed to fight.

"The smaller and lighter the universal music library becomes, the heavier it seems to pull us down," as Geert Lovink has stated.[51]

Aggregation of sounds from a number of online distributors scattered across the internet again stresses that Spotify's data infrastructure needs to be grasped in its heterogeneity and in its capacity to scale. Streaming services would not have been able to gain rapid, global popularity if it had not been for their aggregated, abundant back catalogs of content. In countless interviews, Daniel Ek has emphasized the importance of building a vast music catalog: "With music, rediscovery is a critical part of how you listen to music."[52] Consequently, during the past decade, the number of tracks available from music retailers and streaming sites has been promoted to entice prospective listeners. In many ways, Apple's iTunes Store set the tone by persistently advocating its swelling back catalog. "The iTunes Music Store in the US, UK, France and Germany offers an extensive music library of over 700,000 songs in each country," Apple boasted in 2004.[53] Today, all streaming services on the market make similar claims: Spotify and Apple Music now have well over 30 million songs, Pandora claims to feature 40 million tracks, and SoundCloud gives access to no less than 120 million user-added tracks. More music, indeed, seems to be better music.

Every stream means potentially increased revenue from advertisers in Spotify's ad-supported version. Since Spotify Free operates similarly to commercial radio, more streams are equivalent to more usage, which is what attracts advertisers—an issue to which we will return in chapter 4. We have argued elsewhere that this is one of the reasons why streaming services such as Spotify aggregate almost indiscriminately and are more likely to include, rather than reject, various forms of (semi-)automated music and sounds—especially compared to retailers such as iTunes, from which users purchase individual downloads.[54] One might be surprised to find that Spotify contains tracks with titles such as "Aircraft Lavatory Ambience," "Weight Loss Hypnosis," "Car Alarm on City Side Street," "Beach Rain," and "Spend Less-Stop Wasting Money Subliminal Message Therapy"—not to mention the one-hundred-track album *Correct Wrong Sound Effects*. While these tracks do not attract crowds of listeners, they are an important part of the marketing hype around "more music" and thus part of the "all-you-can-eat" bid that streaming services offer. The multifaceted and unregulated market of music aggregation is the main reason why all these tracks are available.

Figure 2.3
In March 2014, the funk band Vulfpeck released the conceptual album *Sleepify*—
which contained some five minutes of pure silence—in order to crowdfund the
Sleepify Tour. Screenshot provided by authors.

As we have previously described in the intervention on our record
label experiments, current rejection criteria at music aggregators are more
or less arbitrary, depending on whether users pay a fee or not. Aggregators disagree about whether the same tracks and albums even count as
music. The line between music and nonmusic, artist and machine becomes
blurred. Bizarre tracks on Spotify—such as "Overcoming Job Loss – Positive
Affirmations"—might not come across as music, but they have passed an
aggregator. Still, record labels and artists expect Spotify to act as a walled-
off streaming service with professional offerings rather than a semi-open
platform. Consequently, streaming fraud has generated worries within the
music industry, not least since music hacks, pranks, and tricks tend to get

Figure 2.4

public attention. These have included the funk band Vulfpeck and its conceptual album, *Sleepify* (which contains five minutes and sixteen seconds of
pure silence); the band Ohm & Sport and it application Eternify, where—
for a very short time—one could enter the name of a favorite artist and play
songs on repeat in thirty-one-second intervals in order to maximize the
artist's revenue; and the music spammer Matt Farley, who has personally
released over fifteen thousand songs.

The spread of illicit or non-"organic" promotion in the form of automated
listeners on Spotify and other services may be seen as relating to similar
aggregation devaluation mechanisms—and to the paradoxically expanding back catalog of unheard music. Approximately 20 percent of Spotify's
catalog has not been listened to by anyone even once. Thus, more music
always means more unheard music. A site such as Forgotify testifies to the
vast amount of aggregated but undiscovered content. "Millions of songs on
Spotify have been forgotten. Let's give them new life in new ears—yours.
[At Forgotify] we were so shocked to learn that millions of Spotify songs
had been played only partially or never at all. A musical travesty, really.

Figure 2.5
Stills from the promotional YouTube video for the Sleepify Tour, with bandleader
Jack Stratton asking fans to stream the album on repeat (while sleeping!). Reprinted
with permission from Vulfpeck.

So we set out to give these neglected songs another way to reach your ear-
holes"[55] The dark side of aggregation equals plenty of "zombie music" on
Spotify.

The Radio Loop Experiment

When music becomes data and comes to resemble all other kinds of digital
content, it also comes to adhere to all aspects of computational logics, even
the more annoying ones. Therefore, we would like to conclude this chapter by describing one experiment—related to the previous discussion on
aggregation—that we conducted at Humlab. The experiment proposes a set
of methodologies for performing humanist inquiries on "midsize" data and
black-boxed media services, such as Spotify, that increasingly serve as key
delivery mechanisms for cultural goods. As with some of our prior interventions, the experiment used bots as research informants and sought to critically investigate aggregation of music and the prospective lure of infinite
archives via the radio functionality of Spotify.

Through unknown algorithms, Spotify Radio offers users a potentially
unlimited avenue of music discovery due to the service's vast back catalog

of aggregated content. The service, however, has been severely criticized: "Is Spotify Radio broken?"; "How do I get Spotify to stop playing the same few songs for every artists [sic]?"; "How do I teach a Spotify radio station to play a wider array of songs?"; "Is the Spotify streaming radio…purposefully terrible with the intention of trying to get people to upgrade?"[56] As these queries from the website Quora indicate, not only do many users dislike Spotify Radio, they have even accused it of playing the same artists over and over.

We have also discussed similar issues with the poor performance of the Spotify Radio algorithm. Such assumptions reveal a normative claim that the radio algorithm *should* produce apt recommendations. In order to answer at least some of these issues, we decided to set up an experiment that would explore Spotify Radio. Our objective was to uncover why we rarely liked the songs that the radio algorithms suggested we should like. But given normative assumptions about the ways in which Spotify Radio ought to work, the research question also hinted at the ways in which algorithmic music discovery today features and promotes some artists—and obstructs others. Hence, a software-driven cultural analysis of music delivery mechanisms could potentially reveal the algorithmic flaws that regulate music recommendations to the detriment of a more diverse listening experience, making less room for emerging musicians or neglected genres (with economic ramifications).

Our experiment attempted to analyze the possible limitations found within "infinite archives" of music streaming services such as Spotify. For commercial reasons, Spotify Radio claims to be both personalized and never ending. Our hypothesis, however, was that Spotify Radio did not consist of an infinite series of songs. Rather, music seemed to be delivered in limited loop patterns. If our hypothesis held true, what would such loop patterns look like? In order to answer these questions, we set up an experiment with the purpose of examining Spotify Radio loops. Our loops were constructed using 160 "bot listeners." All of our bots were Spotify Free users with literally no track record—they had "heard" no music before they were put into action. Our primarily interest was not the personalized recommendations that Spotify's algorithms offered but rather how Spotify Radio functioned generically. Moreover, providing all of our bots with a personal track record would have been impractical, if not impossible, to accomplish. In addition, as virtual informants, our bots did not explicitly collect information. They were programmed and designed to search for a track, retrieve subsequent songs, partially interact, and (most importantly) log data caused by different "actions."

If one of our aims with the experiment was to study the repetitiveness in loop patterns, another hypothesis was that the size and structure of radio loops might depend on music genres as well as popularity. We decided to let our bots "listen" to both a hit song and a less popular track with some contextual similarity. Then, all of our bots would start a radio channel based on Swedish music from the 1970s and listen for twenty-four hours. A major and a minor experiment were conducted. In the first round, 120 of our bots (although many eventually failed because of various technological problems) started Spotify Radio based on the highly popular ABBA song "Dancing Queen" (1976), which has been streamed some sixty-five million times on Spotify. The second round of bots (40 in all, with a few failures) started a radio channel using the significantly less popular "Queen of Darkness" by Swedish progressive rock band Råg i Ryggen (1975), with approximately ten thousand streams. The bots were to document all subsequent tracks played in the radio loop, as well as to interact differently within the Spotify web client as an "obedient" bot listener, a "liker," a "disliker," or a "skipper." The interactions were documented, including tracks and artists played, as well as breaks for advertisements.

Elsewhere, we have described in detail the results of our Spotify Radio experiment.[57] The first thing to note is that it is possible to measure loop patterns on Spotify Radio. Working with bots as research informants allowed us to monitor the logs they produced and thereby empirically sustain claims of repetitiveness within Spotify Radio. The regularity of patterns was clear, and music loops were definitively not endless. On the contrary, they displayed a repeated pattern with only slight variations according to which artist a radio station was based on. For instance, the specific track that we based our radio stations on kept returning in the bot playlists. If a radio loop started with "Dancing Queen," it was played again by the Spotify Radio algorithms after about fifty tracks. Bots listening to a radio station based on "Queen of Darkness" displayed a similar tendency, but with the difference that the song was not repeated as often as "Dancing Queen" and at longer intervals (regularly after some seventy tracks or so).

A preliminary conclusion to draw from the experiments with Spotify Radio is that similar artists reappeared frequently within all bot playlists.

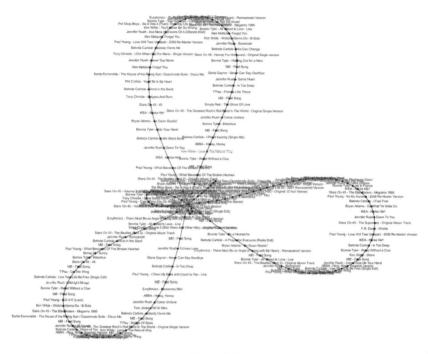

Figure 2.6
Five "song loops" on Spotify Radio, as listened to by one of our preprogrammed
bots. The radio loop began with ABBA's "Dancing Queen" (in the middle)
and repeated the same track an additional five times (during a
twenty-four-hour intervention).

Music recommendation algorithms at Spotify did not really take advantage of the archival infinity of the service. Thus, if Spotify Radio is about
personalization of content, as the company claims, then the recommendation algorithms were a disappointment. An even more troubling result, at
least for Spotify, was that radio loops tended to look more or less the same,
independent of bot characteristics. Giving Spotify Radio the user feedback
of "thumbs up" (like), "thumbs down" (dislike), or skip did not produce
significant differences in the results.

One result of the experiments was therefore that music loop patterns
basically looked the same, regardless of interaction within the Spotify web
client. Another general conclusion was that the recommendation ability of
Spotify Radio is exaggerated. The claim that "the more you personalize, the
better the music gets" should be perceived as a mendacious company claim

used to attract listeners and stir commercial interest in the radio functionality (when the service was new). Yet, since complaints were made right after the launch of Spotify Radio, it is likely that the recommendation functionality was flawed from the start. The public critiques on Quora of the inadequate functionality of Spotify Radio were thus spot on.

Today, the technology seems to have caught up—but not in a radio setting. In recent years, Spotify has put way more emphasis on its "Discover Weekly" and "Release Radar" playlists than on its radio functionality. In short, there seems to be a particular tech-musical recommendation narrative stretching from Spotify Radio (2011) to "Discover Weekly" (2015) and "Release Radar" (2016). The latter is different from "Discover Weekly" in that its tracks are brand new and have no listening data. Instead, Spotify relies on a solution that tries to predict who will enjoy a song by analyzing the audio signal. In the end, it seems that traditional radio recommendations appear to be less significant for Spotify, at least in comparison to other, newer types of suggestions. As streaming music—and not radio—has become the default listening mode, it is hardly surprising that the radio metaphor would gradually lose its popularity and consequently be largely replaced with new computational recommendation formats based on taste profiles, song identification, and digital fingerprints. Music, in other words, is now made of other kinds of files.

Intervention: How We Tracked Streams

In June 2016, a major consumer outburst erupted on several online forums concerned with Spotify. Users were beginning to notice that their Spotify client was running amok and had suddenly started to record large amounts of junk data on their solid-state drives (SSDs), which could potentially slow down—if not destroy—their storage capacities.[1] As the news spread, reports of ever-larger examples of trash generation began to roll in. Journalists at the tech website Ars Technica ran a test and found that their Spotify clients were unwittingly writing five to ten gigabytes of data per hour on their computers—even when the clients were put in idle mode.[2] In cases where the program had been running for months, users reported having terabytes of junk dumped on their hard drives.[3] Blog outlets were calling the debacle an "assault on user's storage devices,"[4] a case of excessive "data gobbling,"[5] and an issue which was "quietly killing" the lifespan of hard drives.[6] It quickly became clear that Spotify had unwantedly turned the computers of thousands of users into garbage dumps. Instead of momentarily diffusing music, the program was spitting out digital trash.[7]

What happens when someone clicks play on Spotify? It is a simple question, yet it is tricky to answer from a technical viewpoint. As we stated in our introduction, one guiding metaphor for this research has been to "follow" streamed music files as they are shuffled across the web. But such an effort is negated by the basic logics according to which streaming operates. First, data is not technically transported—as in being moved from one location to the next—when information is streamed. Instead, data is copied and multiplied. Thus, the question of how streamed files "move" is not only a matter of tracing changed data locations but an issue of tracking how data proliferates. Second, streamed music does not simply concern the replication of audio data. Hundreds, if not thousands, of other types of data transmission occur every time content is streamed. And while it is possible to single out and isolate specific audio content in such floods of data traffic, it makes little sense to do so, since streaming is inevitably bound up in much larger computational processes. The streaming of music, then, is not simply a matter of transportation; it is an intricate data traffic solution that involves connecting multiple actors, networks, and infrastructures that span the globe.

As the example of Spotify's unwanted generation of trash data illustrates, these data transmissions can sometimes have hidden or unintended consequences. In order to explore the nature of such streamed data processes, we set up an experiment that allowed us to monitor the data transmissions that are triggered by a "click" (or play) on Spotify. The experimental setup was simple: By using an open-source program called Wireshark, we were able to eavesdrop on data traffic that occurred between one of our personal computers and the internet when Spotify was used. This allowed us to map what streamed data traffic looks like close up, zooming in on its contents and characteristics.

One of the world's most popular network protocol analyzers, Wireshark is used by programmers to troubleshoot problems in network traffic. The program was first created in 1998 and has since been developed by an impressive 1,316 open-source contributors (and counting). According to its founders, Wireshark "lets you see what's happening on your network at a microscopic level."[8] The program does this by logging and intercepting the transmission of packets—that is, the small units of data that are sent within a network when a computer is hooked up to the internet. This enables a study of the origin, destination, and characteristics of the data that passes to and from selected computers. For this reason, network protocol analysis tools (or "packet sniffers," as they are also called) are frequently used for diagnosing network problems, detecting network intrusion attempts, gathering network statistics, and evaluating the effectiveness of security systems, such as firewalls or spam filters. These tools thus play an important role within the day-to-day business of maintaining and upholding the functions of the internet.

Software programs like Wireshark are also popular with malicious hackers, since they enable sniffing out and eavesdropping on every computer that is hooked up to the same Wi-Fi network. Because these programs translate and present the details of all transmissions occurring between two or more nodes on a computer network, they can be used to spy on unprotected Wi-Fi cohabitants. This is usually done when the program is set to "promiscuous mode," a feature that is available on many network protocol analyzers. Promiscuous mode can be used to gather sensitive information—such as passwords, private email details, credit card numbers, browser histories, and cookies with saved login credentials—from unsuspecting targets, provided that the information is not encrypted.

In our experiment, we did not collect such private communication details concerning other people's internet use. Rather, we repurposed Wireshark as a digital research tool for "listening in" on our personal streamed data traffic.[9] In other words, the intercepted traffic only concerned our own Spotify streams and no one else's. "Eavesdropping," biolinguist John L. Locke suggests, "is a deeply biological trait with ancient roots. Few if any species do *not* eavesdrop—even plants do it."[10] By drawing on this deeply rooted practice of willfully overhearing conversations between others (in our case, computers), our interventionist exercise thus consisted of trying to capture the conversations taking place when music is streamed on Spotify. This gives insight into a sphere of digital communication that is rarely observed by humanist scholars. As Wendy Chun has described it, packet sniffers reveal how "your computer constantly wanders without you."[11] By this, Chun refers to the ways in which computers constantly do stuff without our direct knowledge and how data moves in ways that are not seen at the interface level. Packet sniffers thus challenge the idea that computers are under our control and only act at our request; they reveal the hidden—and sprawling—transmissions that occur within internet networks. In order to understand Spotify as an (organizer of) infrastructure, one has to take such network connections and actors into account.

Consider the scale of data that passes through a service such as Spotify. In 2016, Spotify product manager Ali Sarrafi reported that the company handled more than thirty-eight terabytes of incoming data per day, while permanently storing more than "70 petabytes of…data about songs, playlists, etc."[12] To give a sense of how much data this is, consider that seventy petabytes is roughly equivalent to 930 years—nearly one millennium—of high-quality video. In 2016, Spotify's backend system was said to be capable of singlehandedly pushing "more than 700,000 events per second halfway across the world," where an "event" (as we described in chapter 2) refers to any action being performed by a user on the Spotify client, such as adding a song to a playlist.[13] In order to cope with such data traffic, Spotify has long hosted a fleet of over twelve thousand servers, distributed in four data centers in Stockholm; London; Ashburn, Virginia; and San Jose, California.[14] Since 2015, however, the company has increasingly shipped its data through Google Cloud Platform, which involves using not only Google's global cloud/storage data centers but also other Google services, such as virtual machines and database management systems.[15] In addition, Spotify is hooked up to at least five internet exchange points (IXPs) located in Frankfurt (DEC-IX), Stockholm (Netnod), Amsterdam (AMSIX), London (LINX), and Ashburn (EQIX-ASH). The service is also attached to several content delivery networks (CDNs) and subscriber networks—that is, broadband or mobile providers—which speed up and shorten the distance to their users.[16] Each time Spotify is used, traffic is dynamically pushed through these data channels within a split second, depending on where the connection is best.[17]

What knowledge could we gain about these complex arrangements between cloud providers, internet hubs, and CDNs from using Wireshark? On the evening of May 15, 2017, we intercepted Spotify's network traffic first by using one recently registered Spotify Free account and then by using one old Spotify Premium account. The premium account belonged to one of us researchers and had been in use for many years, while the new account was registered that evening with a personal email address. During the data capture—which lasted for only twenty minutes on each account—we listened to a series of songs, much as one normally does when using Spotify. All plays were triggered manually, and five songs were played in total.[18] While the network traffic was being intercepted, we used the Mac's Activity Monitor to make sure that no programs other than Spotify were active. The traffic was also filtered so that we only monitored ports that Spotify was using: 80, 443, and 4070.[19] The data was first stored in the pcapng format, which enables a dynamic reading of the data in Wireshark, and was later exported to Excel and Google spreadsheets for analysis.

In total, 1,618 Spotify-related packets were captured during the session with the Spotify Premium account, and 11,653 packets were captured during the session with the Spotify Free account. The most likely reason why so many more packets were sent to and from the free account was that this data was collected first, which implies that the music had already been cached (i.e., temporarily stored) on the computer's hard drive by the time we intercepted the data transmitted via the premium account. In addition, two advertisements (one still image and one video ad) appeared during the free session, which caused more data to be sent and received. In many cases, the captured packets turned out to be simple "Can you read me?" requests, that is, short "hello" messages that allow computers to acknowledge one another's existence in case information should be transferred between them in the future. We also found that a long list of erroneous packets had been captured on both of the accounts. In fact, 38 percent of the premium data traffic and 4 percent of the free traffic consisted of failed transmission control protocol (TCP) packet transmissions. These failures were never noticed at the interface level during the data collection; the client never froze, and the music played without lag or interruption. Yet the fact that so many erroneous packets appeared reveals how states of breakdown continuously underlie the seemingly well-functioning interfaces of software programs.

Even if Spotify appeared to be running smoothly, hundreds of minor malfunctions were taking place in its network transmissions. For instance, during the premium session, the Spotify client made 213 attempts to establish contact with an IP address located in San Francisco, without any success. Similarly, during the free session, 215 failed attempts to communicate with an internet protocol (IP) address in New York City occurred when the Spotify account was intercepted. For the purposes of this intervention, we will not get into the details of why these packet transmissions failed. Nor do we claim that failed packet transmissions are exclusive to Spotify. The reality is the opposite: they represent a highly common element in general network

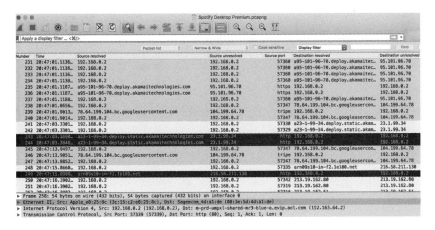

Figure 2.7
Screenshot of Wireshark in action. Black rows indicate failed
TCP packet transmissions.

traffic. The point is that network protocol analysis tools enable consider-ations of how "technology cannot exist without failure."[20] Even in cases when Spotify appears to be functioning seamlessly, what Federica Frabetti calls "quasi-failures" might still lurk below the surface.[21] Tools such as Wire-shark, we argue, can thus be used as entryways for studying the sometimes-troubled communication attempts that take place between computers, as well as the moments when software breaks down and misbehaves.

As Nicole Starosielski notes, a simple "click" on a computer commonly activates vast infrastructures whereby information is pushed through routers, local internet networks, IXPs, long-haul backbone systems, coastal cable sta-tions, undersea cables, and data warehouses at the speed of light.[22] The char-acteristics of such infrastructural connections could also be gleaned from our eavesdropping session. In detail, the data traffic that was intercepted during the experiment could be isolated to twelve different actors located in Europe and the United States, of which only one belonged directly to Spotify:

Actor	Type
AOL Transit Data Network	Tier-1 Backbone Network
Level 3 / Rubicon	Tier-1 Backbone Network
Akamai	Content Delivery Network
Amazon CloudFront	Content Delivery Network
Appnexus	Programmatic advertising
AudienceScience	Programmatic advertising
MediaMath	Programmatic advertising
Turn	Programmatic advertising
Fastly	Cloud platform
Google	Cloud platform
Spotify	Datacenter

Figure 2.8
List of actors that were found when we eavesdropped
on Spotify's network traffic in May 2017.

AOL and Level 3 are two of the world's largest Tier 1 backbone network providers, supplying nodes through which a large portion of the world's internet traffic is connected. The US-based—and sometimes controversial— Level 3 was acquired by CenturyLink in 2017 and is active in more than sixty countries and controls over ten million miles of fiber-optic cables.[23] This is equivalent to about four hundred trips around the world.[24] Several of these fiber-optic cables are subaquatic and link Africa, Asia, Europe, and North America. The company also runs 350 data centers with fifteen thousand CDN servers across the world.[25] Through these cables and data centers, Level 3 has provided network access to several large content providers, such as Pandora, Netflix, and Grooveshark, as well as more delicate customers such as the US Department of Defense.[26] During our eavesdropping session, however, it did not appear as though the primary role of Level 3 was to enable Spotify's transmission of music. Rather, Level 3's IP addresses appeared to be hosted by the Rubicon Project, an online advertising firm that has managed Spotify's programmatic ad sales since 2016, in competition with other actors such as Turn, Appnexus, Audience Science, and MediaMath (to which we will return in chapter 4).[27]

The actual music that was streamed to our computer during the experiment instead appeared to have origins in Google Cloud Platform's data centers in Ashburn, Stockholm, and Mountain View, California. As mentioned in the previous chapter, Spotify's music transmissions are based on the Ogg Vorbis codec, a free open-source solution for lossy audio compression that stands in direct competition with the proprietary—and much more commonly used—MP3 codec.[28] Most of the packets that were sent between Google's data centers and our computer contained Ogg Vorbis–labeled data. These packets were also encrypted with the help of a free, open-source software protocol called TrIPE (or Trivial IP Encryption).[29] (Interestingly, we were able to listen to these distorted versions of music by playing the encrypted files in the program Audacity.) By using TrIPE and Ogg Vorbis, Spotify gains access to encryption and compression technologies without having to pay costly proprietary fees to build its software on top of them. This cost-saving practice is a common thread in the company's software and infrastructure management. "At Spotify we love open source," Noa Resare, one of Spotify's "free software mediators," proclaimed in 2014.[30] The Spotify client, for example, has benefitted significantly from the labor put into more than three hundred different open-source projects.[31] Spotify thus resembles a hybrid of proprietary and open-source software solutions. When looking at the codecs and software on which the service runs, it becomes obvious that Spotify is neither self-built nor self-maintained and instead relies on a vast network of actors for its service to function—another indication that the notion of an enclosed platform is inapt. By hunting among the collected data packets, our eavesdropping session allowed us to study the traces of such actors and to consider their economic and political effects.

From the collected data, we also learned that our Spotify client had been interacting with two different CDNs: Akamai and Amazon CloudFront. As Stephen Graham and Simon Marvin noted in 2001, CDNs are constructions that bypass congested internet infrastructures and instead establish parallel network traffic routes that—against a fee—allow information to reach its destination at a higher speed.[32] Such parallel networks have clear political dimensions. They often run between high-priority cities around the globe (such as capitals) and frequently target areas with a high density of corporate activity. In fact, Akamai has been singled out as providing a private network infrastructure that serves to enhance the unequal distribution of global network connectivity.[33] Because of their practice of selling high-quality internet access to selected customers, CDNs are also known for sidestepping net neutrality orders and regulations, thus counteracting the basic and open end-to-end principles of the internet.[34] Given that we recorded our session in the heart of Stockholm—the most populous city in the Nordic countries—it should come as no surprise that Spotify's data traffic was routed through such CDNs. Yet our experiment exemplifies how a task as mundane as listening to music on Spotify may trigger complex entanglements with internet infrastructures that are tightly linked to controversial debates around digital policy making, network neutrality and the freedom of the web.

"Unlike telegraphy and telephony," Tiziana Terranova once wrote, "the communication of information in computer networks does not start with a sender, a receiver and a line, but with an overall information space, constituted by a tangle of possible directions and routes, where information propagates by autonomously finding the lines of least resistance."[35] "This," she further argues, "produces a space that is not just a 'space of passage' for information, but an informational machine itself—an active and turbulent space."[36] The inconstant, improvisational, and mutable qualities of online information transmissions imply that network traffic is constantly in flux. Therefore, it is not certain that a play on Spotify will activate the same data centers, backbone providers, CDNs, and advertisement brokers mentioned in this intervention. Rather, any snapshot of Spotify's infrastructuring unavoidably links to a position from which the snapshot was taken. Instead of being read as a general depiction of the kinds of data transmissions that a Spotify click triggers, the results of our eavesdropping session must therefore be read as highly situated and context dependent.

The scholarly significance of this intervention is thus not to make general claims regarding how Spotify organizes its data infrastructure but rather to provide an example of its complexities. As Brian Larkin notes, infrastructures play a dual role: they are things that "enable the movement of other matter" while simultaneously also constituting "the relationship between things."[37] As both things and relations, then, Spotify's data infrastructures connect, prompt, and link together various distributed elements across large geographic distances. While this experiment has far from exhausted the kinds of infrastructures that a service such as Spotify relies on, it has provided some insight into the lively, complex, and sometimes downright-failing network transmissions that a simple click can generate. When pushing play on Spotify, music is heard—amid a cacophony of other data.

3 How Does Spotify Package Music?

"Dear Spotify, sometimes I don't know what to listen to." We know what you mean. Sure, having millions of songs in your pocket has changed the way you listen to music, but can you figure out what to play on a lazy Sunday afternoon?[1]

In 2013, those were the words with which Spotify introduced a "new and entirely personal way of discovering music," which aimed to predict user preferences based on previous listening. Followed by the launch of "expert playlists for every mood and moment" a few months later,[2] the new features pointed to a shift in the company's way of attending to both music and its users. Period E—as this phase is referred to in chapter 1—meant a turn toward algorithmic and human-curated recommendations, through which the company promised to offer a personalized experience with "music for everyone." The emphasis on recommendations illustrates how Spotify, similar to other digital content providers, not only delivers music but also actively frames and shapes data. The service thereby promotes certain values and identities over others, with music files being contextualized in a range of different ways: through playlists and other classificatory systems, through visual and textual elements of the interface, and through recommendations delivered to particular groups of users. Such operations are central for turning digital music into goods, but they also constitute a politics of content through which the delivery of music implicates prescriptive notions of the streaming user.

The integration of music files into larger value systems is dependent on two elements: the curatorial processes designed to be carried out behind the scenes (as described in chapter 2) and the interface through which users engage with the perceptible features and materialized effects of these processes. While the previous chapter was centered on the back end and various technical systems beneath the surface of Spotify's desktop client, this chapter is concerned with Spotify's front end. It engages primarily with the level of the interface as part of a larger apparatus that shapes digital music delivery and users' modes of relating to musical content in the forms of various "expert curations."

While scholars such as Nick Montfort and Matthew Kirschenbaum have cautioned against one-sided "screen essentialism[s]" that privilege visual aspects of digital media at the expense of material analysis,[3] any attempt at uncovering the workings and effects of data contextualization must take into account both media-specific properties and representational content. As Johanna Drucker argues, graphical interfaces are in themselves "zone[s] of affordances" that organize data in particular ways and thereby foreground some things rather than others.[4] In this sense, the interplays between users and interfaces—and thus the sprawling system of human and computational actors underlying them—come to constitute particular realities and ways of being.[5]

By drawing on playlists and album recommendations that were observed and collected between 2015 and 2017, this chapter sets out to discuss the inherently political aspects of Spotify's recommendation features and how they (re)instate certain notions of music, of streaming, and of the ideal user. More specifically, the chapter builds on data from a number of case studies in which both manual data collection and bots were deployed to retrieve information about recommendation features as seen from a user angle. The bots were programmed to play particular songs and then capture the response in terms of generated recommendations. Together with manual observations and documentation of 224 playlists from Spotify's mood- and activity-based categories, this has enabled us to perform close readings of visual representations and interface elements while also analyzing processes of personalization in music deliveries.[6] Contextualized through critical analysis of promotional materials, journalistic accounts, and online user discussions, the collected data has provided us with an understanding of the performative effects of Spotify's way of packaging music.

What's in a Playlist?

It is often claimed that the digitization of music distribution involved a disaggregation of the otherwise dominant form of music commodity: the album.[7] Relatedly, the popularization of file sharing by Napster around the turn of the millennium is typically mentioned as the point at which individual tracks were set loose from the album format, lending themselves instead to be mixed and matched according to the preferences of their listeners. Early media player software such as Winamp provided functionality for reaggregating tracks into customized playlists—an approach to music that built on previous assembling practices and technologies, such as broadcast radio, compilation albums, and mixtapes.[8] Playlists thus have a longer history but emerged in their digital form as a way of recommodifying the individual tracks of the disaggregated album. Now a staple of every streaming media service, they are, to cite Jeremy Wade Morris, metacommodities that "rewrap individual commodities into a bundle under the assumption that the new whole is greater than the sum of its old parts and that another new whole is only a recombination away."[9]

The streaming metaphor itself implies a continuous flow of music, reminiscent of a never-ending playlist—and playlists have indeed been one of the main devices by which users have created and managed their personal music collections on Spotify since its launch. As we have charted in detail in chapter 1, Spotify was initially centered around a search-based interface where users would have to enter keywords to find their desired music, unless they had imported their locally stored MP3 files. Tracks could then be added to a personal library or dragged and dropped into sharable and collaborative playlists. In other words, a notion of sociality was built into the service early on, but it has—somewhat paradoxically—come to be backgrounded through the service's continuous transformation toward an increasingly personalized experience. For the purposes of this chapter, the single most important change to Spotify was the so-called curatorial turn, in 2013, from a search-based interface focused on simply accessing music to its current emphasis on delivering crafted music recommendations.

Introducing a range of prepackaged lists for different tastes and occasions, Spotify then consolidated the playlist's status as a privileged object of its streaming universe and also reframed the playlist from being a primarily social and interactive element to being an object of editorial and algorithmic expertise.[10] Both the search box and the recommendation deliveries can be understood as ways of managing overabundance in an archive so vast that it makes other browsing practices—such as shuffling through the entire collection—impossible. Importantly, however, they also represent two quite different notions of the streaming user.[11] As we have argued elsewhere, the former reliance on the search engine made music consumption "dependent on a conscious reflection on the part of the listener, who is forced to ask herself: 'what music do I want to listen to right now?'" This upholds the fictions of individual taste and consumer choice. In contrast to this positioning of streaming listeners as knowledgeable consumers, the reorganization toward a recommendation-based interface—still a form of music navigation largely "characterized by the centrality of text (and image) rather than sound"—imagined the listener as being in urgent need of musical advice and guidance from experts.[12]

More specifically, the 2013 turn toward tailored music recommendations, with Spotify being a producer of "entirely personal" musical experiences, was materialized in the (now slightly rearranged) Discover, Browse, and Follow features. Together, these functionalities allowed users to follow their favorite artists and tastemakers and to check out selected music based on previous listening patterns and editorial decisions.[13] Through such collaboratively filtered album recommendations and prepackaged playlists, Spotify now took on a new role of delivering music "for every moment," thus increasing the service's reliance on both curatorial expertise and algorithmic systems. The latter, however, was typically downplayed in the initial promotion of the new features, as Spotify attempted to invoke a relationship of trust with users: "We'll be your new best friend and offer handpicked recommendations that we think you'll love. We'll give you a full explanation of why we've picked each song too—like any best friend should."[14] Moreover, as discussed by Rob Drew, the trope of the mixtape added a nostalgic and affective value to this supposedly personalized mode of music streaming.[15] Rather than dedicated mixtapes, however, the computational approximations of music preferences and ready-made playlists can be seen to reference commercial mixes, such as compilation albums, as markers of "an increased level of commercialization of the music industry," in which business-related aspects are more important than the creative process.[16]

At present, the Spotify desktop client allows a user to access musical content via four different frames: through the search box in the banner; the menu bar to the left, which contains the Browse and Radio options, as well as links to the user's saved and favorited content; the feed of followers' streams to the right; and the main content frame in the center, which presents search results or automatically selected playlists. The player is found in the footer. For Spotify Free accounts, the otherwise sleek interface typically has a banner area that contains advertisements. Figure 3.1 offers a vivid depiction of the sponsored promotion of artist Selena Gomez, which at first glance is not easily distinguished from the other, Spotify-promoted musical content.[17]

The Browse tab is open by default when logging in to the service, and the home page displays a selection of twelve Featured Playlists, together with a short and typically cheerful greeting: "Have a great day!"; "Focus with Your Favorite Coffee!"; or "New week, new opportunities!" The message and the selected playlists are refreshed several times each day and also vary between countries.[18] As seen in figure 3.1, playlists are visually represented in the form of square-shaped icons—a form of remediated album covers—and they are further framed by catchy titles and short descriptions that add affective value and context to their usage and users.

From the home page, users can move on to explore top charts, new releases, local concerts (based on their internet protocol, or IP, address), and—of special interest in this chapter—the so-called Discover and Genres & Moods features. Discover includes album recommendations based on the user's recent streaming, as well as a weekly updated playlist with supposedly new musical discoveries. Genres & Moods presents a vast number of what seem to be (at least partially) human-curated playlists, divided into a number of categories.[19] These represent both conventional music genres

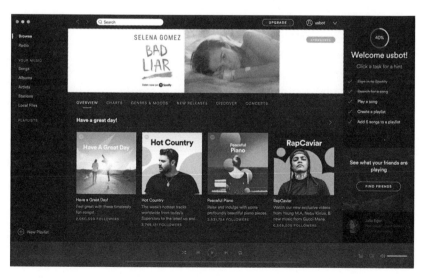

Figure 3.1
Home page of the Spotify desktop client, as seen from a US listener account in May 2017.

(typically broad ones, such as pop, electronic/dance, and hip hop) and generic moods and activities (such as Sleep, Travel, and Chill).

While Spotify provides access to a countless number of public playlists shared by individual users as well as independent curators (e.g., Indiemono, Soundplate, All Things Go), such user-created playlists can only be found through active searches. The playlists that are visually foregrounded in the interface—as Featured Playlists or Genres & Moods playlists—are the official ones compiled either by Spotify's team of curators or by playlist brands connected to Spotify partners, such as Filtr (Sony), Digster (Universal), and Topsify (Warner Music).[20] Not only are the in-house playlists thematically tailored to match advertisers' potential target groups, they can also be sponsored by advertising clients.[21] Moreover, as musical discovery through playlists is a prominent selling point for Spotify, playlists work as promotional devices for record labels and musicians. Because curation "has become a neutralised marketing term for taste-making and gatekeeping,"[22] the selection and inclusion of specific artists on Spotify-curated playlists—some of them with millions of followers—have enormous effects for building a fan base and for increasing the number of streams and generating more revenue.[23] Consequently, record labels work heavily with playlist promotion, aggregators such as CD Baby advise their members on how to best reach out to curators, and online discussions abound among independent artists on how to get their music on popular playlists.[24] Meanwhile, Spotify keeps asserting the independence of its in-house content curators.[25]

In addition to being an important avenue for music marketing, the promotion of prepackaged playlists—as well as specific albums—should be acknowledged as a value-laden practice that is constitutive of certain subjectivities. The emphasis on delivering recommendations in the Spotify interface forges an asymmetrical relation between casual users and musical experts, with the former being understood as requiring assistance to find their way through the overwhelming collections. The implicit and explicit interactivity of the service—such as the possibility for users to share and jointly work on personal playlists, or the collaborative filtering of listening habits on which personalized recommendations are based—suggest that any user could potentially become a tastemaker, knowingly or not. The favoring of Spotify's official playlists by way of the interface design, however, still insists on the significance of expertise in selecting the right, "handpicked" music for every user.

Soundtracking the Lives of Happy Subjects

"You can soundtrack your entire life with Spotify. Whatever you're doing or feeling, we've got the music to make it better."[26] That was the bold declaration on the webpage of Spotify Running, a recently retired mobile functionality that used tempo detection to match "songs you love to the tempo you're running."[27] The Running feature provided an illustrative example of Spotify's attempts at selling a "branded musical experience" oriented toward personal improvement, something that can be seen throughout the service and especially in the promotion of ready-made playlists.[28] In a previous publication, we explored the ideals promoted through the rotation of Featured Playlists and their accompanying greeting messages on the home page.[29] This content category is what users first meet when they sign in to the service, and it provides thematically selected playlists and messages for mornings, afternoons, evenings, and weekends. Because it is refreshed several times a day, its content is essential to how the Spotify client produces a sense of real time–ness through filtering streams by time of day.[30] As we demonstrated in our previous study, the particular notion of temporality presented here is also bound up with chrono-normative prescriptions of "the good life" that instruct users to get out of bed, go to work (in an office), work out in the afternoon, and then socialize with friends, family, and lovers in the evening. Meanwhile, music is presented as a way of increasing productivity and performance in these time-bound activities.[31]

However, the larger collection of Genres & Moods playlists, from which Featured Playlists seem to be retrieved, is not dayparted in the same way. It is currently organized into roughly forty different genre-based and thematic music categories, the exact content of which varies slightly over time and between geographic places. For example, in the spring of 2017, a snapshot comparison showed that some genres were provided to users in only one or a few countries (for example, Dansband in Sweden and Cantopop, Brazilian Music, and Mandopop in Singapore and Hong Kong). A Christian music category was present in many parts of the world but absent in European countries. Latin music, while present in all of the locations we explored, was typically found toward the bottom of the page—except for users registered in Spain and Mexico, to whom it was suggested among the top choices.[32] Judging from language and musical content, a substantial number of the specific playlists found in each category were likewise based

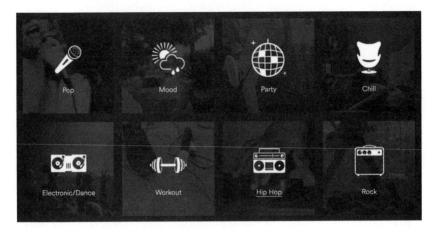

Figure 3.2
Spotify's top eight Genres & Moods categories, as seen from a Swedish account in May 2017.

on a user's country. Unsurprisingly, this illustrates the significance of local music cultures in shaping the appearance of the service, something that arguably could also relate to copyright and licensing issues.

In addition to presenting content according to a conventional, genre-based structure, Genres & Moods also includes ten playlist categories that are specifically related to activities and mind-sets: Mood, Party, Chill, Workout, Focus, Dinner, Sleep, Travel, Romance, and Kids & Family. Some of these categories, as well as their actual playlists, can be traced back to Tunigo—the playlist app discussed in chapter 1—which was acquired by Spotify right before its shift toward a recommendation-based service in 2013. Mundane as it may seem, this taxonomy is noteworthy in its attempt to schematize every aspect of daily life, not least because the music categories correspond to target activities offered to advertising clients.[33]

Looking at the short descriptions that accompany each playlist in these activity-related categories, most lists are promoted as functional tools for accomplishing a task or reaching a certain state of mind. In our manually collected data, for instance, the Workout category included a "Motivation Mix" playlist (with 1.5 million followers at the time), which was full of "Upbeat songs that keep you motivated while doing your cardio." The Focus category held the even more popular "Deep Focus," which encourages users to "Keep calm and focus. This playlist has some great, atmospheric rock to help you relax and concentrate." The Mood category also included more specifically targeted lists, such as "The Writer's Playlist": "Suffering from writer's block? This collection of writerly and literature-inspired songs might help!"

The use of music as a functional device has a long history, especially in terms of productivity requirements in workplaces and the exercise of and resistance to power more broadly.[34] However, while the idea that music can be used to control one's body and mind is not new, the mode of "ubiquitous listening" facilitated by streaming services seems to correlate with a broader turn toward a utilitarian approach to music, whereby music consumption is increasingly understood as situational and functional for certain activities (rather than, for instance, a matter of identity work or an aesthetic experience).[35] This shift is evident not only in Spotify's classification scheme (figure 3.2) but also in other features delivered by the service. The previously mentioned Spotify Running is one example, as well as the short-lived Party feature, which included a mood slider that allowed users to indicate their desired music energy level.[36] More recently, Spotify has called out to users to "Show your mind some love" with new partner Headspace, an app for voice-guided meditations that will "help you feel happier, healthier, and more confident."[37] Whereas these examples suggest that music streaming and listening should be used for utilitarian purposes, they also privilege specific ways of thinking, feeling, and acting. In particular, they insist on self-governance through mood control, which can also be seen in how the Mood and Chill categories are found among the top music categories in all our explored countries, and how supposedly productivity-enhancing playlists are collected under the mood-related label "Focus" rather than, say, "Work."

Mood management is thus a central theme of Spotify's way of delivering music, as we have also noted elsewhere.[38] The same has been said in relation to other music streaming services: Jeremy Wade Morris and Devon Powers, for example, conclude that emphasis on the affective dimensions of music consumption is one of the key components of a shift toward a branded musical experience.[39] In a similar vein, Paul Allen Anderson discusses how streaming services increasingly work to create musical moodscapes in the tradition of older mood-delivery systems such as Muzak. Music recommendations, then, can be understood as products for mood enhancement and the management of psychological capital. According to Anderson,

"Neo-Muzak services encourage listeners as never before to explicitly play with moods, to try out their tonalities and colorings at work, home, and anywhere with network reception."[40] However, complementing Morris and Powers's broad discussion of mood management, and in contrast to Anderson's emphasis on the circulation of and play with different moods, we want to emphasize the singularity of "Mood," as the category is labeled on the Spotify interface. The branded musical experience delivered by Spotify does not seem to involve much playing around with different moods. Instead, it evokes fantasies of one specific state of mind and the moral values that come with it: happiness.

By *happiness*, we refer to contemporary formations of emotional well-being, as well as their improvement through techniques of the self that stem from popular positive psychology. The discourse of positive psychology promotes the idea that happiness is a result of one's cognitive outlook, as well as "a task, a regimen, a daily undertaking in which the individual produces positive emotional states just as a fitness guru might shape a desired muscle group."[41] Looking specifically at the presentation of top playlists delivered in the Mood category of our data, these are almost exclusively devoted to the maximization of positively charged emotions, with descriptions such as the following:

- "Set it off with these epic anthems. Only good vibes here!" ("Good Vibes")
- "The perfectly brewed cup, the perfect songs to match. Your happy place is right here." ("Coffee + Chill")
- "Hits to boost your mood and fill you with happiness." ("Happy Hits!")
- "Let your worries and cares slip away..." ("Relax & Unwind")

Affective responses to and connotations of music are, of course, highly subjective. The same songs can be included in differently themed playlists, and the same playlists are also found in different music categories. However, our interest lies not with the subjective experience of musical content but with the universalizing and homogenizing aspects of its packaging: "Need a burst of inspiration?" "Need to cheer up?" "Feeling tired?" Met with such rhetorical questions in playlist descriptions, users are repeatedly called upon to cultivate their optimism by using music to manipulate or cure their thoughts and behaviors. The promotion of music as a technique for achieving the (most likely unattainable) ideal of happiness is reflected not only in calls to feel "happy-go-lucky to a lush and glossy mix of bouncy and peppy tunes. Stay positive—life is good!" but also in how the service offers help to overcome difficulties in times of emotional hardship:

- "Breathe deep and release that pressure right now with The Stress Buster."
- "When someone you love becomes a memory…find solace in these songs." ("Coping with Loss")
- "The best cure for a broken heart or lost love. Angry or sad songs. You never know when you need comfort for a heart break—breakup songs is here for you!" ("Breakup Songs")

The mood-based recommendations simply promise to provide the conditions necessary for fostering happiness—even in times of utter darkness.[42]

In this sense, the positive thinking characteristic of prepackaged playlists is intimately tied to the privileging of "entrepreneurial subjectivity," as users are encouraged to direct their desire for change inwards and "capably manage difficulties and hide injuries."[43] Spotify, however, also offers a small number of playlists that provide a corrective to the happiness imperative, such as the "Life Sucks" list ("Feeling like everything just plain sucks? We've all been there. These songs will probably only make you feel worse, but at least they'll let you know you're not alone")—or "Down in the Dumps" ("It's a horrible day and nothing can change your mind"). These rare examples of negative sentiment open up spaces for reflection on the compulsory positivity of the interface, precisely because of their otherness in this context.

The general self-help ethos and cheerfulness of playlist descriptions is echoed in the graphical display of playlists, as seen in the (mostly) brightly colored covers of the top Mood playlists. The square-shaped cover icons conform to a visual aesthetic that combines the conventions of stock photography with traits of what Lev Manovich terms "Instagramism." The concept refers to "the aesthetic of the new global digital youth class that emerge[d] in early 2010s," which overlaps in many ways with the currently dominant commercial aesthetic.[44] In addition to the square format, other visual characteristics of Instagramism present in the playlist covers include the privileging of flat rather than deep space and bodies cut by frame rather than symmetrically arranged full figures. This visual form resonates with the lack of denotative excess and contextualization in commercial stock photography,[45] while at the same time constituting what Manovich describes as an "urban/hipster sensibility" by staging unique moments, feelings, and states of being. Props such as bubble gum, sunglasses, or a jetty invoke

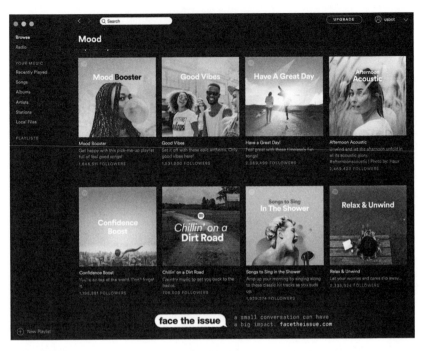

Figure 3.3
Spotify's top eight Mood playlists, as seen from a US account in June 2017.

relaxed and joyful atmospheres through which individuals are turned into cultural stereotypes of the young and happy middle class.

Such visual elements also come to constitute gender and gender relations in specific ways. The visual materializations of curated playlists tend to foreground people presenting as women, especially in the Mood and Chill categories: laughing women, smiling women, bubble gum–chewing women, relaxing women, dreamy-looking women in nature. While the use of women as playlist-marketing instruments might be understood as building on historical gender conventions in advertising, it could also be considered in light of one of our previous case studies. There, we found that an overwhelming majority of Spotify's recommended artists were male, suggesting that Spotify's curatorial authority is deployed in ways that maintain male privilege in the music industries.[46] Pitted against the visual aesthetic of playlists, this indicates that while the service reproduces an often-criticized notion of music production as a domain of masculinity, music consumption—especially for the sake of mood management—is portrayed as a female undertaking. The alluring promise of happiness and positive thinking gleaned from Spotify's mood boards can thus be seen as reproducing a gendered form of neoliberal subjectivity, where young women in particular are invited to identify themselves as entrepreneurial subjects and to embrace the values associated with "consumption, self-transformation and notions of choice."[47] Possibly reflecting the entrepreneurial mind-set demanded of contemporary cultural workers, as discussed by Rosalind Gill, it seems to favor myths of egalitarianism and individual achievement while disavowing structural power relations.[48]

While implicit modes of governance through mood management and calls for self-enhancement are pervasive throughout the service, it should be noted—as we discussed in "Intervention: The Swedish Unicorn"—that Spotify has also been known to occasionally raise traditional and overt political issues. For instance, our collected data included the somewhat controversial "Refugee Playlist," which was published in early 2017 in response to Donald Trump's travel ban.[49] In 2016, Spotify published the "Black Lives Matter" playlist, which was removed shortly after its publication, possibly due to fierce criticism.[50] Furthermore, during the US elections in 2016, Spotify launched "Clarify," a podcast targeted at young voters.[51]

The causes supported in these examples clearly target a specific audience and implicitly position the ideal user as a millennial with progressive values. And while the individual cases might be seen as providing counterpoints to the focus on interiorization in the construction of a happy, entrepreneurial subject, they are at the same time obvious examples of how a media company capitalizes on social injustice and politically charged events. In a similar vein, Spotify presents its updated "Feminist Friday" playlist every week, and the genre category WHM (Women's History Month)—"celebrating women in music and culture"—was highlighted in the spring of 2017 for Swedish users. These content categories serve to emphasize the role of women in music production while simultaneously singling out female artists as *the other* to the male norm. In contrast to the visual association of women with mood management, such explicit references to gender might be said to illustrate the new "post-postfeminist" sensibilities of mainstream media, in which a commercialized version of feminism is constructed as "a desirable, stylish, and decidedly fashionable" identity.[52]

The Unruliness of Algorithmic Profiling

Our analysis of Spotify's ready-made playlists points to the ways in which Spotify's packaging of music comprises elements of gendered consumerism, individualism, and psychologism. The promise of happiness, in short, often invokes the ideal of a self-governing subject (at least potentially) in control of their inner life and social circumstances, so long as they stream the right playlists, with the right attitude. However, user input may also affect what content is being delivered, adding further layers of meaning to the construction of the user and to ways of packaging and conceptualizing music.

Alongside the supposedly human-curated playlists of Genres & Moods, Spotify's Browse menu provides access to the Discover feature, one of the service's main selling points and part of what marked its transition in 2013. The feature has changed over the years, from the initial display of a collage-like presentation of different musical objects (songs, playlists, albums, apps) to today's streamlined organization of content in strips, including the weekly updated playlists "Discover Weekly" and "Release Radar," as well as album recommendations framed as "Top Recommendations for You," "New Releases for You," "Because You Listened to…," "Similar to…," and "Suggested for You Based on…" These tailored recommendations are supposedly based on their resemblance to the user's recently streamed artists, calculated through comparison with other users who appear to have similar taste.[53] Thus, they "organize individuals into collective forms,"[54] and the sheer number of Spotify users (140 million) provides a fertile ground for such collaborative filtering operations.

Based on accumulated data and feedback loops between recommendation deliveries and users' actions, algorithmic systems work prescriptively; they attempt to predict user preferences and therefore also tend to shape user practices. The murky workings of proprietary algorithms have spawned scholarly interest over the last decade, and a large body of work now discusses the ways in which algorithmic systems are constitutive of taste, knowledge, and cultural practices.[55] Software has performative capacities, as algorithms may attribute meaning to patterns of user behavior. Scholars have demonstrated how algorithmic content delivery has implications for the production of gender, race, and other categorizations.[56] Building on Max Weber's and Erving Goffman's notions of the "ideal type," John Cheney-Lippold argues that algorithmic identity can be thought of in terms of "measurable types"—that is, sets of observed data patterns that produce norms against which new user data can be compared and by which users can be categorized. However, as Cheney-Lippold stresses, such measurable types do not necessarily correspond with our nondatafied self-identifications or sociopolitical identities. Instead, they form constantly refreshed classifications that are usually inaccessible to ordinary users—classifications that act as modes of soft biopolitics by defining and governing large populations.[57]

While Spotify's recommendations are based precisely on this type of continuously updated data, we cannot know exactly how user behaviors are classified and sorted into normative measurable types. What we do know is that users are invited—or obliged—to have their listening habits turned into "taste profiles," which record clusters of preferred artists and genres, as well as affinity scores that measure how heavily, actively, and regularly those artists and genres are played and how much is streamed from an artist's full catalog of music.[58] Taste profiles are "mapped against wider 'cultural knowledge' about how those artists are described online, and the characteristics of their music" (such as "mainstreamness," "freshness," "diversity," and "hotness"), as well as against the profiles and listening patterns of other users.[59] Thus, each user becomes part of a larger collective intelligence from which recommendations are derived. As Matthew Ogle, product manager of the "Discover Weekly" playlist, puts it: "It's still humans who are doing the song selection and arranging, but instead of outside experts, it's users like you and me."[60] Currently, these taste profiles are not revealed to users, although there have been requests to make them public, resettable, or exportable between services.[61]

What is not known, then, is the precise content of these profiles and the wider cultural knowledge against which they are measured. Neither do we know whether or how traditional demographics factor into these calculations. Dynamic behavioral data, determined by input, is typically understood as more relevant for marketing purposes or content delivery than strict demographic categories. However, in a series of blog posts, Paul Lamere (The Echo Nest) claimed that certain artists are in fact skewed toward listeners of one gender or a certain age group.[62] More specifically, Lamere argued that "for mainstream listening about 30% of the artists in a typical male's listening rotation won't be found in a typical female listening rotation and vice versa."[63] Similarly, when comparing listeners by age, Lamere stressed that the artist overlap between thirteen-year-olds and sixty-four-year-olds was only about 35 percent. Lamere's blog posts also highlighted that streaming service users aged twenty-four to thirty-five played more music and listened to more artists than younger and older users. A similar argument has been made by Ajay Kalia, Spotify's product owner for taste profiles, who has stated in interviews that, as people get older, they tend to stop keeping up with popular music. By their mid-thirties, users' tastes have matured into a "taste freeze."[64] Despite these patterns, both Lamere and Kalia stress that demography is not as useful as actual listening patterns for predicting preferences, but it is still not clear whether or to what extent it plays a part in Spotify's recommendation deliveries.

What is evident, however, is that before creating a new account, Spotify requires every user to self-identify their gender and age (via their birthdate). The service also detects a user's location based on their IP address, thereby assigning a national identity to each user. At a later stage, users can add details such as postcode, cell phone brand, and carrier to their profile. The drop-down menus of the mandatory gender and (to some extent) birthdate fields testify to the enforced selection of what Lisa Nakamura calls "menu-driven identities," that is, a limited range of simplistic and mutually exclusive identity categories through which users have to make themselves known to a service.[65]

Menu-driven identifications are thus performative acts required for the constitution of intelligible users. The fact that they are mandatory and yet offer only a limited range of options, as Rena Bivens has shown, can be understood as symbolic violence—such as when a binary gender menu (as was included in the Spotify registration form for many years) forces non-binary users to either misrepresent their gender or abstain from using the service.[66] After many years of criticism and discussions in the user community, Spotify rolled out a third gender option ("non-binary") during the fall of 2016—but only in select locations, including Sweden, the United Kingdom, the United States, Australia, and New Zealand.[67] Arguably, the selection of countries relates to market-driven assumptions about cultural and political appropriateness in different national contexts. It illustrates the significance of geography as a main structuring device and geographic difference as a performative effect of the service.

The fact that this third option is only available in a few countries—and that gender registration, within or outside the binary, is still mandatory at the time of writing—indicates that gender is perceived as vital to the

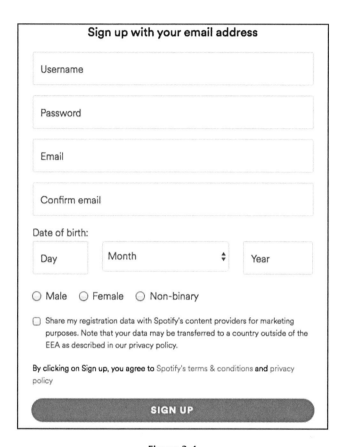

Figure 3.4
Was the introduction of a nonbinary gender option in the fall of 2016 a token of progressiveness or market-driven appropriateness?

functioning of Spotify, at least for marketing purposes.[68] In order to investigate whether demographic self-categorization matters for music delivery, in 2016 and early 2017, we set up two case studies using the previously described bots to explore the meaning of gender and age. The intention was not to reveal the secrets of Spotify's proprietary algorithms—an undertaking obviously beyond the scope of this project—but to gain insights into how the service appears to different users and thus comes to constitute situated notions of music, taste, and listening.

The results of the gender case have been reported elsewhere, and we will therefore mainly focus on some observations from the age case.[69] Here, we created Spotify accounts for thirty-two bots that were identical in all respects—apart from their assigned birthdates. They were divided by birth year into four groups: 1924 (aged ninety-three), 1954 (aged sixty-three), 1984 (aged thirty-three), and 2004 (aged thirteen). Four sets of ten songs were selected, based on one of the *Billboard* charts for the genres Hot Country, Hot Latin, Kids, and Spotify Rewind (music from the 1960s and 1970s), respectively, and two bots of each age were assigned identical music. Each bot was instructed to play its assigned songs and document the albums presented as "Top Recommendations for You." Data collection went on for six weeks, during which recommendations were retrieved on a daily basis. Focusing specifically on the recommended artists (and not albums), the data was analyzed on both the aggregated and individual bot levels. The rationale behind our methodology is discussed at greater length in the forthcoming intervention; suffice it to say, we took a special interest in two questions:

1. To what extent could age-specific artist recommendations be identified?
2. How many unique recommendations were given to bots in each music group?

All in all, we collected over twenty-one thousand recommendations, including 1,809 artists. In other words, many recommendations were repeated; for each individual bot, about 70 percent of the recommendations were duplicates that were offered several times during the course of data collection. The pace at which content changed seemed to match Spotify's claim that Discover content is refreshed every three to five days.[70] However, it should be noted that two of the music types took weeks longer than the others to generate recommendations: Kids and Spotify Rewind. Kids music is a special case in this context, as it is not supposed to affect recommendations. For Spotify Rewind, however, the reason why songs needed many streams to generate recommendations was possibly related to them being more diverse in terms of genre. Thus, the taste profiles of these bots might have been seen as less uniform and predictable. This might also explain the fact that Spotify Rewind bots were provided with the largest number of artists in their recommendations, compared to the other music types.

Generally, the proportion of what we termed "age-specific" artist recommendations was very low—only 0.3 to 2.0 percent of the total recommendations.[71] There was, however, one exception: the pair of ninety-three-year-old

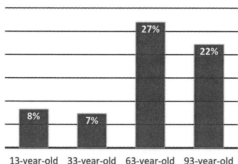

Figure 3.5
Spotify Rewind: unique artist recommendations as a percentage of each age group's total artist recommendations.

bots in the Spotify Rewind group, for which such age-specific recommendations made up just over six percent of their total artist recommendations. Besides attesting to the multifarious musical landscape of this Billboard category, it indicated that there was something special about our old-timer bots, as they were clearly set apart from the others. Looking at the ways in which unique artist recommendations—that is, artists recommended to only one bot, regardless of age—were distributed among the Spotify Rewind age pairs, we found further indications of this status.

The pairs with the oldest bots (ninety-three and sixty-three years) seemed to be provided with a much more diverse set of artists than the younger age pairs (thirty-three years and thirteen years).[72] A similar pattern was seen in the country group, in which the pair of sixty-three-year-olds also received a larger and more varied set of artist recommendations. While the case study was not designed to produce generalizable results, at first glance, the data seemed to indicate that Spotify and its music deliveries—at least at this particular moment in time and for these particular users—attributed meaning to some taste profiles that reproduced the demographically based categories assigned at registration. On the one hand, the results could be taken as a suggestion that our older bots, supposedly suffering from taste freeze, needed special—that is, *more*—help to find music and thus received a greater number of recommended artists. On the other hand, we wondered whether the music defined as similar to the streamed Rewind songs was age skewed in Paul Lamere's sense, so that there were simply more albums to offer older bots listening to this particular music style.[73]

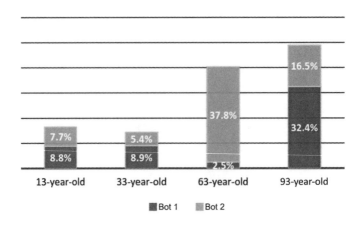

Figure 3.6
Spotify Rewind: unique artist recommendations for individual bots as a percentage
of each bot's total artist recommendations.

However, when delving into the data on an individual level, what had
initially looked like musical diversity in the pair of sixty-three-year-old bots
turned out to be the result of only one of them having received a vast number of unique artists—more than twice the average in this music group.

This was in line with the observations from our previous gender
experiment, in which a large majority of all bots within each music group
were given almost identical artist recommendations (regardless of gender), while a few of them received a much larger and more varied set of
recommendations—similar to our odd sixty-three-year-old.[74] We decided
to call the former *mainstreamers* and the latter *outliers*, although it is not
immediately clear whether the mainstreamers were given more popular
recommendations. From a user perspective, though, being positioned as an
outlier means being attributed a more alternative taste, in contrast to the
crowd of slightly more conformist and generic mainstream listeners.

Another outlier was also found among the sixty-three-year-old country
listeners, and similar constructions of users seemed to be at work in the Kids
music group. We included Kids music in the case study precisely because
children's music is supposed to be *filtered out* in algorithmic calculations
of listening patterns. According to Matthew Ogle, Spotify "made the decision early on in testing that we wouldn't include children's music. A lot
of Spotify users are parents who play Disney tunes for the kids. They do a

pretty good job of telling their parents when a new soundtrack has come out, you don't need us to help with that."[75] During the course of the case study, one of the eight bots in the Kids group (a sixty-three-year-old, again!) actually received a total of 127 different artist recommendations, while the seven other bots received none. This bot, too, was seemingly positioned as an outlier in a group where being mainstream meant not getting any recommendations at all. Notably, the recommended music included album tracks such as "Pokémon (Trap Remix)," music from the TV series *Glee* and *Family Guy*, and music from video games, as well as music by major artists Zara Larsson, Beyoncé, Bon Jovi, Katy Perry, and Christina Aguilera. While presumably aimed at a younger audience, it was still pretty far from the Kidz Bop songs that constituted the original playlist in the Kids group.

Obviously, the number of bots in the age case was too small to make any inferences about the general relationship between outlier status and specific age groups, but the results can provide a backdrop for considering how supposedly personalized recommendations are unruly and beyond the control of individual users—despite ostensibly being based on previous listening. In fact, the very notion of personalization might itself be implausible. As Cheney-Lippold notes, measurable types cannot automatically be mapped onto lived social and political identities, and it might be better to talk about "profilization" as the constantly shifting "intersections of categorical meaning that allow our data, but not necessarily us, to be 'gendered,' 'raced' and 'classed.'"[76] Users, then, are not governed in terms of individuals but as members of populations, or even clusters of correlations.[77] Nevertheless, the results of algorithmic governing are likely to affect how individual users conceive of themselves, the service, and the content delivered. Looking at the way in which recommendations were distributed among users in both the gender and the age case, it would be tempting to describe the algorithmic consequences as somewhat random and arbitrary. While always matching the musical style that our bots had previously listened to, the large variations in content and in the number of recommendations surprised us—in quite the opposite way from how the Spotify Radio function tended to repeat itself and not respond to user interaction, as described in chapter 2. As seen from the angle of our bots, then, Spotify was obviously a different service for each particular user: scant and mainstream for some, and exploratory and dynamic for a few others.

The Politics of Personalization

Despite—or precisely because of—the ongoing profiling, the trope of *personalization* looms large in Spotify's marketing. As users are drawn into a supposedly tailored universe that seeks to provide the right music for "everyone" and "every mood," they are also encouraged to enter into an affective and intimate relationship with the service. This sense of intimacy is invoked partly by phatic cues in terms of cheerful imperatives and real-time exclamations on the home page of the desktop client ("Music for your afternoon," "Get the week started with upbeat music," "Afternoon Energy?"). Moreover, it is promoted by the provision of curated playlists meant to facilitate daily activities and mood management, thereby bringing up topics otherwise understood as belonging to the private sphere.[78] The invocation of intimacy and affect can also be seen in how algorithmically calculated Discover recommendations are framed as being built on the shared collective knowledge of human users—where any user could be seen as a potential tastemaker—rather than on computational processes.[79]

These constructions of intimacy, we argue, form part of a politics of content that seek to map and shape the lives of streaming users. The selling point of Spotify is not necessarily music but music streaming framed as a deeply personal and intimate—even happiness-inducing—practice. More specifically, this chapter has shed light on how the organization and presentation of recommendations privilege certain ways of attending to music and, consequently, to oneself as a subject of contemporary digital media culture. There are at least two types of disciplining logics at play here. First, curated playlists seem to inscribe music streaming in a gendered discourse of positive psychology. While alternative points of identification were present in our collected data, music streaming at large was rendered intelligible through references to neoliberal and capitalist values of individualism, self-fashioning, and self-responsibility. The mode of packaging and (re)presenting music mostly served to reinforce the notion of the user as a happy, entrepreneurial subject—young, urban, middle-class. At the same time, happiness and an entrepreneurial ethos were promoted as the taken-for-granted ideals toward which users should strive.

Second, the profiling of users, on which the delivery of customized album recommendations is based, illustrates the other disciplining logic at play. The molding of users into types or taste profiles can itself be seen as an expression of the "soft biopolitics" that, according to Cheney-Lippold, regulate our lives without us being fully aware of it.[80] While recommendations are marketed as based on a user's previous streaming practices—and thus suggest a notion of user agency—our study indicated that users had limited control over some of the content designated as personal and recommended "for you." In fact, our interrogation of parts of the Genres & Moods and Discover features showed that the apparent personalization of music delivery, brought about by a multitude of actors and algorithmic processes and materialized on the surface of Spotify's interface, was not very personal at all. Instead, music delivery appeared overall to be structured around a combination of broad and universal claims—such as the call to deploy music in order to achieve happiness—and particularities that seem haphazard rather than personal, such as the inconsistently profiled recommendations we found in the age case.

To our knowledge, the features found on Spotify's Discover tab are the only ones that are dependent on a user's past streaming. However, the constant feedback loops of user data are invaluable to the company's business strategy, even if this is not immediately visible to users. Playlists, for instance, occupy a central role in Spotify's strategy for attracting advertisers. Targeting users either according to their moods and activities or to demographic categories ensures that advertisements can be delivered to particular groups of users at particular points in time, as will be discussed in our next chapter. Here, the trope of personalization encourages users to work on their future recommendations by streaming more music and inputting more data into the system. The functional and intimate framings of playlists insist that listeners share data not only about their streaming behavior but, implicitly, also about their state of mind at any given moment, which in turn generates revenue for the service. Hence, while the act of providing playlists for every moment is in itself constitutive of intimacy, this intimate relation is monetized at the very moment when users click play.

Intervention: Too Much Data

"This is really an anticlimax! Last time we met, we were like, 'Wow, we've got *unlimited* data, what should we do with it?' And then it took just a couple of days and we discovered that we still have *too little* data!" This disheartened remark is called out by one of us as we're sitting in front of our laptops, hardly believing what we are seeing in the Excel files. Having compiled the data from our last run of bots, we have just realized that despite tons and tons of data points in the files, none of our ninety-six bots actually got any recommendations at all from Spotify's Discover feature. And the Discover feature is the only thing we're interested in. We have loads of data here, but not the data we wanted.[1]

These short notes, recorded during the implementation of one of our bot experiments—the so-called gender case—point to the perils of navigating and trying to understand the effects of a constantly changing software system such as Spotify. They also raise critical and self-reflective questions about doing humanistic inquiry during what David Berry has termed "the computational turn."[2] What did it mean for us to have "loads of data"? What were the epistemic rationales and subjective investments at work here?[3] These are issues that we have struggled with during the course of our experimental case studies, and they were acutely brought to the fore in the case mentioned above.[4] By drawing on the field notes made during this process, we can go back to the beginning:

In early 2015, we were starting to gain momentum in the research project and were gradually establishing our roles as researchers and developers. One of the first suggestions that came up during an initial brainstorming session was to approach the issue of user profiling by investigating the relation between users' self-categorization and their recommended content. As discussed in chapter 3, gender and age are the two demographic categories required to sign up for the Spotify service. Based on what we knew about gender and age-skewed artists,[5] we were interested in how these categories corresponded to the kind of music that was recommended—and thus, how male and female users were constructed and treated in interaction with the software.

At the outset, we were unsure about how to best design such an investigation. Should data collection be dealt with manually, by creating a few accounts and observing the results in line with an ethnographic tradition, or would it be better to use automated scripts to collect data? Inspired by earlier work on algorithmic auditing,[6] and bearing the public interest in mind, we were interested in potential instances of algorithmic discrimination. We did not intend to cause harm to Spotify's software system nor to collect any personal data about Spotify users.

As researchers coming from fields primarily characterized by qualitative methods and social constructionist stances, we were well experienced in doing research based on close readings, digital ethnography, and rich, contextual data, but we had little previous experience of using quantitative scientific approaches. Notes from our first meetings reveal that we considered the manual approach to be familiar and potentially fruitful. At the same time, the idea of an automated setup was very appealing to us, as we imagined that automation would make it possible to collect structured data that, in turn, would allow more reliable comparisons between users of each gender.

Hence, after some discussion, we opted for the automated approach. We agreed that the developers at Humlab would design a script for running identical user accounts and retrieve their recommended content from the supposedly personalized Discover feature, and we were eager to start working with this type of rule-bound data collection. The developers repeatedly asked us how we wanted the data to be reported (in what format, according to what structure, etc.). Yet at the start of our project, this seemed like an abstract question to us. Furthermore, having been trained to collect empirical material in an open-ended fashion, we did not want to limit ourselves to certain forms before we knew where the study was heading. This meant, in essence, that we had no specific plan as to how we would organize the data after obtaining it.

The first step, once a structure of data capture had been developed, was to run a consistency test to analyze the stability of the system and learn more about the basics of Spotify's recommendations. For instance, we wanted to explore what type of input was needed for recommended content to be displayed to users and whether identically registered bots with identical behaviors were also given identical recommendations. For this purpose, we used seventeen bots. Some of these bots played songs, others followed artists, and some did nothing at all. The resulting amount of data was quite small, and we managed to analyze it manually. It showed that streaming was indeed needed for recommendations to appear and that the bots that streamed the same songs also received the same recommendations. Satisfied to see that the system worked the way we had hoped, we set out to design a small pilot study with sixteen bots that were identical apart from their gender (half were registered as male users and half as female). The bots were divided into four music genre groups, meaning that two bots of each gender streamed the same tracks. This design, we thought, might indicate potential gender and genre differences in the recommendations, and depending on the results of the pilot, we would then proceed with an extended study.

The pilot study went on for five days, with data capture occurring twice a day. The results were presented to us in the form of spreadsheets as well as through an interface built specifically for the project, which enabled us to view the documentation for each individual bot and session but not compare them or aggregate data from several bots.

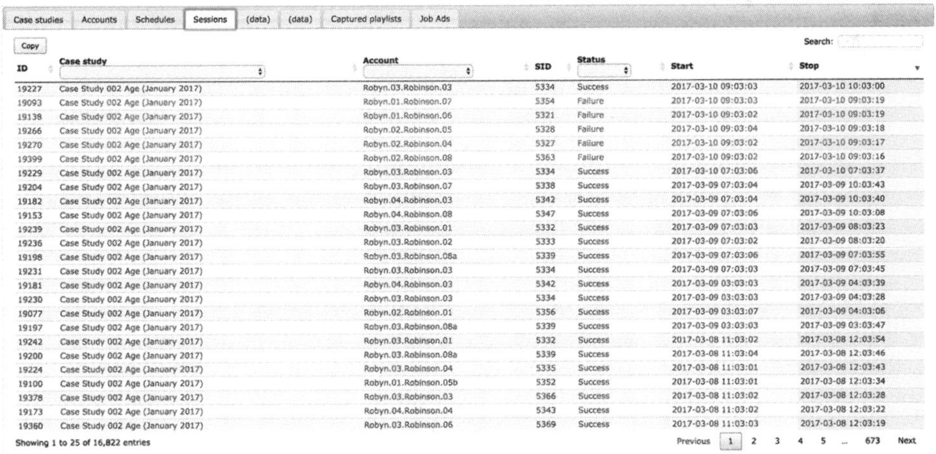

ID	Case study	Account	SID	Status	Start	Stop
19227	Case Study 002 Age (January 2017)	Robyn.03.Robinson.03	5334	Success	2017-03-10 09:03:03	2017-03-10 10:03:00
19093	Case Study 002 Age (January 2017)	Robyn.01.Robinson.07	5354	Failure	2017-03-10 09:03:03	2017-03-10 09:03:19
19138	Case Study 002 Age (January 2017)	Robyn.01.Robinson.06	5321	Failure	2017-03-10 09:03:02	2017-03-10 09:03:19
19266	Case Study 002 Age (January 2017)	Robyn.02.Robinson.05	5328	Failure	2017-03-10 09:03:04	2017-03-10 09:03:18
19270	Case Study 002 Age (January 2017)	Robyn.02.Robinson.04	5327	Failure	2017-03-10 09:03:02	2017-03-10 09:03:17
19399	Case Study 002 Age (January 2017)	Robyn.02.Robinson.08	5363	Failure	2017-03-10 09:03:02	2017-03-10 09:03:16
19229	Case Study 002 Age (January 2017)	Robyn.03.Robinson.03	5334	Success	2017-03-10 07:03:06	2017-03-10 07:03:37
19204	Case Study 002 Age (January 2017)	Robyn.03.Robinson.07	5338	Success	2017-03-09 07:03:04	2017-03-09 10:03:43
19182	Case Study 002 Age (January 2017)	Robyn.04.Robinson.03	5342	Success	2017-03-09 07:03:04	2017-03-09 10:03:40
19153	Case Study 002 Age (January 2017)	Robyn.04.Robinson.08	5347	Success	2017-03-09 07:03:06	2017-03-09 10:03:08
19239	Case Study 002 Age (January 2017)	Robyn.03.Robinson.01	5332	Success	2017-03-09 07:03:03	2017-03-09 08:03:23
19236	Case Study 002 Age (January 2017)	Robyn.03.Robinson.02	5333	Success	2017-03-09 07:03:02	2017-03-09 08:03:20
19198	Case Study 002 Age (January 2017)	Robyn.03.Robinson.08a	5339	Success	2017-03-09 07:03:06	2017-03-09 07:03:55
19231	Case Study 002 Age (January 2017)	Robyn.03.Robinson.03	5334	Success	2017-03-09 07:03:03	2017-03-09 07:03:45
19181	Case Study 002 Age (January 2017)	Robyn.04.Robinson.03	5342	Success	2017-03-09 03:03:03	2017-03-09 04:03:39
19230	Case Study 002 Age (January 2017)	Robyn.03.Robinson.03	5334	Success	2017-03-09 03:03:03	2017-03-09 04:03:28
19077	Case Study 002 Age (January 2017)	Robyn.02.Robinson.01	5356	Success	2017-03-09 03:03:07	2017-03-09 04:03:06
19197	Case Study 002 Age (January 2017)	Robyn.03.Robinson.08a	5339	Success	2017-03-09 03:03:03	2017-03-09 03:03:47
19242	Case Study 002 Age (January 2017)	Robyn.03.Robinson.01	5332	Success	2017-03-08 11:03:02	2017-03-08 12:03:54
19200	Case Study 002 Age (January 2017)	Robyn.03.Robinson.08a	5339	Success	2017-03-08 11:03:04	2017-03-08 12:03:46
19224	Case Study 002 Age (January 2017)	Robyn.03.Robinson.04	5335	Success	2017-03-08 11:03:01	2017-03-08 12:03:43
19100	Case Study 002 Age (January 2017)	Robyn.01.Robinson.05b	5352	Success	2017-03-08 11:03:01	2017-03-08 12:03:34
19378	Case Study 002 Age (January 2017)	Robyn.03.Robinson.03	5366	Success	2017-03-08 11:03:02	2017-03-08 12:03:28
19173	Case Study 002 Age (January 2017)	Robyn.04.Robinson.04	5343	Success	2017-03-08 11:03:03	2017-03-08 12:03:22
19360	Case Study 002 Age (January 2017)	Robyn.03.Robinson.06	5369	Success	2017-03-08 11:03:03	2017-03-08 12:03:19

Showing 1 to 25 of 16,822 entries

Previous 1 2 3 4 5 ... 673 Next

Figure 3.7
The interface used to facilitate research in some of the case studies.

Although captivated by the structured feel of the data presentation—where bot IDs, time stamps, input data, and output data were recorded—we were not able to get close enough to the data to detect any gendered patterns in the recommendations. Had the pilot study not been running long enough? Did we approach the data in the wrong way by only doing synchronic comparisons between recommendations provided at the same point in time? Or were there simply no gender differences—something that, we reassuringly told one another, would be an important result in itself? As we were beginning to experience frustration, one of the developers demonstrated some simple network visualizations of the data. This presentation enabled us to see that there were indeed variations in which artists were recommended to male and female registered bots—differences that we had not previously been able to identify manually and that were noticeable only when aggregating and comparing all recommendations for each gender.

With these preliminary results in mind, we decided to scale up the test. Aware of the opacity and potential bias of algorithmic recommendations and the way these are subject to constant change, we wanted to confirm the results from the pilot study. Having embarked on a project that involved structured data collection and quantification of results, we also felt a simultaneous urge and duty to continue on this chosen methodological path. By using more bots and capturing more data, we assumed that we would generate more valid results. Thus, we eventually decided to use ninety-six bots for the next round. And instead of only targeting selected elements of the web client, such as the Discover recommendations in the pilot study, we now wanted to capture as much as possible. Notes and recordings from our meetings reveal how every nook and cranny of the client was perceived as a possible source of knowledge about music streaming: What if we missed something? Why not capture everything when we had the means to do so? We realized that this would result in quite a lot of data and that we had no definite plan for how to manage it, but we agreed that we'd cross that bridge when we came to it.

Thus, a system was set up where roughly fifteen thousand data points would be collected daily.[7] Using both the web client and the Spotify application programming interface (API), we received screenshots, HTML documents, and logs of each instance of data capture. When one week's worth of data had been collected, we consequently found ourselves in the midst of a flood of data detailing different aspects of music recommendations. While we were thrilled, it also felt slightly unsettling. What now? What would we do with all of this information? How does one even begin to sift through all of these entries? We had a hundred thousand data points to consider, and we were not even well experienced in working with spreadsheets.

In other words, we were immersed in data, but not in the ethnographic sense. The data lacked the richness and deep contextualization that we were used to, and the immersion did not help us get any closer to understanding the potentially gendered dimensions of Spotify's recommendations. And while our notes, reflections, and documentation from project meetings provided a much-needed context to our methodological decisions, they did not shed light on our actual research question. At the same time, we felt truly excited that we had managed to extract such tremendous loads of data. In a meeting with the project team, we discussed how smoothly the process of data collection had run and that "there's simply too much damn data" for us to work with.[8] A few of us promised to look further into it and get back to the team a week later with some initial observations.

Because we realized that we could not review this mass of data from the existing interface, we asked the developers to design a tool for comparing input data between bots. With this solution in our hands, we sat down together and began scrolling through the entry list in the drop-down menu. Even though we had known from the start that we would end up with a large amount of data, the seeming endlessness of the list was almost shocking. Slightly overwhelmed by the massive records, we collected ourselves enough to start running comparisons between male and female registered bots in each of the four music genres. As playlist recommendations popped up on our screen, highlighted by bold colors, we gradually noted that they only referred to the country-specific Featured Playlists and Genres & Moods features. The specific recommendation category that we were interested in, Spotify's supposedly personalized Discover feature, did not show up on the screen at all. Perplexed by this fact, we double-checked it with the developers, who confirmed our worries. There were simply no Discover recommendations in the huge database.

This realization, then, takes us back to the opening quote of this section. Despite our successful capture of substantial amounts of data, we still lacked the specific data points that we were after. More precisely, none of our ninety-six bots had received any personalized recommendations during the course of data collection—not one single bot! We could track the greetings they had received at different times during the week, as well as new album releases and the prepackaged playlists delivered to them through the Genres & Moods feature. But we already knew that these elements were broadcast to larger populations and not tailored to individuals. This was not the data needed to explore patterns of gendering. The data that lay before us was useless for our purposes.

This insight left us disappointed, of course, but we were also puzzled as to why the Discover recommendations were absent in the first place. Trying to figure out where things had gone wrong, we speculated together with the developers: Had we somehow accidentally managed to create a setup that made the bots immune to user profiling? Could the lack of personalized recommendations be related to the weeks that passed between registration of the bot accounts and implementation of the actual test? Perhaps Spotify had categorized our bots as lazy and unworthy of recommendations because they didn't use the service immediately after registration? Was it possible that the service had identified our bots as bots and therefore blocked their recommendations? But then again, why not block them from the service as a whole if that was the case? Perhaps our bots had simply not streamed enough music? Even if ten played songs had been sufficient to generate recommendations in the pilot study, Spotify could have changed its requirements so that the study was no longer reproducible. A thousand theories like these were running through our heads as we traced the historical details of each data capture, making sure that our bots had behaved as intended.

For comparison, we then ran a series of manual tests using fresh Spotify accounts. Here, to our great surprise, recommendations appeared shortly after streaming began, sometimes after as few as two played songs and after at most eleven streamed tracks. It did not make sense. If that was the approximate range of streams needed, then at least some of our bots—having streamed seven times ten tracks each—should have received some recommendations. Annoyed by this result, we repeated the automated setup with sixteen gendered bots, letting them stream songs for yet another week. During this period, personalized recommendations finally began to roll out for some but not in any coherent manner. Instead, there were quite large variations between the bots as to the number of streams needed to generate recommendations. Was it all simply a matter of performance on the part of the service, with recommendations being partially scheduled to avoid overloading the systems? Frustrated by the lack of consistency, we found ourselves struggling to find a rational—and, in particular, causal—explanation for what seemed to be entirely random patterns of recommendations.

Without any clear answer, we began to think of the gender case as an outright methodological failure. Scrutinizing our setup, we also started doubting if the number of bots was sufficient for answering our initial research question. We had not fully assessed different ways of approaching the data—for instance, whether it would be useful to have an in-depth, interpretative look at the musical content delivered to our bots—but simply found ourselves oriented toward statistical comparison ever since deciding on the automated setup. Having initiated this automated approach, we felt as if we were also compelled to engage in a form of knowledge production that required quantification, and we began to think that the bots might be too few to generate any valid results. To address this problem, we scaled up the test to 144 bots of each gender, which was the limit of what our systems could handle. This time, we let it run until we had made sure that all bots received some personalized recommendations. Finally, it all proceeded without major difficulties. (The results, by the way, did not indicate any significant differences in how male and female users were treated by the client.[9])

So, why are we telling this story of an initially failed case study? It is not because of some masochistic desire to put our mistakes and ignorance on display but because we want to intervene with our own assumptions and stress the need to reflect on how research could always have been done otherwise. Our narrative describes the complications of trying to capture the outcomes of a constantly changing system, as well as the ways in which digital skills and disciplinary backgrounds on the part of researchers may impede (or facilitate) such endeavors. Furthermore, it sheds light on how scientific identities and methodologies are not only bound up with different ontologies and epistemologies but also "built around emotionally charged constructs" or fantasies.[10]

By *fantasy*, we refer to Jason Glynos's Lacanian use of the term as a way of critically explaining why people become invested in certain discourses. More specifically, Glynos describes "a narrative structure involving some reference to an idealized scenario promising an imaginary fullness or wholeness (the beatific side of fantasy) and, by implication, a disaster scenario (the horrific side of fantasy)."[11] From an ethnographic point of view, as Anna Johansson and Anna Sofia Lundgren demonstrate, the use of digital technology for research purposes has historically been construed both in terms of an imaginary fullness and a threatening disaster: the former because it provides ethnography with methodological rigor, order, and distance, and the latter because it might be seen to threaten traditional values in ethnographic research, such as empirical immersion, creativity, and personal involvement. Such fantasies of digital technology thus build on a longer history of perceived oppositions between technology and culture—oppositions that tie in with persistent tensions between explicit and less explicit methodologies; between computers as orderly and fieldwork as messy; between computer-driven and human-driven modes of analysis; between quantitative and qualitative analysis; and between distance and closeness to data.[12] In other words, while digital technology has sometimes been conceptualized as a threat to the foundational values of qualitative research, it is also linked to dominant notions of objectivity and "scientificity."[13] Engaging with computational methods as an ethnographer—or, in a broader sense, as a humanistic or social science scholar—hence implies that one is drawn into (and possibly subordinated by) already established power relations between different scientific epistemologies.

In hindsight, our methodological choices and experiences during the experiment on Spotify's gendered recommendations were—at least to some extent—structured precisely by a beatific fantasy of digital technology. Our first tests did not include a large number of bots; manual observations and collection of data in this context would indeed have been possible in practice. Still, we opted for the automated setup, having great hopes for what it would help us achieve. Our hopes were fueled by the idea that automated bot methods would provide the rigor and systematicness necessary for a scientifically valid analysis of algorithmic effects—an idea that was, in turn, related to unspoken assumptions about digital data as being possible to master through standardization (and, at a later stage, quantification).

Jason Glynos's notion of fantasy involves a promise of "imaginary fullness," but as this fullness is inherently unattainable, any fantasy also involves the construction of "obstacles" that explain why fullness is not yet achieved.[14] In the gender case, our choice of methods seems to have been guided by a fantasy in which digital technology symbolized a fullness to come in the form of a quantified and well-organized scientificity. However, as demonstrated in our narration of the process, the paths and detours taken en route to the end result proved to be far from the systematic and well-ordered scientific endeavor we had imagined. The frustration and unease that we experienced during this process was caused not only by the actual system failures—or even by our own troubles in making sense of the large amounts of data. Rather, our ambivalent feelings toward our methodological approach were related to our initial fantasy of what the bot setup would help us achieve: a systematic and well-ordered analysis of structured and easily comparable data.

Invested in this fantasy, we were oblivious to the fact that our frustration and perceived methodological failures were indeed reminiscent of how qualitative, and especially ethnographic, research is always expected to unfold: as an unpredictable, open-ended, and messy process. Instead of recognizing this complexity as a valuable aspect of the research setup—an aspect that could tell us something about the incoherent and constantly shifting ways in which algorithmic systems work—we perceived it as an obstacle to attaining a certain form of desired scientificity. By discussing these methodological slips and scrutinizing our own decisions and experiences along the way, we want to remind ourselves and others of the need for reflexivity throughout the research process. We need to account for not only the methodological and interpretative choices made along the way but the subjective "desires, identifications, and investments"[15] that permeate any research process and its actual outcomes.

4 What Is the Value of Free?

Sitting amid a large crowd of agitated press representatives and industry executives, it is hard to overlook the work that has gone into staging this event. It begins, of course, with the loud playback of a funky Spotify playlist, attracting much excitement on Twitter and Periscope, where the event is being transmitted live. Neon red lights are shooting up the walls. Then the music is turned down and the lights are dimmed. An ad is screened, showing hip millennials enjoying music while pursuing activities such as running or doing laundry, ending with the tagline "For you. For now." A sweaty, pale Ek takes the stage and begins unpacking statistics, emphasizing Spotify's global claim on scale. Slides with numbers, arrows, and country icons pass in the background behind him, vividly changing colors. A product called Now, which offers personalized playlists, is launched by Spotify's vice president of user experience. Video is introduced as being part of Now. Comedians Abbi Jacobson and Ilana Glazer, creators of Comedy Central's television series Broad City, *join the VP on stage. Hilarity ensues. The comedians leave and Ek rushes back on stage, still pale and sweating, announcing video content partnerships. Another executive comes up, announcing music for running. Musician Tiësto appears and acts as if he is having an informal chat with the VP about composing music for running. The event culminates with a wall suddenly being removed, revealing D'Angelo on a previously hidden stage, with Questlove on drums. Fog machine, two songs played live, cheers from the audience. End of show.*

During fieldwork in New York City in May 2015, we got access to a media event organized by Spotify to present plans for expanding its services in response to increasing competition from YouTube, Tidal, and (most importantly) Apple Music. Addressing the press, industry executives, and investors, CEO Daniel Ek introduced major additions to Spotify's core business. These included the integration of short-form videos, podcasts, and radio, representing a shift from manually selected genres to automatically

Figure 4.1

Figure 4.2

Figure 4.3

Figure 4.4

Spotify media event, New York, May 20, 2015. Photographs by the authors.

personalized playlists, as well as "more targeted advertising."[1] Based on a trove of behavioral user data collected over the years—and on content deals with the BBC, Comedy Central, and multichannel networks such as Fullscreen, Maker Studios, and Rightster—Ek offered a top-down curated media buffet as a precondition for programmatic advertising, a mechanism using personal data and algorithms to buy and sell ads. Promising to "soundtrack your entire day, and then your entire life" and to give "new meaning to the phrase, 'stay tuned,'" Ek consistently evoked scale. Referring to "25 billion hours of listening" since launch, growing numbers of subscribers, and devices such as social tools and discovery features for further scaling the service, his presentation culminated in the claim that "Spotify is the growth in streaming, and that means so much to us!"[2]

Reading these field notes three years later, we reflect that the 2015 product launch left at least two questions open. First, what was the actual product being launched? While commentators largely took it to be about the introduction of video series programming and related content deals with Vice, Comedy Central, and Maker Studios, this content never made a lasting impression, with view counts as low as "hundreds" per video.[3] However, the curated playlists that match what listeners are doing at certain parts of the day (described in chapter 3) remain a prominent feature of Spotify. Second, to whom was this product launch addressed?

In order to answer these and related questions, this chapter begins by briefly contextualizing Spotify within a broader history of "free" access to internet services. The chapter then adopts a conceptual framework provided by economic sociology, a field of empirical research that challenges the tradition of neoclassical and mainstream economics.[4] Based on such a definition, the chapter focuses on the one element of Spotify's music market that has been at the very center of internet culture's *free* debate for almost two decades: advertising. Providing a detailed empirical and experimental study of Spotify's programmatic advertising—and ad-tech networks—we will show that targeting is part of a process that considerably exceeds the mere dissemination of digitized sounds. We also argue that Spotify's platform or interface is not where its main market materializes. While there is, of course, relevant economic input and output managed via Spotify's back end and interface, this market is in itself embedded in a more significant one that is not directly observable on or via Spotify. The chapter concludes by suggesting that the study of digital "free culture" needs to include a focus on the embedding of markets into other markets and consequently on the negative externalities usually not considered in platform studies. The real "value of free" is that it helped scale Spotify's marketplaces, the most important of which (finance) extends far beyond music.

A Brief History of *Free*

Free is the most common way of imagining the delivery of information via the internet today. In this view, digital culture largely owes its cultural specificity to the absence of a commercial revenue model for—and private ownership of—global communication infrastructure. Theorists such as Larry Downes, Philip Howard, Jeff Jarvis, Charles Leadbeater, Jeremy Rifkin, Clay Shirky, Don Tapscott, and Anthony Williams have vividly described the internet as ending the rule of monopolies and inspiring decentralized media flows.[5] A decade ago, using examples such as Wikipedia or the free and open-source software movement, Yochai Benkler famously argued for the internet as a free information ecology, where the "outputs" are "usually nonproprietary" and where "free access to a set of the basic instrumentalities of economic opportunity" is provided. "From the perspective of a society's welfare," Benkler stated, "the most efficient thing would be for those who possess information to give it away for free—or rather, for the cost of communicating it and no more."[6] Subsequently, the ideas of the internet as a common carrier of freedom of speech and of gratis access to all sorts of cultural production have often come to be conflated. In daily parlance, *free* now equals a price tag of zero for online services or products that are—or appear to be—free to use and free of charge. This price tag is variously attached to email, blogs, software, news, games, social networking, online storage, scholarship, books, film, television, and music.

Historically, in the case of music, the advent of *free* can been traced to unauthorized services such as Napster and peer-to-peer file sharing, as well as to a subsequent cultural shift from ownership of recorded music to authorized access of vast music catalogs. Since 2012, this conceptual shift from ownership to access has been accompanied by Spotify's attempt to engineer a shift "from access to context,"[7] in the sense of using music as such a context for developing a business model based on advertising revenue and subscriptions. The history of these conceptual shifts is significant and worth closer scrutiny.

The idea of free access to information is often traced back to the famous 1980s hacker slogan "Information wants to be free."[8] By the mid-1990s, however, it had already turned into a cyber-libertarian market proposition that not only envisioned a "toll-free" cyberspace for "netizens"—to recall the then-prominent jargon—but also an explicit trade-off between users and advertisers.[9] In opting for free access, users were increasingly asked to agree to a model that would exchange their personal data for the "enhanced targeting of online ads."[10] While targeting capabilities have massively increased since the advent of the social web in 2000, display ad targeting already existed in the mid-1990s.[11] Such personalized ad targeting was seen as a major promise of the internet, marking a break with earlier mass advertising principles. Also, initial attempts in 1996 by the *Wall Street Journal* and *Slate* to introduce subscriptions after a period of free access had failed dramatically.[12] The consensus was, in short, that if the internet wanted to grow, it had to be "ad-supported."

The shift from ownership to access, in other words, went along with an economies-of-scale approach to cultural content distribution, based on projected new revenue streams from ad targeting. The term *economies of scale* refers to an economic system based on diminishing marginal costs, that is, an expected decrease in the cost of production for any additional copy or unit of an item produced. Newspapers, films, and songs were envisioned as markets with unlimited scalability, since copies could be made available at no cost per copy—after the first one had been produced—premised on global access as a precondition for such unlimited growth.[13]

Turned into a market model for the emerging digital economy, *free* thus came to signify a curious shift from what it had meant previously, that is, public economies and nonprofit organizations.[14] *Free* also came to mean both gratis and voluntary, in the sense of being free to the consumer and voluntarily given to the advertiser. For instance, in 1996, the webmail service Hotmail was widely touted as an innovation for exchanging a free web-based email account for the free or "viral promotion" of its very own service by automatically adding a tagline to each email. Subsequently, companies such as Google, YouTube, Facebook, and Spotify came to be known as building on a similar "two-sided market" model, whereby a platform establishes an exchange between two different types of users that value each other's presence, without this relation being one of buyers and sellers.[15]

In theory, it is the platform that incentivizes valuable behavior between formerly disconnected parties—like "a space where people meet and not just where trade takes place."[16] In practice, this has often amounted to a model similar to ad-financed newspapers or television, wherein free programming allows the sale of audiences to advertisers. For YouTube, Facebook, Spotify, and many other services, this is what the shift from access to context has implied. Hence, understood as a market model, *free* was premised on the assumption that the exchange value of cultural production itself could be neglected. Videos, books, music, and personal data could be given away without charge, in order to enable platform owners to capitalize on the markets they had created. Although copyright infringement claims were brought up in the early histories of YouTube and Spotify,[17] these and other services quickly succeeded in establishing themselves as mediators between free users and advertisers. As we discussed in chapter 1, the hype around Spotify intensified during 2008, when it was rumored that the new service would "make music free" by relying on advertising. Thus, Spotify is often singled out as a company that positively affected supply and demand by bringing more music to more listeners, decreasing marginal and fixed costs, and exploiting the so-called indirect positive externalities between different sides of the market.[18]

In this view, Spotify has enabled advertisers to benefit from the presence of many consumers, while consumers now benefit in their discovery of products and services from many advertisers. But what are the benefits for musicians—or cultural producers more generally—whose content is the incentive attracting both sides? Chris Anderson, probably the most ardent proponent of the model that identified two-sided markets with ad-supported media, claimed that technology had made gratis access to culture inevitable. Announcing a major revival and "shift to ad-supported content" in his book, *Free: The Future of a Radical Price* (2009), Anderson found that *free* was now simply a given, not least of all for music: "Music is nothing to pay for … it's something they do for other reasons, from fun to creative expression. Which, of course, has always been true for most musicians anyway."[19]

Over the past decade, such views and the economic models on which they rely have been widely criticized. When it comes to Spotify, a substantial part of this criticism has been directed against low royalty rates caused by the company's so-called pro rata revenue share approach. *Pro rata* means that revenues received by the streaming service are divided to the rights holders based on how many approved plays a certain track has in relation to all the other tracks played at the same time. Popularity, catalog size, and catalog ownership matter, and the approach consequently benefits major labels—not independent musicians.[20] Listeners have also never valued the presence of advertisers in the way suggested by economics, as documented by continuous complaints within the Spotify community regarding the frequency, repetitiveness, and loudness of audio ads—especially in regard to the lack of proper ad targeting.[21]

Furthermore, advertising never fully supported Spotify's free tier, since it failed to generate sufficient revenue to pay for gratis access.[22] In 2015, Spotify's declared "best year ever," ad revenue accounted for only 10.1 percent of total income, with the remaining 89.9 percent coming from people paying for premium accounts.[23] Spotify has long experimented with various "freemium" models that combine free with subscription access. In 2008, for instance, the company offered four distinct tiers of service, two of which involved free access.[24] Yet the notion of freemium also largely fell short of expectations, with the result that Spotify still lost money for more than a decade.[25]

The Spotify context makes clear the limitations of the two-sided market model itself, which envisioned and then structured market activities in the first place.[26] Anderson and his many followers in business and academia strategically downplayed the possible negative externalities that have, in a somewhat ironic twist, now turned into the most widely observed consequences of this development, such as private data brokerage, platform capitalism, and the unregulated global proliferation of intermediaries.[27] If it is fair to say that the two-sided market model has failed to account for the dynamics that have come to drive the digital economy, what are its flaws? Within economics, the answer has been to adjust and to expand the two-sided market model by suggesting the need for conceptual extensions for describing various platforms or by extending from a two- or three-sided market approach to a multisided one. While such adjusted models keep enabling entrepreneurs to operationalize network economics and other theories, they fail to account for anything that is not contained in the model. It is the abstraction of the market itself that confines an understanding of digital economies to forms of platform-mediated exchange.

What is needed, in other words, is a proper empirical description of digital markets. How is music put on the market today? A growing body of work in communication and media studies attempts to answer this question about music's commodification. On the one hand, this includes industry-oriented scholarship based on interviews with music industry professionals that focus on how the music commodity can be successfully monetized.[28]

On the other hand, media historians such as Jonathan Sterne and Jeremy Wade Morris have provided more critical views on the digitization of music, focusing on particular media formats, interfaces, affordances, and social practices.[29] Morris has provided a particularly detailed account of what he describes as the "digital music commodity," arguing that once digitized, music always remains the same type of commodity. From this perspective, differences between streaming and downloading are neglected and the interfaces of Spotify or iTunes are merely understood as an arena where an already commodified object appears.[30] Although the commodification of music is not entirely determined by the techno-economic setting of a given platform, differences in the interaction design, business models, corporate strategies, or actors involved in Spotify, or any other media company's service, matter considerably.

When Morris and other scholars take it for granted that it is the same commodity that is made available by "iTunes, Spotify, and many other digital retailers,"[31] the underlying notion is that Spotify is indeed a retailer, or distributor of commodities produced elsewhere. The retail business is based on the buying and reselling of identical goods. Any company that sells commodities that are substantially different from those it has bought is evidently also engaged in some form of production. As this chapter demonstrates, Spotify indeed changes the substance and form of music as a commodity to such a degree that it cannot be seen as a mere distributor. As we have shown previously in this book, the turning point came with the introduction of personalized music recommendations in 2012 and 2013. At the same time, Spotify is also involved in market activities related to the dissemination of music. How is one to empirically grasp Spotify's twisted market realities? Where is the market, and what is actually being sold?

Entering the Market

The best way to begin an empirical encounter with market actors is to define what is meant by the notion of the *market*. In drawing from various works within economic sociology, Patrik Aspers suggests this simple definition: "A market is a social structure for the exchange of rights in which offers are evaluated and priced, and compete with one another."[32] Key here is the notion of market as a form of order, for "it is only when there is order that we can speak of a market."[33] As a form of ordering of economic knowledge and activities, markets imply a place (or forum) where goods of any kind

can be exchanged in a voluntary, peaceful, and transparent way, based on
legitimate property rights, free choice, and public prices. Markets also tend
to go by some name, indicating that they are about one kind of thing and
not another and that there is stability or extension over time—a market for
used books today will not turn into a market for fish tomorrow. Such stability, or institutionalization of a given market, even pertains to recurring
social roles where the market identity of each actor is either tied to only one
side of the market or where the roles of buyers and sellers may be switched.
In this way, most markets are "fixed role markets," according to Aspers: a
car manufacturer has an identity tied to the role of the seller of cars in the
consumer market, while in a stock exchange (or "switch-role market") buyers and sellers change places over the day.[34] In short, for a market to exist it
must be clear what is traded in the market; there must be rules governing
what (and what not) to do and by whom; and offers must obtain economic
value in the market through procedures of competition and evaluation.

This conceptual framework thus posits that markets are primarily coordination devices. Markets correlate and arrange economic interest in many
ways: by locating market activity at a certain site (virtual or real) and through
pricing, the definition of roles, and mutual agreement on what is being
traded. Coordination can also take on different forms. Apart from markets
themselves, economic behavior can be coordinated through forms of reci-
procity, or networks, and through redistribution, or hierarchy. While a market has buyers and sellers, a network implies open and reciprocal interaction
without central control within a larger cultural setting, as opposed to a hierarchy (or decision-based asymmetrical order), such as a corporate organization. Market, network, and hierarchy are ideal-type abstractions to describe
various degrees of formalization and control; they are regularly mixed in
the real world. Markets thus may take on the character of networks or hier-
archies, as implied in the notion of the two-sided or networked market.[35]
Markets also never exist in isolation: one market is always embedded in
other markets, as when a car manufacturer sells vehicles in a consumer
market while buying labor in a different market.

While providing a useful approach for describing markets in general, the
idea of markets as socioeconomic coordination devices is not easily translated into the realities of music streaming and the Spotify marketplace.
Aspers's simple questions—"What is the market about?" and "How are things
done?"—do not lead to equally straightforward answers.[36] Given the absence

of public pricing for any song, for instance, is Spotify's subscription service indeed a retailer, as opposed to iTunes' unit-based download model? Obviously not. In Spotify's early years, even property rights were lacking, as the service's cofounders did not hold the rights to the music they distributed.

So what is exchanged via Spotify? A growing number of subscribers buy access to a music catalog, but the majority of listeners still neither buy nor sell. This has prompted platform scholars to assume that, rather than being a market, Spotify is more like a network embedded in digital culture's gift-giving or "sharing" habits, based on reciprocal interests between parties.[37] Here, platform theory seems implausible, given the explicit commercial interests on both the marketers' side and the intermediary or platform's side. One could easily argue that Spotify even contains elements of a hierarchical ordering, as it redistributes music in ways that do not adequately reflect the interests of all the actors in the network. And where is all this happening? If advertisers form a key "side" of Spotify Free's networked market, the interface cannot be assumed to be the marketplace, as no evaluation or competition related to the "audience commodity" is observable.[38] So where are listeners—and listening—commodified? Who is trading?

Any answers to these questions will be only temporary, given that the entire setting of the exchange, or platform, is constantly changing, as we previously described in chapter 1. We therefore have to tackle these questions differently. In order to do so, we may come back to economic sociology's observation that markets are always embedded in other markets. Harrison White (on whose work the observation is based) argued that many markets are "mobilizers of production in networks of continuing flows," rather than isolated sites for transactions between parties.[39] Markets come in families, and what counts are the relations they entertain. In White's view, markets can be seen as located in a production chain, so that we can talk of markets in "upstream" and "downstream" relations. In fact, what we call an industry is nothing but a set of markets, of which one is the core or leading market to which other markets are auxiliary.[40]

Scaling Markets

It is helpful to think of Spotify as a market whose actors' behavior depends on what actors in other markets do. Turning away from Spotify's interface and the issue of advertising itself, it thus becomes possible to circumscribe the service marketplace from the outside—that is, by studying its environment, which also includes markets. And here the empirical work begins.

Returning to our field notes and the New York City event in May 2015, it is important to note that most commentators understood the launch of Spotify's new features as an offer made on consumer markets. But Ek's staged performance holds additional implications. In mobilizing graphs and statistics alongside music, talent, and the attending audience, Spotify engaged in a form of "data work," betting on the affective properties of data visualization.[41] Such data work comes with the routine setting of showcases and tech demos in which big data rhetoric is employed to conjure up scale. For consumers, there is no need to evoke global scales, nor is there such a need for distributors. There is no logical reason for any delivery infrastructure to make claims about scale; after all, roads are built without the promise of "25 billion" cars using them. Scale making, however, is regular practice among financial investors. As Anna Tsing notes in a study on internet investments, finance needs to conjure up scale: It is "a regular feature of the search for financial capital. ... Profit must be imagined before it can be extracted; the possibility of economic performance must be conjured like a spirit to draw an audience of potential investors."[42] Tsing's observation holds particular valence for internet economics, in which economies of scale are a key ideological framework.

Back in 2015, Spotify had to stage a "performative drama of financial conjuring" because the company attempted to grow into its $8.5 billion valuation before planning an eventual IPO, which the company finally filed for on April 3, 2018.[43] Every feature added to the service was thus also about commodifying the service itself, a service that despite its valuation had not generated any revenue. The market on which this commodity was going to be traded was not the market for music, entertainment video, or ad targets. In the decade-long buildup to its IPO and possible acquisition by Facebook, which was long rumored to be Ek's end game,[44] Spotify—like Facebook—had literally become capital or "financialized stock."[45]

As we charted in chapter 1, between October 2008 and June 2015, the company raised $1.6 billion in seven rounds of investment from twenty-six investors, including Coca-Cola, Goldman Sachs, and Palo Alto–based Technology Crossover Ventures. In 2012, Spotify had begun trading securities on the US financial market; in 2015, it raised $500 million in the form of a loan convertible into Spotify shares; and in 2016, it raised another

$1 billion in convertible debt with "devilish terms" that subsequently enforced a rapid joint stock exchange listing in Sweden and the United States.[46] Further strengthening ties to both finance and other media, Technology Crossover Ventures partner and former Netflix board member Barry McCarthy was appointed Spotify's chief financial officer in 2015, replacing Ek in key leadership functions at subsidiaries such as Spotify Ltd., Spotify Service AB, Spotify Europe AB, and Spotify Sweden AB. Spotify, in short, had turned online music distribution into a media company and then into stock options, a market over which Spotify itself had no control.

While *free* was central for scaling Spotify in the early years, by 2015, finance had become the leading market from which Spotify's other markets and their actors were governed. Using White's analogy, one might say that the markets for ads and music were located in a downstream relation to financial capital, given the money-losing company's dependence on such capital. If we describe Spotify as a production chain, then songs, videos, audiences, and ads appear as auxiliary markets, despite the company's promotional claims to the contrary when facing consumers.

As Spotify's case is not an isolated one, critics usually attribute such market structures to a "financialization" of media. Financialization, according to Max Haivens, is a broad cultural and social phenomenon, referring to a "contagious" expansion of financial "themes, ideas, tropes, measurements, metaphors and influence into spheres seemingly in no way related to the core operations of the financial economy."[47] Financial interest seems evident in the way Spotify evokes scale through reference to a potentially boundless horizontal expansion of the music streaming market—more content, more users, more data, more ads—and to the vertical scaling up across different sectors, where losses in one market may create assets in another. For instance, constantly shrinking revenues for independent musicians, caused by the effects of scale on Spotify's proportional revenue model, are projected to go along with increasing corporate treasury trading elsewhere. In this view, its market resembles a *stack*—where trading sites are stacked into or on top of one another, in often opaque, unaccountable, and unsustainable ways—rather than a two- or multisided platform.

Yet while there is reason to see Spotify's claims about scale as an effect, or symptom, of a far wider-reaching financialization of media, a focus on processes of "infrastructuring" here speaks rather to Mary Poovey's reminder that financialization "cannot be understood and should not be theorized apart from an analysis of the infrastructure that supports financial transactions."[48] Put differently, we need a still more thorough empirical examination of how Spotify's markets interrelate—or are embedded into one another—while ordering economic knowledge and activities. Here, advertising makes for a relevant case, given how it contributes to produce value from data, metrics, interactions, and patterns of listening behavior, thus contributing to the ways the world of streaming is made accessible. Advertising is key for infrastructuring the digital media ecology, as it creates the "practical ontologies" that shape the ways music looks, sounds, and feels.[49] Advertising was also key for scaling up Spotify Free. If the observation is correct that Spotify's ad market is embedded in the financial market, then it should be possible, we argue, to present evidence that financial ideas, tropes, devices, and processes matter for the way advertising is implemented and practiced on Spotify. While such an empirical approach falls short of matching the data standards of economic modeling, it correlates well with the sociological, historical, and ethnographic methods that formed this book's starting point.

Embedded in Finance

What is the advertising market about? Which goods are traded, and by whom? And how are things done? What are the beliefs, norms, tools, rules, and behaviors considered appropriate to the setting by market actors? Taking up the latter issue first, Spotify's ad market has to be seen in light of a broader corporate culture that has evolved through practices of *brokerage* and *arbitrage*. Introducing the financial concepts of brokerage and arbitrage as analytical terms, we suggest that coordination within Spotify's production chain followed and appropriated models from the financial world.

Internet critics often note that the overabundant catalogs of songs, videos, books, and academic papers that have come to epitomize platform culture would devalue content in order to maximize corporate gains. If "value depends on scarcity," scaling up seems to imply devaluing audiences, content, and ad rates.[50] While not owning, producing, or servicing anything, the argument goes, Facebook, Uber, Airbnb, YouTube, Alibaba, and Spotify are "indescribably thin layers that sit on top of vast supply systems (where the costs are) and interface with a huge number of people (where the money is)."[51] Scale, then, seems to depend both on the allegedly infinite "shelf space" of the internet and on a type of intermediary that would be able—or ruthless enough—to clear that shelf: a broker. As a theoretical figure and sociological type, the broker has a long history whose importance reemerges in contexts of state crisis.[52] Brokerage not only relates to weakening ties between state and market, as well as the increase of transnational flows, but also to entrepreneurs with both a "special expertise in manipulating boundaries: between legal and illegal, commercial and noncommercial, formal and informal" and with the talent to relocate "transactions from one side to the other."[53] The broker is a specific type of middleman: an actor who gains from the mediation of valued resources that he or she does not control. According to a well-known distinction by Bruno Latour, what distinguishes the broker as a mediator from an intermediary in the broader sense is that while the latter transports meaning without transformation, mediators "transform, translate, distort, and modify the meaning of the elements they are supposed to carry."[54] Brokerage has always been morally ambiguous, especially where inequality forms the basis for brokerage opportunities and where the broker is seen to exploit an exclusive, central location in a given network and thus becomes identified with a structural function of regulating the circulation of values.

Spotify was founded with the stated aim of mediating the interests of two conflicting parties: the music industry on the one hand and unauthorized file sharers on the other. Spotting an opportunity in the structural hole between these two disconnected groups, the company's brokerage role developed as that of a market maker.[55] Although Ek and his engineering colleagues themselves did not have anything of value to offer—neither a cultural good nor valuable contacts in the field of cultural production—they successfully began promoting trade by reducing the physical, social, and temporal distance between an industry (largely US based) and its economic free riders (mostly via Sweden's Pirate Bay). In order to do so, they transformed the meaning of online music listening by shifting focus "from access to context," so that a business model based on advertising revenue could take hold.

Bridging the gap between industry and piracy, Spotify's initially situational role as a broker soon turned into a structural brokerage function in line with the company's intensifying relations to finance. In this respect, Spotify's prevalent classification as a tech company is somewhat obscure, since—from its very start—the company was unequivocally in the business of providing content to audiences while selling those audiences to advertisers. These are defining characteristics of the media sector that put Spotify in line with cable television and satellite industries. The firm's original articles of association list "Internet-based services within digital media such as music, games, and television, and related activities," and its first subsidiaries—Spotify Sweden AB (2009) and Spotify Service AB (2012)—were established to expand advertising sales and media buying, as well as public relations and communication, respectively.[56] Spotify still came to be identified with technological innovation rather than as a traditionally operating media firm, however, because "being thought of as a tech company brings with it the potential for much higher valuations from the investment community."[57] Venture investing requires an industrial self-categorization such as Spotify's—"data processing, hosting, web portals," according to the Swedish Tax Agency's industrial classification standard (SNI)—since investors see way more potential in the technology sector than the media sector.[58] And they especially did so throughout Spotify's two initial series of venture capital funding, granted during the global financial crisis of 2007 to 2009, a period when the availability of such capital decreased—except for internet startups.[59]

Today, Spotify is neither particularly Swedish nor particularly about music. While invocations of the company's "Swedishness" are needed to sustain the venture capital vision of "European unicorns,"[60] and to position Spotify at the sexy, cool end of digital innovation, the company now acts as a digital broker whose history of equity rounds, market and debt capitalization, and board of directors firmly ties its brokerage strategies to US-based financial interests. As illustrated by the 2015 addition of television content, Spotify now operates increasingly like a conventional American media company while retaining the benefits of financial and regulatory loopholes granted to European tech firms.[61] The bet on advertising—and on what was introduced as programmatic advertising (or behavioral targeting) at the 2015 New York event—has to be seen in light of these transnational flows. As a digital broker Spotify has, in short, contributed to reconfiguring the relationship between state, market, and music.

But brokerage is not the only financial practice to be found in the way the service coordinates economic activity on and off its interfaces. Of equal importance, we argue, is *arbitrage*. Arbitrage, in market practice, is a form of trading "that aims to make low-risk profits by exploiting discrepancies in the price of the same asset or in the relative prices of similar assets."[62] Not only is arbitrage a widespread form of trading, it also builds markets and determines their scope and the extent to which they become global. When Daniel Ek, Martin Lorentzon, and others first developed Spotify, they famously did so by building on a collection of music they did not hold any rights to themselves. The history of music streaming thus begins with an act of free riding—or arbitrage. As arbitrageurs of music, Ek and his colleagues would obtain scarce goods at no cost, with the aim of making revenue through advertising and later subscriptions, while others involved in the transaction—the composers, musicians, music publishers, artists, and repertoire owners—experienced an implicit loss, at least initially (the majors), if not still today (the independents). While arbitrage loopholes may gradually be closing, what remains is an "art of association" that consists in constructing the equivalence of properties across different assets.[63] In other words, the art of making one thing the measure of something else.

Arbitrage thus creates a sense of comparability—that one may measure the value of music against the value of audience segments or subscriptions. But what counts when it comes to cultural goods, and how can they be counted? Although companies such as MyPlay.com experimented with the conversion of music into targets starting in the late 1990s,[64] they did not develop a business model for this conversion to scale. In order to properly establish a scaled exchange, Spotify had to define a unit of what is measured—a measurement standard—and a forum where exchange could take place. The evolution of Spotify's graphical user interface documents how this definition came to materialize.

Think, for instance, of the relation between playlists and the ad banners that have been a key feature of the user interface since the earliest versions of Spotify Free. If arbitrage is not about identifying the essential or relational characteristics of two assets so much as testing ideas about their correspondence based on isolated qualities of each, then playlists and call-to-action banner ads have come to mark this correspondence between music and advertising over the years. As we described in chapter 3, associating mood-oriented playlists with psychographically targeted display ads means focusing on a quality of music described as "neo-Muzak," or as a turn from sounds toward "personal care products for affect management and mood elevation."[65] Spotify is "buying" such products increasingly under value, because prices for most of its (non–major label) music continue to fall due to the effects of scale on its proportional revenue model. And it is "selling" at an increasingly higher price—or is at least attempting to drive up costs for advertisers in order to do so. While such arbitrage trading is usually deemed unfair and is expected to end as soon as the buying and selling sides match up, Spotify's pro rata share model and resulting royalty payments are unlikely to change.[66]

Brokerage and arbitrage thus provide us with an analytical framework to describe Spotify's corporate practices as tied into the logics of financial markets. Broader tendencies within company culture suggest that key decision-making incidents relate to a governing market and actors that are not primarily or solely about music. Finance is thus not simply another side of the same market, as implied by the notion of the two-sided or multisided market. Rather, it is a form of internally ordering the production chain that ranks finance above other considerations. We now need to examine what the advertising market is about, who is involved in that market, and what relations it holds to the financial logic assumed to govern the entire chain.

Automation—or Programmatic Advertising

Programmatic—the industry shorthand for *programmatic advertising*—is an obvious case to be considered in a context of financialization, given that its practices were directly and literally modeled on those of the stock exchange. Introduced in 2008, programmatic is a new transactional procedure of media buying that is projected to replace manual insertion-order (IO) inventory by 2018.[67] Put simply, it is a mechanism for using personal data and algorithms to buy and sell ads. This includes the automation of online ad buys via interconnected online "trading desks" that allow the auctioning off of inventory within milliseconds. Such trading desks are not accessible via Spotify's desktop or mobile interfaces but come as separate interfaces connecting buyers and sellers directly via real-time bidding procedures. This means that the entire ad buy market remains entirely invisible to consumers and musicians—and, importantly, that pricing is never made public. Programmatic is a matter of coordination between marketers, ad-tech firms, and Spotify, with anonymity on some sides of the market, as marketers often do not know on which platform they bet.

In principle, such automated trading of ad buys yields several advantages. It allows the sale of overabundant inventory that human sales teams have failed to sell. Thus, ad auctioning is a clear indicator that the economic value of the offer (the ads on Spotify) has not been settled and cannot be settled without an auction. While Spotify had ads long before programmatic, it is only through auctioning that a functioning market could be established. Programmatic also creates larger scales more efficiently by allowing advertisers to aggregate interactions with audiences across the web without first having to select audiences manually across thousands of publisher sites. For ad agencies and media planners, establishing automated trading desks was a defensive measure against Google and other players that ensured their own relevancy in a field where brands were able to buy directly from ad networks.[68] Low barriers of entry and high profitability created additional incentives that fueled ad-tech market growth.

Spotify promotes its platform to advertisers as an innovative setting for programmatic targeting techniques. The company's 2015 New York media event gives an idea about the value it saw, and sees, in "more targeted advertising." Ad targeting techniques include both demographic targeting and targeting content at users with particular habits, mindsets, and tastes that align with a predefined target persona. Playlists tailored to specific urban activities (such as "Morning Commute") and moods (such as "Life Sucks") are combined with data on genre preferences, age, gender, geography, language, and streaming habits, alongside information from third-party data providers about broader interests and lifestyle and shopping behaviors. It is, in short, a business model based on technologically aided information exchanges—not music. Music is rather promoted as merely functional for defining and microtargeting audience segments. The main promise of programmatic advertising is its competitive edge when it comes to demonstrating advertising's new "relevance to the consumer."[69]

While Spotify upholds the success of its efforts to match ad content to listening behaviors, members of the Spotify community regularly criticize the service for its lack of accurate targeting. They note, for example, that some ads do not match basic data sets, including the user's age, gender, location, language, genre preferences, and listening context. Such criticism is partly misdirected, however, as it wrongly puts the blame on publishers for what are, in effect, decisions made by advertisers, most of whom do not microtarget their ads but instead opt for broad media reach, always depending on overall ad campaign goals and disposable budget. Spotify itself has pointed out that ads serve the dual purpose of generating a revenue stream and encouraging advertising-adverse users to pay for Spotify Premium, a goal demonstrated by the fact that, as of August 2016, the most repetitive and frequent audio and display ads indeed promoted Spotify's own ad-free service.[70]

In order to develop a more tenable critical position vis-à-vis the market coordination enacted through programmatic advertising procedures, better empirical data are needed. Occasionally, Spotify employees leak such data in semipublic contexts, but industry leakages are seldom helpful for developing industry-critical perspectives.[71] Between August and October 2016, we therefore conducted a number of simple experiments in collaboration with programmer Roger Mähler at Humlab. Our objective was to gain insight into the ad-tech market, an issue not reliably covered via trade journals or interviews.[72] The experiments used the Ghostery browser plugin for Spotify's web player, which allowed us to map various stakeholders involved in placing ads, and Fiddler, a tool for capturing network data.[73] By establishing a Facebook user ID connected to Spotify, we were able to identify some of the advertising supply-chain vendors involved in the placing of ads related to that specific user profile. While these findings are indeed limited, they allowed us to confirm a few assertions about Spotify's production chain.

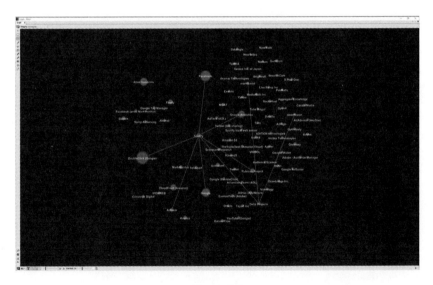

Figure 4.5
Fiddler in action, sniffing out communication between Spotify and its ad-supplying partners.

Ghostery and Fiddler provided us with a list of various companies that take part in networked interaction when browsing through a user's playlist stats. Some of these companies provide trackers, widgets, and analytics, while others measure performance. However, most are related to advertising, including (but not limited to) the following groups of actors to be found in programmatic ad sales:

Supply-Side Platforms (SSPs): AdScale, PubMatic, Rubicon, and YieldLab

Demand-Side Platforms (DSPs): AdRiver and Sociomantic

Ad Exchanges: Admeta, AppNexus, Facebook Exchange (FBX), OpenX, and Yahoo Ad Exchange

Ad Networks: Adkontekst

Ad Servers: Adtech

Data Suppliers: Seed Scientific and the Echo Nest

Data Management Platforms (DMP): BlueKai and Krux

Measurement: Moat and Google

Verification: ComScore and Nielsen

As in an actual stock exchange, the auction of Spotify audience segments is constant and continuous. Real-time bidding is managed via ad exchanges and digital marketplaces. In this brokerage setting, a publisher such as Spotify partners with one or several yield-optimization or supply-side platforms (SSPs). This partnership is designed to maximize the sale price for Spotify's impressions and to aggregate and manage Spotify's relationships with ad buyers as well as with ad exchanges and ad networks. Through the SSP, the publisher may determine whom it wants its inventory bought by, the type of ads it wants displayed, and the range of pricing: preferences that are set before trading starts. Once a publisher's sales partner or SSP (such as Rubicon) begins throwing available ad impressions into automated ad exchanges (e.g., Admeta), demand-side platforms (DSPs), such as AdRiver, analyze and purchase them on behalf of marketers and brands based on attributes such as location or specific targets, with the objective of buying ad impressions as cheaply and efficiently as possible. In addition, publishers may also presell part of their inventory at a fixed price to one or several ad networks (e.g., Adkontekst) for a particular targeted audience. From a marketer or brand perspective, the exchange may start differently: by simply buying a "whitelisted" inventory, which would also include Spotify; by accessing Spotify's inventory through a DSP for open auction bidding; or by directly contacting Spotify in case something more than just inventory is wanted, such as when first-party data are required in order to target a brand in relation to content or demographic data, as in so-called private (prenegotiated) marketplaces.[74]

Trading is fueled by consumer data that are extracted by various data suppliers and aggregated by one or several data management platforms (e.g., BlueKai). As soon as the inventory has been sold, several media- and for-mat-specializing ad servers (e.g., Adtech) will deliver the ad units to the website, while the viewability and effectiveness of the ads are monitored (by Moat or Comscore). Although the basic currency of the exchange is cost-per-mille, buyers and sellers measure differently: a marketer may optimize toward viewability or click-through settings in the DSP platform, and a publisher toward number of buyers or revenue per thousand impressions. The entire exchange process from the client's initial linking up to the publisher content server to the final placing of the ads takes less than thirty milliseconds.

Somewhat complicating the picture, several of the aforementioned firms perform multiple roles in the supply chain and may be directed toward either publishers or marketers, or both (e.g., AppNexus). None of them is exclusively working with Spotify. Spotify claims to partner exclusively with Rubicon as SSP, but in our experiment, Ghostery listed a number of special-ized SSPs that may serve specific ad format- or region-related purposes.[75] Dozens of firms, clustered in digital space but operating from often remote countries, offer highly specialized, competing or complementary services that are partly tailored to regional ad markets, subject to a constant trans-formation of technology and industry, and always actualized in their rela-tions depending on a given brand and target. Automation thus entails a *super-intermediation* of media buying. In the words of the Internet Advertis-ing Bureau, it leads to an "exploding number of ad technology products and services, new cost models, and an evolving patchwork of bundled buy-side offerings and solutions."[76] As Jana Jakovljevic, Spotify's head of program-matic advertising, admits in an interview, it is a "lot of middle-men…, defi-nitely confusing, even more so for the buy side."[77]

Our exploratory and experimental mapping of Spotify's ad-tech infra-structure allowed us to draw a few tentative conclusions about the company's ad market. For consumers and musicians, this is indeed an opaque market. Even for actors representing the advertising side, the ad market has a peculiar form of order. Its technical environment and network of involved actors are highly unstable, not only because they involve a constant switching of roles but also because of the constant expansion and accretion of the network itself. Ad tech coordinates the market through auction procedures, yet the idea of a stock exchange is misleading when it comes to the distribution of costs and benefits between actors. Ad tech increases the costs for publishers and marketers, instead of reducing them. Programmatic media buying is more expensive (especially regarding costs per exposure) than insertion-order advertising, adding an "ad tech tax" to the budget, often without transparent pricing.[78] It also disrupts long-established relations between ad agencies, media planners, and publishers. Here, automation may serve to dispose of human intermediaries and to restructure and renegotiate the input of any actor. It is, in short, not so much a form of trade modeled on the stock exchange as a form of incrementally stacked exchanges.

This chapter has shown that Spotify's ad targeting is one element in a process that goes beyond the mere dissemination of digitized sound. Spotify is a mediator, rather than an intermediary, that actively reproduces the meaning of the songs it is supposed to distribute. This reproduction is engineered through a music classification and recommender system whose output is data for advertising. The ad market constitutes but one in a family of markets connected by the Spotify brand. Given the opacity of some of these markets, the internal ordering among them remains speculative. It is likely, however, that the financial market governs all others, given the valuation reached for Spotify and the way corporate practice seems tied up into the logics of finance. None of its markets build primarily on network effects, but there are implications of hierarchy in the way songs, ads, and targets are subsumed under such logics. Somewhat ironically, these logics even put wealthy publishers such as Spotify in a precarious position, because it turns them into brokers depending on other brokers for realizing globalized claims on scale—middlemen on top of middlemen.

As a more general result of this empirical market study, future research is needed to highlight the way digital markets are always embedded in other markets.[79] We have argued that such mutual embedding, or relatedness of markets, is exactly what defines an industry. So far, Spotify, Facebook, and Google have often been studied primarily as platforms in the sense of techno-economic configurations somehow isolated from or elevated above the manifold activities that constitute markets on- and offline. Platform studies emphasize that digital markets are ontologically distinctive and multisided,

imbuing internet businesses with ideas of newness and networked egalitarianism. As the ad market case study has shown, there certainly are positive effects in the interaction between Spotify's various market actors, such
as increasing ad revenue. But when considered as a media industry, Spotify
and other services constitute production chains that also cause a number of
negative externalities. While programmatic advertising has only spread since
2008, the experience is of a higher volume of ads everywhere. Its spread has
disrupted established relations between ad agencies, media planners, and
publishers. With its millisecond processing of personal data and predictive
behavioral targeting capacities, programmatic also engineers a new, uncanny
intimacy between publishers, cultural content, and audiences.

"Finance can only spread as far as its own magic,"[80] Anna Tsing has
observed. Our research has shown that Spotify's magic indeed exists and cannot be discounted as fake. This includes a new belief in the magic of music
as commodity, despite music as a business having been declared dead on
numerous occasions. It includes the wonders of *free* and Spotify's subsequent
conversion of free listening into scale and value. Spotify's magic also invokes
acts of corporate staging, cultural border crossing, and the manipulation of
boundaries in ways that connect the world of finance to our own imagination. The value of *free*, in this context, may rest on us imagining other forms
of freedom.

Intervention: Introducing Songblocker

In February 2017, during the thirtieth transmediale festival for art and digital culture in Berlin, a new application was launched: Songblocker.[1] In line with classic tech startup jargon, the app was introduced as a "groundbreaking application" that would "revolutionize the way people listen to and enjoy ads." Functioning as a Microsoft Windows and Mac OS X plugin, Songblocker's declared allure was its ability to automatically mute songs on Spotify and instead allow its users to enjoy "100% awesome ads." Following startup lingo, Songblocker was claimed to be "more than just a blocker." Indeed, company representatives insisted on Songblocker's capacity to make the world a better place by "empowering users and unleashing their inner advertisers." Set against what was described as an ongoing (and scandalous) act of antiadvertising terrorism against the music industries, Songblocker presented itself as the morally correct opposite of ad blocking: a service that would put an end to the uncontrolled financial bleed that torments online content providers.

Before the transmediale event, stickers, T-shirts, and coffee cups with the Songblocker logo had been specially ordered, along with a glossy video ad that featured happy teens swimming and riding bikes, accompanied by taglines such as "connect," "friendship," and "curiosity."[2] Songblocker did not just claim to have reversed the functions of two previously existing ad blockers, "putting their technology to much better use," it also allegedly catered to a generation of internet users who had yet to experience the truly amazing qualities of ads. At the core of Songblocker's corporate ethics lay a strong belief in the potential of supporting online content publishers by exposing oneself to ads—and ads alone. "No music. No disturbance," as the business jingle would have it. Songblocker's corporate model was presented as easily scalable and capable of supporting an "entire media industry

Figure 4.6

under attack by adblockers." At the transmediale launch, one cofounder even exclaimed—with increasing enthusiasm—that: "Songblocker is just the start. Imagine what comes next. Newsblocker! Filmblocker! Bookblocker! Artblocker! Pornblocker! Wikiblocker! Tweetblocker! Blogblocker! Friendblocker! Cashblocker! And, you know … Foodblocker! Whatever! The opportunities for supporting high-quality content are unlimited."[3]

Songblocker, in short, envisioned a future where everyone would be happy to pay for access to ads—and just the ads. By calling this a strategy for "turning commercial speech into economies of scale," the company was explicit about seeing advertising as one of the largest untapped resources on the planet. Painting a dreamy (and dollar-laden) image of times ahead, Songblocker's representatives were aggressively fishing for venture capital investors who were prepared to open their wallets for the newest—and presumably hottest—tech startup to emerge out of Sweden. Finally, the audience was told, "Songblocker will do for Spotify what Spotify did for the music industry!"

In due time, Songblocker established a presence on Twitter (@songblocker), with this account description: "Tech startup reconceptualizing the experience of listening. Songblocker gives you 100% ads when listening to Spotify. No music. No disturbance. Full support."[4] The company also set up a Facebook page and engaged in a social media campaign that culminated

Songblocker
More than just a blocker

Figure 4.7
Stills from the Songblocker promotion video, uploaded to YouTube
during the spring of 2017.

in Songblocker's promotional video on YouTube receiving more than sixteen thousand views. However, doubts were also raised. As one commentator, HampStamp, stated on YouTube: "This has to be a joke."[5]

HampStamp was correct. As readers might suspect, Songblocker was nothing but a hoax: a fictitious startup designed by us researchers to intervene, discuss, and problematize some of the moral imperatives that have begun to emerge around online content and its monetization by ads. We ourselves portrayed the startup prophets at transmediale (poorly disguised in Songblocker T-shirts). The sixteen thousand views of the YouTube promotional video were obtained by buying fake likes and views from specially selected click farms in Indonesia. Moreover, while the Songblocker plugin is downloadable, fully functional, and available at songblocker.com,[6] the company's promise of a premium version was never meant to materialize— most likely to the great disappointment of those who wanted to "skip all silence between ads, listen to ads in an offline mode, share ads with the people you love, and receive free ad recommendations based on moods, genres, and your personal taste."[7]

Within our research project, we approached the Songblocker intervention as a form of ethnographic speculation. The aim of the experiment was not to generate results. Rather, we wanted to engage in the kinds of speculative methods we discussed in the introduction to this book, methods that have been proposed by Luciana Parisi, Nina Wakeford, Celia Lury, and others.[8] Such methods privilege imagination, narrational mutations, and adventurous methodological journeys on the path toward exploring digital technologies and triggering discussions. The presentation at transmediale prompted some critical conversations, both at the actual launch and within media. One of us researchers was, for example, interviewed by NPR Berlin. "Our research project is designed to be playful in some ways. That kind of hackerish attitude is necessary if you want to get information about these [secretive] companies," we stated. "The academic...team is using 'Songblocker' as a metaphor to describe the strange new economic conditions of streaming music in the digital age, and the role of advertising and ad-blocking."[9]

Songblocker thus became a tool for us to not only map and describe but also intervene in the ad-tech infrastructures that are built around streamed music. Rather than simply depicting the kinds of data traffic that advertising on streaming platforms gives rise to, we wanted to find ways of participating in that traffic while simultaneously problematizing its basic premises. In short, we committed to an agenda that was both skeptical and interventionist. Integrating the construction of an actual digital tool—the Songblocker plugin—with autoethnographic observations (as we took on the characters of startup prophets) and a performance at transmediale, we wanted to explore the role of ads in processes of commodification around streamed music. We also sought to directly engage with the ethics and subjectivities that current ad-tech markets rely on and foster.

Ad blockers have challenged visions of how content provision on the web can become financially profitable. They have been a hot topic for years, with ad-blocker developers arguing that any ad-supported medium is "abusing its readers." Publishers, in turn, have repeatedly stated that blocking ads is "tantamount to theft." Both sides have, in cat-and-mouse fashion, "experimented with blocks and counter-blocks, culminating in sites simply blocking all users with an adblocker turned on."[10] Ad blockers are often free plugins that work by filtering out distracting ads on websites or in desktop clients. But ad blockers also serve other purposes. For example, they help save bandwidth so that web pages can load faster and with less battery usage. In the Swedish context, it has been argued that the latter is a distinct benefit for online public service media (without advertisements) compared to commercial news sites, since the former load much more quickly. Most ad blockers also protect privacy, since they prohibit the transmission of personal information to third-party ad agencies. In addition, ad blockers may provide security, since they filter out ads that nowadays may contain malicious code. Ad blocking thus goes beyond simply filtering out unwanted ads and instead taps into wider concerns about integrity, surveillance, and usability on the web.

As we have already stated, the introduction of ad blockers has been controversial. In May 2015, for example, Martin Bryant openly stated that "adblockers are immoral."[11] Bryant voiced strong resentment for people who "starve" content providers by using ad blockers and called such behavior snobbish, shameful, and a display of "either sociopathic tendencies or ignorance of economic realities."[12] Bryant is not alone in his critique. Ad blocking has been likened to theft, eliciting the claim that "every time you block an ad, what you're really blocking is food from entering a child's mouth."[13] Similarly, ad blocking has been described as a deeply violent practice that could cause a "bloodbath of independent media."[14] In the autumn of 2015, Marco Arment—the creator of a highly popular ad blocker called Peace—even removed his software from Apple's App Store, followed by a public announcement on his blog stating that he did not "feel good" about being responsible for an app that could potentially "hurt" content providers from gaining ad revenue.[15]

Ad blocking, then, is far from an uncontested solution for modifying how web content is displayed. It is a technology that is deeply entangled in moralistic arguments about our rights and obligations as consumers of online content. At the heart of these conflicts lies the question of whether advertising buyers have the right to expect that their content will reach all the way to its aimed destination (i.e., the eyes or ears of individual humans). In other words, ad blocking touches on issues concerning property owners' right to be seen or—in the case of audio ads—the right to be heard.[16]

However, with respect to ads, the internet is still akin to the Wild West, at least compared to the physical media world. Advertising regulations stipulate, for example, that "zones between the billboard and the roadway [should be] kept free of visual obstructions" in order to ensure that advertisements can work effectively in analog space.[17] These kinds of regulations prevent governments and corporations from planting trees or building houses that could visually block advertisements. But similar regulations do not yet exist in digital space, thus leaving room for various kinds of ad blockers. In February 2017, the anti-ad-blocking company PageFair estimated that software for blocking ads is put to use on over 600 million mobile and desktop devices globally.[18]

In recent years, ad blocking has also opened up a kind of arms race, in which a number of companies have begun to offer anti-ad-blocking software to the publishing industries.[19] Companies such as Admiral and Sourcepoint sell various kinds of analytics packages for tracking ad-blocking losses, and they also supply solutions for circumventing ad blockers.[20] In turn, these have given rise to anti-anti-ad-blocking measures, which have then been subverted, and so on. To some extent, the battle has been set between major hardware and software companies such as Apple and Google.[21] Apple, on the one hand, has reasons to promote the use of ad blockers, which cater to its users' desires and make Apple's hardware devices run faster (and with less battery usage). Actors such as Google, on the other hand, naturally want to ban ad blocking, since they rely heavily on ad revenues.

To further complicate the matter, some ad-blocking companies have started to take on ambiguous and somewhat corrupt roles. Companies such as the German based Eyeo, which runs the highly popular ad blocker Adblock Plus, has been likened to an extortion racket because it lets advertising companies pay to pass through its filters. By launching a controversial "acceptable ads program"—which allows "some advertisements through its adblocking software, often in exchange for a cut of the revenue received from the ads"[22]—Eyeo has attracted substantial criticism. Here, ad blockers have become yet another part of the ad-tech industry. Indeed, they function like new kinds of advertising middlemen who bring to the fore the controversies and conflicts of interest within the current ad-tech business.

Our Songblocker intervention tapped into these controversial debates around ad blockers. Importantly, the plugin could be built because of Spotify's surprisingly straightforward ways of disclosing metadata about its streamed content. As it turns out, each of Spotify's data streams includes a special metadata indicator that discloses whether an advertisement or a musical track is being transmitted. We cannot say why Spotify makes ad blocking so simple, but the ease does indicate that if Spotify found ad blocking to be a real problem, it most likely would have fought back by not giving away such metadata. Unlike many news outlets, then, Spotify does not currently appear to consider ad blocking to be a serious threat to its business model.

Online there are plenty of tutorials on how to block and override the domain name servers (DNS) that are hosting Spotify advertisment. Broadly speaking, there are two possible types of ad blockers: those that hinder the dissemination of ads by blocking the servers from which such content originates, and those that single out ads from other types of content on the web and then simply hide them from the user. Ad blockers that work by blocking servers largely exist because digital services outsource the function of publishing ads to third-party ad-tech companies. This means that if, say, news content is delivered to users from one server, the ads might originate from entirely different servers. Some ad blockers take advantage of this by simply identifying and whitelisting servers that distribute the desired content, while blacklisting or blocking servers that distribute ads. The second type of ad blockers—to which Songblocker belongs—basically works because metadata transfers make it possible to single out ads from other types of content. In order for this to work, a computer has to be able to locate and recognize advertising content, often in real time. This is tricky—unless content providers directly disclose if content consists of ads or not.

In building our blocker for audio content, all we did was to use Spotify's metadata to locate advertisements (and music), and then tell a computer to turn the volume up or down based on the results. Together with the programmers at Humlab, we created Songblocker based on two currently existing Spotify ad blockers (EZblocker and Spotifree) and simply adjusted their open-source code so that the volume was put on mute when music was played, instead of the other way around.[23] The Songblocker plugin was thus an inverted ad blocker, the result of pushing anti-ad-blocking logics and measures to their extreme. The process of building it involved a number of questions: Would it be possible to create a means for users to support content providers by fully and singlehandedly consuming their ads? What could we learn from different ad blockers' attempts to rewire the functions and economic organizations of online services? And how could we reuse their software to ask other types of questions about the commodification of streamed music and its usage?

When discussing Spotify's advertising scheme, it is important to know that it represents a form of programmatic advertising (explained in chapter 4). To be a Songblocker user thus implies linking up to a vast infrastructure of automated ad sales, but with no evident aesthetic gain, since all music has been silenced. Thereby, Songblocker users are encouraged to engage in "full adtech immersion." In a digital climate where advertising is aggressively pushed toward users, this would involve consuming *ads for the sake of ads* as an act of solidarity with online content producers and providers.

Thus, what Songblocker brings forward is a kind of advertising dystopia—or utopia, depending on one's perspective—in which conventional, quality content (films, books, news, music) and its digital distributors (Spotify, YouTube, Facebook, and so on) are rewarded but simultaneously also pushed to the side to the benefit of advertising per se. Importantly, the aim of creating such a situation was not to generate images of an alternative present that would appear as wholly true and believable. Instead, Songblocker's apparent artifice was designed to give rise to reflection and discussion. To what extent are we obliged to read, view, and listen to the content that streaming services and other online content distributors provide to us? And what informal and moral contracts between users and distributors are currently forming in the digital sphere? Indeed, the absurdity of Songblocker's promotional materials was cliché enough to avoid any misconceptions: Songblocker was, and continues to be, a parody of itself and a critique of ad tech, as well as startup culture. The commentator HampStamp on YouTube was indeed correct: "This has to be a joke."

As a whole, the Songblocker intervention can thus be read as a methodological provocation that, in the words of John-David Dewsbury, is "productive, that proliferates, and [that] creates … interferences"—interferences with the moral imperatives of digital monetization strategies and interferences with Spotify's technical structure and software affordances.[24] The intervention also reveals how research may not only reflect and comment on contemporary affairs but also, much like anecdotes, serve as an "instrumentation and a feature of, the making of 'out theres.'"[25] This new "out there" may be purely fictional and speculative, yet it also invites contemplation of our cultural and historical condition. In the end, the Songblocker intervention represents more than just an example of how other people's attempts to tamper with, and transform, Spotify's original features can be repurposed for critical media research. It has also opened up a context for broadly (re)considering the kinds of advertisement logics that streamed music relies on.

Conclusion

This book—and the project on which it is based—proactively engaged with a well-known problem of access to media industries. Media companies whose main outputs are defined as information goods protected by intellectual property standards understandably prefer secrecy over public scrutiny, especially when heavily investing up front in the development of such property, as in the film industry. In order to avoid potential harm to their products and brands, these companies regularly use gatekeeping arrangements when interacting with scholars. Research interest is sometimes ignored, but it is also often welcomed, provided that it can be vetted, filtered, and guided in order to impose symmetry or at least balance between the legal and ethical interests of both the researcher and the researched. Sometimes, this balance of interest is secured in strictly formal ways and includes nondisclosure agreements, endorsements, or method sanctioning. Sometimes, it develops more informally, built on trust, mutual respect, and the fact that many, if not most, media executives have both an academic background and a vested interest in studies of their operations that differ from business consultancy. A host of remarkable academic studies and recent industry-academic cooperations testify to the potential and prospects of this research.[1]

While digital industries are not necessarily an exception to this rule, it is hard to overlook the fact that the dynamics surrounding the issue of access have developed on somewhat different terms. Generally speaking, companies like Spotify obtain existing copyrighted content from sources they do not directly control, distribute this content, and produce customer data based on the interest the content generates. Spotify USA's Terms and Conditions of Use organize this arrangement by granting users a "limited, non-exclusive, revocable license to make personal, non-commercial, entertainment use of the Content."[2] Users, in turn, have to grant Spotify a "non-exclusive, transferable, sub-licensable, royalty-free, perpetual,...irrevocable, fully paid, worldwide license to use, reproduce, make available to the public,...publish, translate, modify, create derivative works from, and distribute any of your User Content in connection with the Service through any medium." Users also are required to allow the service to use the processor, bandwidth, and storage hardware on their devices, to "provide advertising and other information," and "to allow our business partners to do the same."[3]

There are no specific regulations for academic researchers or journalists defined in Spotify's terms of service, but the user guidelines do not permit, "for any reason whatsoever," any "reverse-engineering, decompiling, disassembling, modifying" of the service; "artificially increasing play count or otherwise manipulating the Services by using a script or other automated process"; or any "crawling" of the Spotify service "or otherwise using any automated means (including bots, scrapers, and spiders) to collect information from Spotify."[4] Facebook's Statement of Rights and Responsibilities, in contrast, allows for the possibility of informed consent when it comes to the use of bots or scrapers.[5] Likewise, Twitter suggests the possibility of prior consent in regard to bots and scraping and explicitly allows crawling the service.[6]

On the one hand, the process of getting access to Spotify was framed through these strictly formal, comparatively restrictive, and user-unspecific guidelines. Although the legal status of such guidelines remains unclear, they firmly articulate the company lawyers' position regarding user rights. On the other hand, when we initiated this research project, Spotify employees were open to conversations probing mutual interests. An early suggestion made in this context was to engage in writing the company's history while access to data was denied. Spotify's suggestion resonated with an implied division of labor between a humanities project such as the one presented in this book and the company's long-term engagement with engineers and computer scientists working at the KTH Royal Institute of Technology. For the four-year duration of the project, access to Spotify employees was individually granted for thematically specified interviews, but establishing rapport on an organizational level failed.

The process of accessing Spotify remained a constant topic of self-reflective inquiries within the project itself. For instance, after a meeting in May 2014, a team member noted the following in an autoethnographic field diary:

Seems as we all agree that it's important to establish a contact with Spotify, but we also feel the need to protect the integrity of the project. I don't really have a clear position on the issue. I'm used to thinking about research ethics, but in this case, there are no human subjects involved (unless we contact Spotify's employees), and the other project members seem more experienced with this type of research. We acknowledge that there are certain criticisms within the music industries against our project, which is seen as an anti-industry project. ... We have been in touch with a head of department at Spotify. There's also a professor and a PhD student connected to Spotify that we might get in touch with. But how should we go about it? After some discussions, we decide to take the official path to Spotify, try to arrange a meeting where we will let them introduce themselves, and then possibly we can get a chance of doing interviews, etc. We decide to draft an email asking if they can meet us before summer to present their work.

The research group subsequently learned that the Norwegian music streaming service WiMP (now Tidal) had shared its data with researchers in an academic project hosted at the University of Oslo, "Clouds & Concerts: Trends in Music Culture."[7] Compared with WiMP's willingness to provide access to streaming and search logs from anonymized users of the service in Norway over a total of seventy-two weeks, Spotify's uncompromising rejection of uncommissioned research seemed all the more debatable.

We have heard from other researchers that they have tried to interview Spotify but that there was no particular interest from Spotify's side. On the other hand, we know that the Norwegian project managed to cooperate with WiMP, getting data from the company.

Spotify is moving towards an IPO. This determines how they may interact with researchers, and we mull over the question of why they are inaccessible. WiMP wants to contribute to Norwegian cultural life and to promote Norwegian artists. But Apple, Google, and Spotify are perhaps more characterized by being closed off. Could we appeal to their social responsibility?

In the early fall of 2014, we also discussed the following:

Nothing seems to happen with the formal email, and we tend to get back to the question about contacting Spotify whenever we meet, but no one seems particularly eager to approach them. I don't know if it is simply because it is more of a challenge to do research "from the outside" or if there are other reasons. In Berlin in August, we discussed whether it would be better to avoid the formal contacts and let project members approach them individually rather than "the project" approaching "the company." The reluctance towards approaching Spotify is also related to our need to be able to show some basic knowledge of what they are doing, which we believe can be gained from working with digital methods.

In November of 2014, one of us got in touch with a Spotify representative after having inquired about participating in a tech meetup event organized by Spotify in November. By joining this event and conducting interviews afterwards, we received valuable information about Spotify's peer-to-peer architecture, but overall the findings from interviews remained meager. Simultaneously, the group had a first meeting with programmers at Humlab, Umeå University's digital humanities lab, which increased the interest in developing a complementary perspective based on digital methods.

> It's our first meeting with the Humlab programmers. The programmers ask if we have been in touch with Spotify. We consider that it is difficult because of business secrecy, requiring us to design alternative means of access to this system (e.g., by throwing our own material into the system). How to upload files, what kind of metadata, which requirements exist for that? Spotify defines explicit frameworks for music distribution, but there is so far not much documentation available about these frameworks. We plan to begin like amateur musicians, loading up music via aggregators manually. Then we aim to register a record label more formally. We have tested one aggregator already. One initial finding is that uploaded songs have to be at least twenty seconds long. Another topic of discussion is our interest in technology and how we have been in touch with a department head at Spotify who is interested in getting the company history written but unwilling to share any data. Now there is a possible contact via another university. By gaining access via an API [application programming interface], we might be able to compare and see directly the difference between what is publicly communicated and what the company keeps for itself.

As these fieldnotes illustrate, negotiating and conceptualizing forms of access was vital to the project. The forms of rapport that result from such access always have strong ethical implications. Traditionally, the ethics of building rapport have been guided by the imperative of informed consent, and access implies that the research subject will not only be respected but also fully protected in its integrity by the researcher. But what happens when researchers encounter a subject that, at some point, begins to threaten their own integrity?

Methods, Law, and Ethics

Shortly after receiving Spotify's notice ("You are hereby asked to confirm by 26th of May 2017, in written form, that you have received this notice and that the group of researchers has ended such actions in violation of

Spotify's Terms of Use"), the project group mailed a detailed response. The letter expressed understanding of Spotify's concerns and assured the company that any action that could potentially have violated its terms of use had ended. The letter also pointed to our previous attempts at engaging directly with Spotify and offered to open a conversation about methods and results. Since the project's plans and methods had been public since 2013, including early press coverage,[8] the letter served as a reminder of the project's research design and the fact that the project would soon be over.

While awaiting Spotify's response, the project group discussed Spotify's reasons to establish rapport at this specific and late point in time. Research interests had been communicated for four years, and project publications were still pending. Why the sudden urge to get in touch and restrict the methodology? The most likely answer was an interview that team member Rasmus Fleischer had given to *Dagens Industri*, a leading Swedish industry and business newspaper, a few days earlier on May 7, 2017. The story was quickly picked up by *Torrentfreak* and *Digital Music News* before spreading widely across the web.[9] Referring to Fleischer as an "investigator" who was "funded by the Swedish government," *Digital Music News* translated one of the *Dagens industri* interview "nuggets" as follows:

> The entire Spotify beta period and its early launch was propelled by the Pirate Bay, Fleischer explained. ... "They'd never have had that much attention without the Pirate Bay happening. The company's early history coincides with the Pirate Party emerging as a hot topic, with the trial of the Pirate Bay in Stockholm District Court." But the connection goes far deeper than that. In fact, Fleischer alleges that Spotify directly connected with the Pirate Bay. Literally. "Spotify's beta version was originally a pirate service," Fleischer said.[10]

Instead of disputing Rasmus Fleischer's claims as quoted in the news media, Spotify used the occasion to inquire about the "methods used by the responsible group of researchers in this project," implying that the company anticipated that more sensitive information about its services might be revealed.

In addition, and unbeknownst to the research group, Spotify's legal counsel had contacted the Swedish Research Council—the government agency that provides funding for basic research, including this project—with a second, more specific request:

> As far as Spotify understands, the project has received financial support from the Swedish Research Council. Spotify is particularly concerned about the information that has emerged regarding the research group's methods in the project.

The available information indicates that the research team has deliberately taken action that is explicitly in violation of Spotify's Terms of Use and by means of technical methods sought to conceal this violation. The research group has attempted, among other things, to artificially increase the number of plays and manipulate Spotify's services using scripts or other automated processes. Spotify assumes that this systematic violation of terms has not been known to the Swedish Research Council and is convinced that the Swedish Research Council aims to ensure that all research undertaken with its support in all respects conforms to ethical guidelines and is carried out properly and in accordance with applicable law. Spotify invites the Swedish Research Council to contact Spotify for a discussion about the above matter. It is Spotify's hope that the Swedish Research Council acts resolutely in order to ensure that unruly or illegal practices cease immediately. Spotify anticipates the Swedish Research Council's immediate response.[11]

While there were not yet journal or book publications that could have substantialized Spotify's claims, these allegations rested on the premise that the project systematically attempted to use digital methods against the service's interest. Speculating that such covert research had been conducted behind the Swedish Research Council's back, the letter more specifically suggested that the project had acted in direct violation of both "ethical guidelines" and "applicable law." It ended with an explicit call to action against the project.

As this book has documented, research within the project used digital methods in an inventive and probing, rather than systematic, way. Only a part of the overall research activity engaged digital methods, and these methods were partly adapted from existing tools developed by the Digital Methods Initiative (University of Amsterdam) and other research groups. No part of the research concerned human subjects; the project did not violate the integrity of any Spotify user, collect any personal data related to Spotify users, or illegally share copyrighted content via Spotify. Spotify's own corporate or competitive interests and the integrity of its service and brand were respected. Not only was the research design, with its covert or "gonzo" strategy, described in detail in the project application, but it was precisely the reason the project had succeeded in receiving funding in the first place.[12] Adopting the idea of inventive methods against a background of previous work that had struggled with creative workarounds to gatekeeper access for decades, one overall aim of the project had been to proactively engage Spotify in a conversation about its culture. Spotify's letter could be read as precisely that. Its confluence of ethical, methodical, and legal standards therefore deserves closer scrutiny.

"Impact Culture"

In the interdisciplinary and proliferating field of research on the internet, digital methods—and views on the "digital *as* method"—are widespread.[13] Apart from regularly scraping and crawling platforms such as Facebook, Google, and Twitter, researchers have previously engaged with algorithmic bias and other critical issues that require systematic approaches such as those deemed illegal by Spotify. This includes, for instance, a platform audit of hotel-rating platform Booking.com that revealed an "algorithmic system bias" based on the confluence of inputs and users, resulting in good reviews for bad hotels.[14] Other researchers have established automated user profiles as inputs to algorithms as a form of audit. One example of this work employed simulated users in order to detect gender bias in online advertising, another conducted experiments to analyze Uber's surge pricing algorithm by emulating Uber accounts, and yet another created multiple Airbnb accounts in order to identify racial discrimination against black users.[15] One of the most consistent and prolific advocate of this kind of research is Christian Sandvig, who has repeatedly argued for what he calls a "consequentialist ethics of algorithms."[16] Together with the American Civil Liberties Union and journalists working for the *Intercept*, Sandvig has sued the US government to challenge the constitutionality of the Computer Fraud and Abuse Act (CFAA), a law that criminalizes any user activity "exceeding authorized access." As Sandvig observes, "Terms of Service sometimes prohibit people from using Web sites for research, they prohibit users from saying bad things about the corporation that runs the Web site, they prohibit users from writing things down. They should not be made into criminal violations of the law."[17] Audit tests like those suggested by Sandvig have been regularly conducted in the offline world.

The project on which this book is based did include forms of platform auditing, yet only as part of a mixed-method approach. At the time of this writing, the applicability of contract law to an online service's terms of service remains an issue of debate, as are these terms generally, with some scholars suggesting that companies ought to pay users for reading them.[18] In October 2017, the Swedish Research Council declared Spotify's accusations to be baseless and rejected the company's call to action against our project.

In terms of research ethics, the project could hardly be accused of violating existing norms, as such norms are inconsistent and still being actively debated. Privacy concerns have been and still are paramount in ethics discussions among internet researchers—discussions that developed before Google, Facebook, and Twitter were founded. Given the traditional focus on how people use the internet, critical ethical concerns primarily relate to research on human subjects, especially on informed consent, and they foreground the needs and safety of vulnerable users.[19] With the growing control of platforms such as Facebook, Spotify, and Google over the infrastructure enabling the recording and analyzing of social and cultural life, however, the question has been raised "how researchers are to maintain rigorous standards of scientific integrity, objectivity, accuracy, and so on, vis-à-vis corporate and government agendas that may run contrary to these standards."[20] The ethics committee of the Special Interest Group on Computer-Human Interaction (SIGCHI) recommends critical industry researchers to argue

> that violating TOS [terms of service] is not only ethically possible, but might even be ethically required in some circumstances. The issue is far reaching: if we abide by overly restrictive TOS, are we giving up the ability to reflect on systems that are increasingly shaping society? If we only work with permission of Large Corporation, can we ever be critical of Large Corporation? If the products and services of Large Corporation are having a profound impact, what is the obligation of the research community to understand that impact?[21]

A similar position is articulated in the Code of Conduct issued by the Association for Computing Machinery's Committee on Professional Ethics. While some groups such as the Council for Big Data, Ethics, and Society and the Association of Internet Researchers (AOIR) are so far lagging behind, to "get your hands dirty" has become not only an accepted but a recommended research practice. When it comes to digital industries, it is "not always feasible or desirable to comply with the consent requirement."[22]

At this point, it is worthwhile to turn from Spotify's inaccurate rendering of the project's methodological, legal, and ethical standards to Spotify's own norms and standards. Its letter appears as written on behalf of a formal organization, but the company in fact has a long history of moving across the entire formal-informal spectrum. For instance, think of its early unauthorized music distribution practices (described in chapter 1) or its reliance on peer-to-peer infrastructure and user devices (discussed in chapter 2). On December 29, 2017, Wixen Music Publishing, whose clients include Neil

Young, Tom Petty, and many other famous musicians, filed a $1.6 billion copyright lawsuit against Spotify in a California federal court.[23] Tax evasion practices and political lobbying efforts are well documented, as are Spotify's attempts to change its Privacy Policy to gain access to users' smartphone sensor information, GPS coordinates, and camera in order to share this information with business partners.[24] In this context, Spotify's conflation of legal, methodological, and ethical issues should not be seen as accidental. Whatever the intent of sending the letter, it effectively negotiated a new cultural norm. Given the company's declared desire to "impact culture,"[25] its action taken against the freedom of academic research should be taken seriously.

Toward a New Ethics of Internet Research

In his book, *Mining Capitalism: The Relationship between Corporations and their Critics*, anthropologist Stuart Kirsch shows how major companies establish and maintain their own order of knowledge. While not engaging in the negative tactics of oil firms or pharmaceutical companies, digital companies such as Spotify, Microsoft, Google, and Facebook certainly manage their relationships with academia. They promote themselves as responsible, encourage diversity, and enhance their reputation through forging strategic partnerships or establishing research divisions, yet occasionally, they also spread uncertainty and doubt.[26] A threat of litigation can be a way to prevent unwanted studies from being conducted or published.

The basic difference between Spotify's corporate behavior and the work of the research team presented in this book is that such critical academic research has no financial interest, is constantly assessed by critics through peer review, and is public. Spotify itself deals in secrecy, as it draws researchers into its private domain while simultaneously claiming to be of public benefit and in the interest of those communities on whose practices its services were built. In balancing the ethical responsibilities of this project against those of a multibillion-dollar company, the project's ethical challenges appear mundane and inflated—part of a situated approach rather than global strategy. While not entirely successful in all of its undertakings, the project has worked out the boundaries of ethics in practice.

Covert research, as this book has attempted to show, may thus help "to get where others get not."[27] The book has made a case for a type of research that avoids routines and being boxed in between institutional ethics boards and corporate interests, opening a space for the unpredictable. But this is not to claim that all research should be covert. Not only did overt and more conventional methods form a significant part of this project, alternative approaches to digital industries are equally productive. For instance, in his anthropological dissertation on developers of music recommendation systems, Nick Seaver pitches Laura Nader's idea of an "imbalanced power dynamic" between researcher and subject against his own findings of an environment largely shaped by cultural factors and "subjective dynamics" that feel not only much less strategic and rational than is often assumed but also much closer to home. While Seaver emphasizes his own similarity to and sympathy for "techies,"[28] this book has insisted on acknowledging difference and has taken an attitude of outsideness.[29]

Although this book has probably left more questions open than answered, we may be considered successful in forcing Spotify to read it, if only to test its own hypothesis of what ethical, legal, and methodological confluences are about. In the meantime, and probably opening a new chapter elsewhere, the research team has drafted a letter of its own, dated May 25, 2017, and addressed to the Swedish Data Protection Agency:

> To: datainspektionen@datainspektionen.se
> Hej!
>
> We would like to inquire about Spotify's compliance with the new General Data Protection regulation issued by the European Union in 2016. In particular, this relates to the Regulation's provisions on profiling. According to the definition of "profiling," as stipulated in article 4 point 4, "profiling" means any form of automated processing of personal data consisting of the use of personal data to evaluate certain personal aspects relating to a natural person, in particular to analyze or predict aspects concerning that natural person's performance at work, economic situation, health, personal preferences, interests, reliability, behavior, location, or movements. Article 22 (1) explicitly provides rules on profiling as follows: "The data subject shall have the right not to be subject to a decision based solely on automated processing, including profiling, which produces legal effects concerning him or her or similarly significantly affects him or her." However, there are exceptions to this rule, outlined in the paragraph 2, 3, and 4 of Article 22. The data subject (i.e., a physical person) shall also have (albeit limited) right to object to profiling (see article 21).
>
> Spotify has, since at least 2015, begun to invest into systems to gather so-called "contextual data" that allows them to track, and predict, user behavior. This is also called behavioral profiling in social psychology and Internet marketing. Such

profiling activities seem to be in direct violation of upcoming EU regulation. They also are not made clear in any of Spotify's offerings to users. Spotify sells its service as music streaming. We therefore would like to inquire about Datainspektionen's view on Spotify's activities, especially in regard to the compliance with upcoming EU legislation. We have already been in touch with EU legal bodies and would be glad to hear from you, in order to complement the information we have received. Thank you in advance.[30]

Intervention: Work at Spotify!

Is it possible to determine—or at least tentatively predict—where Spotify is heading in the near future? If Spotify's IPO in April 2018 was both a success (at least in terms of investors' economic faith) as well as an uncertain forecast for the future of music (can Spotify really contine to grow?), similar questions around the fate of the company have been posed for years. Such speculations have been driven by the paradox that the music industry needs streaming services like Spotify just as much as the streaming business relies on record labels. However, there have also been less speculative propositions. A year before the IPO, in April 2017 for example, the site *Zatz Not Funny!* imagined it was possible to determine Spotify's trajectory and presented a number of recent job announcements from Spotify to substantiate its claim that the company was on an "unexpected foray into hardware."[1] Several job listings—"Senior Product Manager-Hardware," "Product Manager-Voice" and "Director of Product, Natural Language Understanding"—seemingly provided clues that Spotify was working (or would work) on developing its own music hardware. "It seems safe to assume that, in some fashion, Spotify is interested in making a device that's capable of playing music," the *Verge* confidently reported.[2] Based on a series of job listings, it was deduced that Spotify was following in the footsteps of many of its tech siblings, who had recently started to produce their own tangible computer products.[3]

Even if these speculations were based on actual job listings, they turned out not to be true. The job postings managed to trigger the imaginations of the tech press and were used as a source for generating prophecies about Spotify's future advancements—which in the end did not happen. These days, however, job-based speculation is part of a broader trend in labor market intelligence that involves using large collections of job listings to study local and global hiring tendencies—with the goal of potentially offering better recruiting opportunities or even predictions about where markets are moving. The company Wanted Analytics, for example, boasts of being a leading provider of real-time employment market analytics and is said to maintain a database of more than one billion unique job listings from 150 countries.[4]

In our final intervention, then, we were inspired by such efforts to "read" markets and companies through job ads. We decided to scrape our own data set of job postings from Spotify to speculate about the company's prospects for the coming years. We knew that job listings would neither give clues regarding the imminent IPO nor would they provide any substantial evidence about Spotify's general commercial strategy, which—as the recent IPO made clear—would be focused on growth and scale rather than on becoming a profitable company. Nevertheless, Spotify job listings became an empirical source of information about the service, and we have occasionally used them as such throughout our book. Our scraped data set of job listings, in particular, gave us explicit insights into Spotify's corporate ideology and organization. In addition, we wanted to learn more about Spotify's business lingo and how the company "speaks." While analyzing the job postings, we were particularly interested in the kinds of spaces that Spotify carves out for its human employees, as compared to the machines and algorithms that form the core of the company. Job postings, we argue, represent an undervalued source of insight into media industries. As empirical evidence, they provide important clues about how corporations organize, allocate resources, and both perceive and brand themselves.[5] So in order to map Spotify's current and future priorities, we decided to monitor the company's recruitment history.

In detail, the interventionist exercise resulted in the collection of some 800 job postings from Spotify's global website between November 2016 and April 2017.[6] A number of these job listings were duplicates or slight variations of one another, and after removing such ads, we were left with 563 unique Spotify job listings from all around the world. Such listings are not only crucial for a company in the midst of a rapid global expansion—they also provide fodder for publicity stunts. For instance, in January 2017, shortly before Barack Obama's tenure as president of the United States ended, Spotify CEO Daniel Ek tweeted, "Hey @BarackObama, I heard you were interested in a role at Spotify. Have you seen this one?" Ek added a link to an alluring posting for the position "President of Playlists."[7] Ek's tweet was in response to a remark that Obama had allegedly made to Natalia Brzezinski, the wife of the former US ambassador to Sweden, at a White House reception. In an Instagram post,[8] Brzezinski recalled Obama joking, "I'm still waiting for my job at Spotify…Cuz' I know y'all loved my playlist."[9] While Ek's job posting did not mention Obama by name, it required a curriculum vitae that narrowed the talent pool to essentially one person with "at least eight years' experience of running a highly-regarded nation."[10] Thus, job listings are not only vehicles for attracting qualified employees but can also be tools for improving a corporate image. Ek's tweet was liked more than fourteen thousand times and retweeted more than seven thousand times.

Upon closer inspection, we found that Spotify had divided the job postings into three broad categories: business, technology, and product. Among the announced jobs, nearly 60 percent belonged to the first category and nearly 30 percent to the second. Thus, while Spotify may still frame itself as a tech company, business was by far the largest category in our data set for which Spotify sought new employees. Overall, our collected job positions could be traced to thirty-four different cities in eighteen countries, from Bogotá, Colombia, to Taipei, Taiwan, to Antwerp, Belgium. The majority of positions that Spotify sought to fill, however, were located in only two cities: New York (about 37 percent of the postings) and Stockholm (about

Figure 5.1
A world map of Spotify job listings, with New York and Stockholm offering the greatest number of positions. Image courtesy by OpenStreetMapContributors.

25 percent). Half of all listed positions were in the United States, with an additional 27 percent located in Sweden. By contrast, only 1 to 2 percent of the positions were in countries such as Germany, Brazil, and Japan. In other words, even though Spotify appeared to be increasing or at least maintaining its workforce in several of its satellite offices, the bulk of the positions it sought to fill were located in either the United States or Sweden.

The positions in business, technology, and product were divided into further subcategories. For instance, the business category comprised positions in content, sales, finance, label relations, and content & PR. Technology, in turn, included jobs in areas such as IT, software, infrastructure, and mobile, and the product category boasted jobs in product development, analytics, and design & user experience. The wording here is interesting to consider. Based on Spotify's own job categorization, the product that the company is essentially selling could be narrowed down to user experiences (i.e., encounters with cultural artifacts), design (i.e., an attractive and well-functioning interface), analytics and user research (i.e., big data studies concerning customer behaviors), and operations and growth (i.e., Spotify's speculative promise to generate potential profit in order to attract venture capital, as discussed in chapter 1). Some subcategories also fit into more than one main category, such as data & machine learning (both product and technology) and analytics (both business and technology), thus indicating how some of Spotify's positions may float between or span departments.

When trying to attract new employees for these different positions, Spotify is in a comparatively privileged position. In rankings of Sweden's most attractive employer, for instance, Spotify usually comes second to Google and usually ranks among the top five companies.[11] Advanced skills are required to land almost any job at Spotify. A number of positions, for instance, require "an advanced degree, preferably a PhD" and occasionally up to "10+ years of experience." Even more mundane positions—such as "Music Programmer" in Berlin—require substantial skills: "We are looking for a broadly experienced Editor/Music Programmer to join Spotify's curation/programming and editorial team in Germany.... You will curate for first rate music playlist listening and programming experiences for a multitude of our moods, moments, and genres, demonstrate a passion for performance-oriented analytics." In order to perform this work, the applicant ought to have an "ear to the ground in the music community, focusing on Germany" and at least five years of "experience in the music industry,

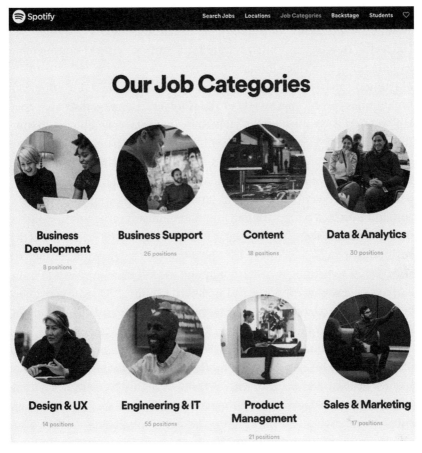

Figure 5.2
Screenshot of Spotify's "Our Job Categories" web page as of June 2017.

programming music for TV, radio or other media networks, working with a broad range of music content."

Job descriptions within the categories of business or technology are similarly demanding. "You have experience implementing machine learning systems at scale in Java, Scala, Python or similar (not just R or Matlab)," a "Machine Learning Engineer" posting states. Other job positions are more niched, such as "Head of Christian Music," who will "make sure that all Christian Music artists see Spotify as the first choice [and] strategic partner when it comes to launching their new music." The "Data Curator" position requires that applicants "have a deep understanding of Latin American music (strongly preferred)." And for a single week in December 2016, it was even possible to apply for a Spotify job in Los Angeles as a "Writer: What you'll do? Develop and pitch scripts for a variety of short and medium length non-fiction video formats."

Our job data sets allowed us to study Spotify's corporate lingo in detail. Job postings can be approached as snapshots of corporate discourse; they tell readers how Spotify "speaks" of itself as an employer and how it pictures and perceives its (potential) employees. In this way, job descriptions reflect attempts at self-branding, as well as expectations of future employees. Most job listings, for example, featured a company assertion—underneath the actual job description, often in italics or bold—stating that Spotify is "proud to foster a workplace free from discrimination. We strongly believe that diversity of experience, perspectives, and background will lead to a better environment for our employees and a better product for our users and our creators. This is something we value deeply and we encourage everyone to come be a part of changing the way the world listens to music." Following company jargon, diversity among employees becomes both a desired quality among personnel and a commercial concept for making better products.

Spotify's assertion regarding diversity is but one of many semantic examples of how job listings shed light on the narratives that the company creates about itself and its labor force. While some media research has gone into studying the ways in which users and audiences are engaged in different kinds of digital (and even unpaid and exploitative) labor,[12] fewer scholars have focused on the working environments of those who build and maintain today's digital services. There are some exceptions, such as a number of studies conducted within the field of corporate ethnography, with anthropologists as "company insiders" who examined product design and branding, the use of information technologies, workplace practices, and the culture of the organization itself.[13] While our collected job ads say little about the actual situation of Spotify's workers, they do tell us something about the kinds of work they are expected to perform.

In trying to hire people, Spotify resembles other tech startups with a hipster-business appeal. "We're pioneers," the "Backstage" page on spotifyjobs.com proclaims. "Our industry sector didn't exist before we arrived. Nowadays, when people think music streaming, they think Spotify. And we're not done yet, nowhere near."[14] We were thus not surprised to find out that the three most common nouns that appeared in the job postings data set were *team*, *experience*, and *product*. All three indicate how Spotify perceives its corporate organization (as made up of collaborative teams), what main trait it values in its employees (experience), and what the company perceives itself as doing (building and maintaining a product).

Following these three terms, word frequencies differ somewhat between countries. Comparing the two countries where most of the jobs were located—the United States and Sweden—we could for example see that *skill* was ranked as the sixteenth most common noun in US job postings, while in Sweden, it was only ranked as number thirty-three. Similarly, *ability* was ranked as the twenty-third most common noun in the US postings but only number forty-five in the Sweden. This does not necessarily imply that Spotify considers it less important that its Swedish employees are able or skilled. It does indicate, however, that considerable regional differences exist in terms of how Spotify expresses its desire for particular skills and personality traits from its employees. Spotify is not recruiting in the same way everywhere; the company implements its own global division of labor.

Analyzing word frequencies also provided us with indications of how such divisions of labor are allocated. Focusing again on the two countries where Spotify wanted to hire the most people (Sweden and the United States), we could detect some noticeable differences. In the United States, for example, *marketing* was the twelfth most frequently occurring noun, but it was only ranked eighty-seventh in the Swedish case. On the other hand, *software* was the twenty-fourth most frequently occurring noun in the Swedish postings but only came in eighty-third in the United States. In Sweden, *IT* was also ranked as number fifty-three, but it did not even make it onto the short list of the one hundred most commonly used nouns in the United States— much like *sales*, which was the sixty-third most commonly used noun in the US postings but did not appear at all on the Swedish short list.

Judging from our collected job listings, Spotify's sales and marketing operations seemed to be primarily located in the United States, while more technical tasks such as IT and software engineering were run from the Swedish offices. This hypothesis was also backed up by an overview of exactly where Spotify's three large job categories (business, product, and technology) were located, as shown in figure 5.3.

The table shows that a majority of Spotify's business-oriented positions were located in the United States, while Sweden hosted a comparatively large portion of tech-oriented jobs. It also becomes apparent that all of the

Row Labels	Business	Product	Technology	Grand Total
Australia	5			5
Belgium	2			2
Brazil	6			6
Canada	4			4
Colombia	2			2
France	5			5
Germany	11			11
Italy	4			4
Japan	10			10
Mexico	5			5
Netherlands	1			1
Norway	2			2
Singapore	16		1	17
Spain	5			5
Sweden	48	30	76	154
Sweden/UK	4			4
Sweden/US	3	1	2	6
Taiwan	1			1
UK	29	1	4	34
US	159	50	74	283
US/UK	2			2
Grand Total	324	82	157	563

Figure 5.3
Distribution of job postings among different countries, with shading indicating
locations with the greatest number of jobs, comparatively.

open positions in countries such Norway, Italy and Mexico were on the
business side. Job openings in the product and technology sectors were
only available in two other locations besides the United States and Sweden:
the United Kingdom and Singapore.

When Spotify describes the personality traits of its employees and/or
the work atmosphere, the company most frequently uses verbs such as
lead, change, develop, value, believe, listen, encourage, build, and *foster.* Moreover, some of the most commonly used adjectives were *better, strong, free,
proud, new, global, creative,* and *excellent.* A majority (about 50 percent) of the
scraped job listings related to higher positions within the company, such as

director, manager, or *vice president.* This is surprising, given that one would expect Spotify to headhunt for more senior job placements, instead of relying on applications from open job listings. Apart from that, Spotify was looking for a comparatively large number of software engineers, specialists, planners, analysts, coordinators, product owners, and data scientists. More low-level jobs, such as assistant jobs and office coordination positions, were much less numerous.

If the site *Zatz Not Funny!* could predict that Spotify would venture into the domain of music hardware based on *three* job announcements, what can our data set of 563 job listings ultimately tell us about Spotify's future? First, we noted a range of practical and material issues concerning Spotify's rapid growth. For example, several job positions—particularly those in New York City—addressed the housing market. "Spotify will expand its U.S. headquarters and relocate to 4 World Trade Center and create 1,000 new jobs, according to New York Governor Andrew Cuomo," *Business Insider* reported in February 2017.[15] A couple of months later, in May 2017, Spotify was hiring a "Senior Real Estate Analyst" who would "lead the forecasting and planning process" of the company's "global real estate portfolio," spending 30 percent of his or her time on global traveling in order to "monitor and track large office space built out projects." A similar ad for a job in "Real Estate Strategic Planning" included tasks such as creating "short and long term occupancy scenarios" and assisting "in the management of lease transactions and executed lease documents." For this position, Spotify requested a "solid business judgement." The fact that Spotify was in dire need of expertise in the New York real estate market suggested that the company planned to move headquarters to the United States, which did not turn out to be true.

If the New York housing speculations based on our scraped job listings turned out negative, another aspect of Spotify's growth that we found striking—and a surmise more accurate—was the relation between *humans* and *machines* in the job listings, hinting at the use of artificial intelligence and other computational methods to give music customers the best music-discovery experience. In thirty-four of the job postings, the notion of "machine learning" was present in different ways. Hence, although Business evolved into the major organizational category at Spotify, its tech identity was still its corporate trademark.

Spotify has frequently branded itself as a *software-driven company* that relies on machine learning and algorithmic data mining in order to generate music recommendations and create music experiences. While streaming services such as Apple Music have taken public pride in their humanly curated playlists, Spotify has instead hallmarked itself as the techy alternative—vividly illustrated by the catchphrase, "music + math = epic," presented in a slideshow by Ching-Wei Chen and Vidhya Murali (both employed in Spotify's machine learning department).[16]

Spotify's aim to hire people to teach machines is a frequent feature among the job listings, hinting at a profound belief in computational capacity: "A Lead Ad Tech Machine Learning Engineer to help us build a modern and dynamic ad stack which can efficiently serve ads to our [listeners]"; "a Machine Learning Engineering Manager (Chapter Lead) to drive the machine learning and data engineering practice within the Revenue mission"; "a data engineer to help us build data-driven solutions"; "We are hiring software engineers who are very enthusiastic about data to focus on building structured, high-quality data solutions"; and so on. Spotify's apparent desires to automate and let machines handle its business is also shown in many of its startup acquisitions. In the spring of 2017, the company Sonalytic was acquired for to its sophisticated audio feature detection, as was the much-hyped French company Niland, which specializes in artificial intelligence.[17]

Yet despite its focus on machine learning and software-aided music curation, Spotify is of course also in need of human bodies and human labor. Even if machine-learning algorithms are capable of performing a large amount of work on their own, they are not capable of designing, monitoring, or directing themselves. Then again, the many job positions regarding machine learning and company acquisitions of cutting-edge tech companies are a strong indication that, in the near future, both machines and computational solutions will have an increased presence at Spotify. When looking at job listings within the general category of Technology, positions in the Software Engineering and Data & Machine Learning subcategories were common in our data set.

Finally, we were not able to perceive any significant changes or alterations—that is, a potential increase (or decrease) in certain Spotify job subcategories—over the half year we scraped our listings. On the contrary, when speculating about Spotify's future, it should be stressed that a number of positions were always listed during the six-month period. It seems as though Spotify is always looking for, say, skilled software engineers—and probably has been for the past decade. Even within the general category of business, a nearly equal number of jobs were being offered within the subcategories of subscription business, finance, and sales. One conclusion from this final intervention is that job listings can give some indications and evidence of where a company is heading. A larger, longitudinal data set is needed, however, especially since a more precise forecast would have to take into account job alterations over time—that is, how the positions themselves fluctuate.

Notes

Introduction

1. All dollar figures are in American currency, unless stated otherwise.

2. The research project, "Streaming Heritage: Following Files in Digital Music Distribution," has involved system developers Fredrik Palm, Roger Mähler, Andreas Marklund, and Johan von Boer (at Humlab, Umeå University), as well as researchers Pelle Snickars, Maria Eriksson, and Anna Johansson (at Umeå University), Rasmus Fleischer (at Stockholm and Umeå Universities), and Patrick Vonderau (at Stockholm University).

3. An early inspiration for this project was Lane DeNicola, "EULA, Codec, API: On the Opacity of Digital Culture," in *Moving Data: The iPhone and the Future of Media*, ed. Pelle Snickars and Patrick Vonderau (New York: Columbia University Press, 2012), 265–277.

4. See, for example, Matilda Svensson Glaser, "De ska studera Spotify inifrån," [They will study Spotify from within], *SVT Nyheter*, November 1, 2013, https://www.svt.se/kultur/musik/de-ska-studera-spotify-inifran; Mattias Berg, "Forskare startar fiktivt skivbolag," [Researchers start a fabricated record label], *Sveriges Radio*, May 7, 2014, http://sverigesradio.se/sida/artikel.aspx?programid=478&artikel=5855117; Maria Brändström, "Forskare blir skivbolagsboss," [Researcher becomes record label boss], *SVT Nyheter*, May 12, 2014, https://www.svt.se/nyheter/lokalt/vasterbotten/forskare-blir-skivbolagsboss; and Carin Mannberg-Zackari, "Forskare följer musikfiler på nätet," [Researchers follow music files online], *Curie*, August 19, 2014, https://www.tidningencurie.se/nyheter/2014/08/19/forskare-foljer-musikfiler-pa-natet/. For further coverage of our project, see the "Streaming Heritage" project website (http://streamingheritage.se) and the two blogs maintained by project members Rasmus Fleischer (https://copyriot.se) and Pelle Snickars (http://pellesnickars.se).

5. Richard Rogers, *Digital Methods* (Cambridge, MA: MIT Press, 2013).

6. For an overview, see Jennifer Holt and Alisa Perren, eds., *Media Industries: History, Theory, and Method* (Malden, MA: Blackwell, 2009); and Amanda D. Lotz and Timothy Havens, *Understanding Media Industries*, 2nd ed. (Oxford: Oxford University Press, 2016).

7. John Thornton Caldwell, *Production Culture: Industrial Reflexivity and Critical Practice in Film and Television* (Durham, NC: Duke University Press, 2008).

8. Jonas Andersson Schwarz, *Online File Sharing: Innovations in Media Consumption* (London: Routledge, 2013); Michael D. Smith and Rahul Telang, *Streaming, Sharing, Stealing: Big Data and the Future of Entertainment* (Cambridge, MA: MIT Press, 2016); Patrik Wikström, *The Music Industry: Music in the Cloud* (Cambridge: Polity Press, 2009); and Patrik Wikström and Robert DeFillippi, eds., *Business Innovation and Disruption in the Music Industry* (Cheltenham, UK: Edward Elgar, 2016).

9. For a discussion, see Andrew Edgecliffe-Johnson, "Lunch with the FT: Daniel Ek," *Financial Times*, September 27, 2013, https://www.ft.com/content/ca45f6b8-25bd-11e3 -aee8-00144feab7de.

10. Anita Elberse, *Blockbusters: Why Big Hits—and Big Risks—Are the Future of the Entertainment Business* (London: Faber & Faber, 2014).

11. Philip Napoli and Robyn Caplan, "Why Media Companies Insist They're Not Media Companies, Why They're Wrong, and Why It Matters," *First Monday* 22, no. 5 (2017), doi:10.5210/fm.v22i15.7051.

12. Jonathan Sterne, *MP3: The Meaning of a Format* (Durham, NC: Duke University Press, 2012), 131.

13. Tim Nudd, "Spotify Crunches User Data in Fun Ways for This New Global Outdoor Ad Campaign," *Adweek*, November 29, 2016, http://www.adweek.com /creativity/spotify-crunches-user-data-fun-ways-new-global-outdoor-ad-campaign -174826/.

14. See Regulation (EU) 2016/679 of the European Parliament and of the Council of 27 April 2016 on the Protection of Natural Persons with Regard to the Processing of Personal Data and on the Free Movement of Such Data and Repealing Directive 95/46/EC, 2016 O.J. (L 119) 1, http://data.europa.eu/eli/reg/2016/679/oj. See especially article 22, 2016 O.J. (L 119) 1, 4.

15. David Turner, "Yes, Spotify Fills Mood Playlists with Fake Artists," *TrackRecord*, November 21, 2016, https://trackrecord.net/spotify-does-in-fact-fill-mood-playlists -with-fake-ar-1820642310.

16. See, for example, Nitasha Tiku, "Get Ready for the Next Big Privacy Backlash against Facebook," *Wired*, May 21, 2017, https://www.wired.com/2017/05/welcome -next-phase-facebook-backlash/.

17. See Cambridge Analytica, https://cambridgeanalytica.org.

18. David M. Greenberg et al., "The Song Is You: Preferences for Musical Attribute Dimensions Reflect Personality," *Social Psychology and Personality Science* 7, no. 6 (2016): 597–605, doi:10.1177/1948550616641473.

19. Adrian Mackenzie et al., "Digital Sociology in the Field of Devices," in *Routledge International Handbook of the Sociology of Art and Culture*, ed. Laurie Hanquinet and Mike Savage (London: Routledge, 2016), 367–382.

20. Esha Bhandari and Rachel Goodman, "Data Journalism and the Computer Fraud and Abuse Act: Tips for Moving Forward in an Uncertain Landscape" (paper, Computation + Journalism Symposium 2017, Northwestern University, Evanston, IL, October 13–14, 2017), https://northwestern.box.com/s/mnyympjp2a7iqau9o73 v4f9mrt1satoc.

21. Laura Nader, "Up the Anthropologist—Perspectives Gained from Studying Up," in *Reinventing Anthropology*, ed. Dell Hymes (New York: Vintage Books, 1974), 284–311; and Hugh Gusterson, "Studying Up Revisited," *PoLAR: Political and Anthropological Review* 20, no. 1 (1997): 114–119, doi: 10.1525/pol.1997.20.1.114.

22. Noortje Marres, *Digital Sociology: The Reinvention of Social Research* (Cambridge: Polity Press, 2017), 182–183.

23. Michel Callon and Bruno Latour, "Unscrewing the Big Leviathan: How Actors Macro-structure Reality and How Sociologists Help Them to Do So," in *Advances in Social Theory and Methodology: Toward an Integration of Micro- and Macro-sociologies*, ed. Karen Knorr-Cetina and Aaron V. Cicourel (Boston: Routledge & Kegan Paul, 1981), 280.

24. Some have criticized the metaphor as worn out, but it is still productive for our purposes. For a critical view, see Christopher M. Kelty, "Against Networks," *Spheres: Journal for Digital Cultures*, no. 1 (2014), http://spheres-journal.org/against-networks/.

25. Gideon Kunda, *Engineering Culture: Control and Commitment in a High-Tech Corporation*, rev. ed. (Philadelphia: Temple University Press, 2006), 7.

26. Evelyn Ruppert, John Law, and Mike Savage, "Reassembling Social Science Methods: The Challenge of Digital Devices," *Theory, Culture & Society* 30, no. 4 (2013): 22–46, doi:10.1177/0263276413484941.

27. Matthew J. Salganik, *Bit by Bit: Social Research in the Digital Age* (Princeton, NJ: Princeton University Press, 2018), 304. For an in-depth discussion of the ethical issues related to our research, see the conclusion.

28. Bronisław Malinowski, *Argonauts of the Western Pacific: An Account of Native Enterprise and Adventure in the Archipelagos of Melanesian New Guinea* (London: Routledge & Kegan Paul, 1922), 25.

29. Barbara Czarniawska, *Shadowing, and Other Techniques for Doing Fieldwork in Modern Societies* (Malmö, Sweden: Liber, 2007), 35. See also Barbara Czarniawska, *Cyberfactories: How News Agencies Produce News* (Cheltenham, UK: Edward Elgar, 2011).

30. Howard Garfinkel, *Studies in Ethnomethodology* (Englewood Cliffs, NJ: Prentice Hall, 1967).

31. Arjun Appadurai, ed., *The Social Life of Things: Commodities in Cultural Perspective* (Cambridge: Cambridge University Press, 1986).

32. David Calvey, *Covert Research: The Art, Politics and Ethics of Undercover Fieldwork* (London: SAGE, 2017). For a longer discussion of corporate research ethics, see the conclusion.

33. Celia Lury and Nina Wakeford, "Introduction: A Perpetual Inventory," in *Inventive Methods: The Happening of the Social*, ed. Celia Lury and Nina Wakeford (London: Routledge, 2012), 6.

34. Callon and Latour, "Unscrewing the Big Leviathan," 292.

35. Christian Sandvig and Eszter Hargittai, "How to Think about Digital Research," in *Digital Research Confidential: The Secrets of Studying Behavior Online*, edited by Eszter Hargittai and Christian Sandvig (Cambridge, MA: MIT Press, 2015), 3.

36. Rogers, *Digital Methods*, 4.

37. Klaus Bruhn Jensen, "New Media, Old Methods—Internet Methodologies and the Online/Offline Divide," in *The Handbook of Internet Studies*, ed. Mia Consalvo and Charles Ess (Chichester, UK: Wiley-Blackwell, 2011), 43–68.

38. Amit Datta, Michael Carl Tschantz, and Anupam Datta, "Automated Experiments on Ad Privacy Settings: A Tale of Opacity, Choice, and Discrimination," *Proceedings on Privacy Enhancing Technologies*, no. 1 (2015): 92, doi:10.1515/popets-2015-0007.

39. Leonid Bershidsky, "European Ruling Buries Uber's Platform Myth," *Bloomberg View*, December 20, 2017, https://www.bloomberg.com/view/articles/2017-12-20/european-ruling-buries-uber-s-platform-myth.

40. One of the most plausible descriptions of digital companies is to be found in Katharina Hölck, "Beyond the Single Platform: An Assessment of the Functioning and Regulatory Challenges of Multi-layered Platform Systems in the Media and Communications Sector" (PhD diss., Vrije Universiteit Brussel, 2016), https://ssrn.com/abstract=2992487. Here, Hölck describes the uncanny dynamics of "platform systems."

41. Jean Burgess, "From 'Broadcast Yourself' to 'Follow Your Interests': Making Over Social Media," *International Journal of Cultural Studies* 18, no. 3 (2015): 281–285, doi:10.1177/1367877913513684.

42. Jean-Christophe Plantin et al., "Infrastructure Studies Meet Platform Studies in the Age of Google and Facebook," *New Media & Society* 20, no. 1 (2018): 293–310, doi:10.1177/1461444816661553.

43. Ian Bogost and Nick Montfort, "Platform Studies: Frequently Questioned Answers" (paper, Digital Arts and Culture Conference, Irvine, California, December 12–15, 2009), http://pdf.textfiles.com/academics/bogost_montfort_dac_2009.pdf.

44. Benjamin H. Bratton, in his own attempt to develop a platform theory, notes the "lack of sufficient theories." Bratton, *The Stack: On Software and Sovereignty* (Cambridge, MA: MIT Press, 2015), 41. For a seminal article on the issue, later followed up with recurring blog entries posted on *Culture Digitally* (http://culturedigitally.org/), see Tarleton Gillespie, "The Politics of 'Platforms,'" *New Media & Society* 12, no. 3 (2010): 347–364, doi:10.1177/1461444809342738.

45. See Bratton, *The Stack*, 141–142; and José van Dijck, *The Culture of Connectivity: A Critical History of Social Media* (New York: Oxford University Press, 2013), 35.

46. Anne Helmond, "The Platformization of the Web: Making Web Data Platform Ready," *Social Media + Society* 1, no. 2 (2015), doi:10.1177/2056305115603080.

47. Carolin Gerlitz and Anne Helmond, "The Like Economy: Social Buttons and the Data-Intensive Web," *New Media & Society* 15, no. 8 (2013): 1348–1365, doi:10.1177/1461444812472322.

48. Jean-Charles Rochet and Jean Tirole, "Platform Competition in Two-Sided Markets," *Journal of the European Economic Association* 1, no. 4 (2003): 990–1029, doi:10.1162/154247603322493212; and Annabelle Gawer, "Bridging Differing Perspectives on Technological Platforms: Toward an Integrative Framework," *Research Policy* 43, no. 7 (2014): 1239–1249, doi:10.1016/j.respol.2014.03.006.

49. Ruth Towse and Christian Handke, eds., *Handbook on the Digital Creative Economy* (Cheltenham, UK: Edward Elgar, 2013); and Ruth Towse, "Economics of Music Publishing: Copyright and the Market," *Journal of Cultural Economics* 41, no. 4 (2017): 403–420, doi:10.1007/s10824-016-9268-7.

50. Dirk Auer and Nicolas Petit, "Two-Sided Markets and the Challenge of Turning Economic Theory into Antitrust Policy," *Antitrust Bulletin* 60, no. 4 (2015): 426–461, doi:10.1177/0003603X15607155.

51. Van Dijck, *Culture of Connectivity*, 25.

52. Some proponents of the platform view, such as David S. Evans and Richard Schmalensee, certainly acknowledge that multisidedness always existed in the offline world as well. Yet, this does not change the course of their analysis. Evans and Schmalensee, "The Industrial Organization of Markets with Two-Sided Platforms," *Competition Policy International* 3, no. 1 (2007): 151–179.

53. Jonathan Zittrain, "The Generative Internet," *Harvard Law Review* 119, no. 7 (2006): 1974–2040, doi:10.1145/1435417.1435426; and Jonathan Zittrain, *The Future of the Internet and How to Stop It* (New Haven, CT: Yale University Press, 2008).

54. Benjamin J. Birkinbine, Rodrigo Gómez, and Janet Wasko, eds., *Global Media Giants* (London: Routledge, 2017).

55. Nora Draper, "Fail Fast: The Value of Studying Unsuccessful Technology Companies," *Media Industries Journal* 4, no. 1 (2017), doi:10.3998/mij.15031809.0004.101.

56. Karine Nahon, "Toward a View of Platforms as Ecosystems" (paper, "Digital Imaginaries," 16th Association of Internet Researchers Conference, Phoenix, AZ, October 21–24, 2015).

57. For a brief introduction on this issue, see Michel Callon, "An Essay on Framing and Overflowing: Economic Externalities Revisited by Sociology," in "The Laws of Markets," ed. Michael Callon, supplement, *Sociological Review* 46, no. S1 (1998): 244–269, doi:10.1111/j.1467-954X.1998.tb03477.x.

58. For instance, see Nick Srnicek, *Platform Capitalism* (Cambridge: Polity Press, 2017); Brooke Erin Duffy, *(Not) Getting Paid to Do What You Love: Gender, Social Media, and Aspirational Work* (New Haven: Yale University Press, 2017); and Michael Curtin and Kevin Sanson, eds., *Precarious Creativity: Global Media, Local Labor* (Berkeley: University of California Press, 2016).

59. Tarleton Gillespie, "Platforms Intervene," *Social Media + Society* 1, no. 1 (2015), doi:10.1177/2056305115580479.

60. Barbara Czarniawska, "On Time, Space, and Action Nets," *Organization* 11, no. 6 (2004): 780–782, doi:10.1177/1350508404047251.

61. Czarniawska, "On Time," 779.

62. Bruno Latour, *Reassembling the Social: An Introduction to Actor-Network-Theory* (Oxford: Oxford University Press, 2005), 39.

63. See, for instance, Joseph C. Palamountain, *The Politics of Distribution* (Cambridge, MA: Harvard University Press, 1955); Helmond, "Platformization of the Web"; and, most importantly, Hölck, "Beyond the Single Platform."

64. Allaine Cerwonka and Liisa H. Malkki, *Improvising Theory: Process and Temporality in Ethnographic Fieldwork* (Chicago: University of Chicago Press, 2007).

Intervention: The Swedish Unicorn

1. Erik Nilson, "Kritiken växer efter Spotifys brev: 'Det är bedrövligt,'" [Criticism grows after Spotify's letter: "It's sad."], *Svenska Dagbladet*, April 12, 2016, https://www.svd.se/kritiken-vaxer-efter-spotifys-brev-det-ar-bedrovligt/om/naringsliv:digitalt.

2. Marcel Broersma and Todd Graham, "Social Media as Beat: Tweets as a News Source during the 2010 British and Dutch Elections," *Journalism Practice* 6, no. 3 (2012): 403–419, doi:10.1080/17512786.2012.663626.

3. See, for example, Jonas Andersson Schwarz and Johan Hammarlund, "Kontextförlust och kontextkollaps: Metodproblem vid innehållsanalys av sociala medier," [Contextual loss and collapse: Methodological problems in content analysis of social media], *Nordicom-Information* 38, no. 3 (2016): 41–55; and Bruno Latour et al., "'The Whole Is Always Smaller than Its Parts'—A Digital Test

of Gabriel Tardes' Monads," *British Journal of Sociology* 63, no. 4 (2012): 590–615, doi:10.1111/j.1468-4446.2012.01428.x.

4. For a detailed discussion and analysis of the Twitter campaign, see Rasmus Fleischer and Christopher Kullenberg, "The Political Significance of Spotify in Sweden— Analysing the #backaspotify Campaign using Twitter Data," *Culture Unbound* 11, no. 1 (2018).

5. Pamela Davidsson and Olle Findahl, *Svenskarna och internet 2017: Undersökning om svenskarnas internetvanor*, [Swedes and the internet 2017: Report on Swedish internet habits], ed. Marianne Ahlgren, v. 1.1 (Stockholm: Internetstiftelsen i Sverige, 2017), 67, https://www.iis.se/docs/Svenskarna_och_internet_2017.pdf.

6. Our search for "Spotify" in the Swedish parliamentary minutes—which are publicly available online—generated 127 results. Search results for "Spotify," Sveriges riksdag, accessed June 9, 2017, http://www.riksdagen.se/sv/global/sok/?q=spotify.

7. Stefan Löfven, speech at the Royal Swedish Academy of Engineering Sciences, Stockholm, January 31, 2017, Government Offices of Sweden, http://www.government.se/speeches/2017/01/speech-by-prime-minister-stefan-lofven-at-iva/.

8. Bridget de Maine, "Inside Spotify's Insanely Cool Stockholm Offices," *Collective Hub*, August 22, 2016, http://collectivehub.com/2016/08/inside-spotifys-insanely-cool-stockholm-offices/.

9. Sebastian Orre, "Spotify har egen bostadskö," [Spotify has its own housing queue], *Svenska Dagbladet*, March 13, 2016, https://www.svd.se/spotify-har-egen-bostadsko.

10. Daniel Ek and Martin Lorentzon (@SpotifySE), "Vi måste agera eller bli omsprungna!" [We must act or be overtaken!], *Medium*, April 11, 2016, https://medium.com/@SpotifySE/vi-måste-agera-eller-bli-omsprungna-383bb0b808eb.

11. Ek and Lorentzon, "Vi måste agera."

12. Andreas Sjostrom (@AndreasSjostrom), Twitter, April 12, 2016, https://twitter.com/AndreasSjostrom/status/719935155549380608.

13. Anthony Cuthbertson, "Swedish Startups Protest as Spotify Threatens to Leave Country," *Newsweek*, April 13, 2016, http://www.newsweek.com/swedish-startups-protest-spotify-threatens-leave-country-447460.

14. Nilson, "Kritiken växer."

15. Hugh McIntyre, "Spotify May Soon Leave Sweden, According to Its CEO," *Forbes*, April 19, 2016, https://www.forbes.com/sites/hughmcintyre/2016/04/19/spotify-may-soon-leave-sweden-according-to-its-ceo/.

16. Annie Lööf and Emil Källström, "Vi behöver Spotify mer än Spotify behöver oss" [We need Spotify more than Spotify needs us], *Expressen*, April 15, 2016,

https://www.expressen.se/debatt/vi-behover-spotify-mer-an-spotify-behover-oss/
(our translation).

17. Miltton Labs (website), accessed June 9, 2017, https://www.milttonlabs.com/.

18. Annie Lööf (@annieloof), "Sverige behöver de snabbväxande tillväxtbolagen mer än vad de behöver Sverige. #backaspotify" [Sweden needs fast-growing companies more than they need Sweden. #backaspotify], Twitter photo, April 15, 2016, https://twitter.com/annieloof/status/720873633426452480.

19. Linda Nordlund (@lindanordlund), "Kötid för hyresrätt: Berlin - 0 v, NYC - 0 v, Bryssel - 0 v, Stockholm (länet) - 208 veckor. Gissa varför företag flyttar? #backaspotify," [Waiting time for apartment rental: Berlin - 0 weeks, Brussels - 0 weeks, Stockholm (county) - 208 weeks. Guess why companies leave? #backaspotify], Twitter, April 12, 2016, https://twitter.com/lindanordlund/status/719931051041243137.

20. Rödgrön röra (@rodgronrora), "#backaspotify," Twitter photo, April 12, 2016, https://twitter.com/Rodgronrora/status/719953388100796416/.

21. Linus Larsson, "Spotify nobbade nya lägenheter," [Spotify rejected new apartments], Dagens Nyheter, April 21, 2016, https://www.dn.se/ekonomi/spotify-nobbade -nya-lagenheter/.

22. Tobias Holdstock (@tobiasholdstock), "Pinsamt när nyrekryterade till Stockholm från New York etc erbjuds boende ute i Järfälla #bokris #backaspotify," [Embarrassment as new recruits to Stockholm from New York and elsewhere are offered apartments out in Järfälla #bokris #backaspotify], Twitter photo, May 17, 2016, https://twitter.com/TobiasHoldstock/status/732806510343032836.

23. "Snurr på Stockholm," [Turn on Stockholm], Ledare, Dagens Nyheter, May 18, 2016, https://www.dn.se/ledare/huvudledare/snurr-pa-stockholm/.

Chapter 1: Where Is Spotify?

1. Ek was called the most important person in the music business by Forbes in 2012, but it was in 2017 that he surpassed the boss of Universal Music Group to become number one on Billboard's famous "Power 100" list. See Steven Bertoni, "Spotify's Daniel Ek: The Most Important Man in Music," Forbes, January 4, 2012, https://www .forbes.com/sites/stevenbertoni/2012/01/04/spotifys-daniel-ek-the-most-important -man-in-music/; and Robert Levine, "Billboard Power 100's New No. 1: Spotify Streaming Pioneer Daniel Ek," Billboard, February 9, 2017, https://www.billboard.com /articles/business/7685308/no-1-power-100-daniel-ek-spotify.

2. Sam Gustin, "Daniel Ek, Spotify," TIME Tech 40: The Most Influential Minds in Tech, Time, May 15, 2013, http://business.time.com/2013/05/01/time-tech-40-the -ten-most-influential-tech-ceos/slide/daniel-ek-spotify/.

3. Ed Sheeran, "Daniel Ek," The 100 Most Influential People, *Time*, May 1, 2017, http://time.com/collection/2017-time-100/4742746/daniel-ek/.

4. Henrik Huldschiner, "26-åringen som sätter skräck i nätgiganterna," [The 26-year-old who puts fear into the net giants], *Dagens Industri*, March 28, 2009, https://www.di.se/artiklar/2009/3/28/26-aringen-som-satter-skrack-i-natgiganterna/.

5. Jens Beckert, "Imagined Futures: Fictional Expectations in the Economy," *Theory and Society* 42, no. 3 (2013): 219–240, doi:10.1007/s11186-013-9191-2.

6. On the historical development of rights in sound recordings, see Rasmus Fleischer, "Protecting the Musicians and/or the Record Industry? On the History of 'Neighbouring Rights' and the Role of Fascist Italy," *Queen Mary Journal of Intellectual Property* 5, no. 3 (2015): 327–343, doi:10.4337/qmjip.2015.03.05.

7. Sally Wyatt, "Danger! Metaphors at Work in Economics, Geophysiology, and the Internet," *Science, Technology, & Human Values* 29, no. 2 (2004): 242–261, doi:10.1177/0162243903261947.

8. See, for instance, Megan Sapnar Ankerson, "Historicizing Web Design: Software, Style, and the Look of the Web," in *Convergence Media History*, ed. Janet Staiger and Sabine Hake (New York: Routledge, 2009), 192–203.

9. William Uricchio, "Historicizing Media in Transition," in *Rethinking Media Change: The Aesthetics of Transition*, ed. David Thorburn and Henry Jenkins (Cambridge, MA: MIT Press, 2004), 23–38.

10. Chris Lorenz and Berber Bevernage, eds., *Breaking Up Time: Negotiating the Borders between Present, Past and Future* (Göttingen, Germany: Vandenhoeck & Ruprecht, 2013).

11. Spotify, "Spotify—The Story," Vimeo, October 6, 2008, video, 1:00, https://vimeo.com/1900024.

12. Frances Moore, introduction to *Global Music Report 2017: Annual State of the Industry*, by International Federation of the Phonographic Industry (IFPI, 2017), 7, http://www.ifpi.org/downloads/GMR2017.pdf.

13. See, for example, Tiziana Terranova, "New Economy, Financialization and Social Production in the Web 2.0," in *Crisis in the Global Economy: Financial Markets, Social Struggles, and New Political Scenarios*, ed. Andrea Fumagalli and Sandro Mezzadra (Los Angeles: Semiotext(e), 2010), 153–170.

14. Jonathan Sterne, *MP3: The Meaning of a Format* (Durham, NC: Duke University Press, 2012); and Jeremy Wade Morris, *Selling Digital Music, Formatting Culture* (Berkeley: University of California Press, 2015). For a critical discussion of Morris, see Rasmus Fleischer, "If the Song Has No Price, Is It Still a Commodity? Rethinking the Commodification of Digital Music," *Culture Unbound* 9, no. 2 (2017): 146–162, doi:10.3384/cu.2000.1525.1792146.

15. John Thornton Caldwell, *Production Culture: Industrial Reflexivity and Critical Practice in Film and Television* (Durham, NC: Duke University Press, 2008), 5.

16. Gideon Kunda, *Engineering Culture: Control and Commitment in a High-Tech Corporation*, rev. ed. (Philadelphia: Temple University Press, 2006), 7.

17. Annette Ruef and Jochen Markard, "What Happens after a Hype? How Changing Expectations Affected Innovation Activities in the Case of Stationary Fuel Cells," *Technology Analysis & Strategic Management* 22, no. 3 (2010): 317–338, doi:10.1080/09537321003647354.

18. Richard Barbrook, *Imaginary Futures: From Thinking Machines to the Global Village* (London: Pluto Press, 2007).

19. In general, we have used the practice of selecting articles through the simple use of the search term "Spotify."

20. For example, we wanted to find reports from those Swedish bloggers who were the very first to try out the beta version of Spotify in 2007. Most of those blogs are no longer online. In some cases, the content is available via the Internet Archive (https://archive.org/) but is not directly searchable, so it is necessary to first identify links to the specific blog entries. There was once a popular site named Delicious (https://del.icio.us) that was used for social "bookmarking." There we found a public account used by the Swedish tech entrepreneur Henrik Torstensson, who was one of Spotify's very first beta testers. As early as 2007, he collected some links tagged with "Spotify," producing a link list (https://del.icio.us/torstensson/spotify) that we found very useful for our research. Many of the links pointed to dead websites, but the content could sometimes be found through the Internet Archive, giving examples of the early reception of Spotify. The short life of many websites is a good reason why the history of digital culture must be written sooner rather than later. In addition, Spotify's official blog should not to be overlooked as a source of information on the many changes to the service, as well as how these were communicated to users. The Twitter accounts of the company and its executives are also useful. Daniel Ek, for instance, has been tweeting as @eldsjal since late 2007. We found no indication that Spotify has engaged in retroactive deletion of tweets or blog posts but cannot be sure; this is an issue of source criticism that any kind of business historian will confront.

21. J. Jasper Deuten and Arie Rip, "Narrative Infrastructure in Product Creation Processes," *Organization* 7, no. 1 (2000): 69–93, doi:10.1177/135050840071005.

22. IFPI, *Global Music Report 2017*, 10.

23. IFPI, *Global Music Report 2017*, 10.

24. Rasmus Fleischer, "Swedish Music Export: The Making of a Miracle," in *Made in Sweden: Studies in Popular Music*, ed. Alf Björnberg and Thomas Bossius (New York: Routledge, 2017), 153–162.

25. Fraser Smith, "Spotify Losing in UK but Profitable in Sweden," *Next Web*, November 25, 2010, https://thenextweb.com/apps/2010/11/25/spotify-losing-in-uk -but-profitable-in-sweden/.

26. Szu Ping Chan, "Spotify In and Sat-Navs Out: Take a Look at the New Inflation Basket," *Telegraph*, March 17, 2015, https://www.telegraph.co.uk/finance/econom ics/11476930/Spotify-in-and-sat-navs-out-take-a-look-at-the-new-inflation-basket .html; and "Measuring Economies: The Trouble with GDP," *Economist*, April 30, 2016, https://www.economist.com/news/briefing/21697845-gross-domestic-product -gdp-increasingly-poor-measure-prosperity-it-not-even.

27. Erik Brynjolfsson, Felix Eggers, and Avinash Gannamaneni, "Using massive online choice experiments to measure changes in well-being," NBER Working Paper No. 24514, National Bureau of Economic Research, April 2018, http://www.nber.org /papers/w24514

28. Anna Felländer, "The Opportunities and Challenges of Digitalisation," in *Digital Opportunities*, by Digitalisation Commission (Stockholm: Swedish Government Inquiries, 2015), 65, http://docplayer.net/11228775-Digital-opportunities.html; and Charles Bean, *Independent Review of UK Economic Statistics* (HM Treasury, 2016), 3, https://www.gov.uk/government/publications/independent-review-of-uk-economic -statistics-final-report.

29. Rasmus Fleischer, "Från lagringskultur till streamingkultur: Om att skriva sam-tidens näthistoria" [From storage culture to streaming culture: Writing the story of contemporary times], in *Återkopplingar* [Feedback], ed. Marie Cronqvist, Patrik Lun-dell, and Pelle Snickars, Mediehistoriskt arkiv 28 (Lund, Sweden: Lunds universitet, 2014), 219–234.

30. Rasmus Fleischer, "Nätutopier och nätdystopier: Om 2000-talets sökande efter internets väsen" [Net utopia and dystopia: Searching for the soul of the internet during the early 2000s], in *Samtider: Perspektiv på 2000-talets idéhistoria* [The Present: perspectives on the history of ideas during the early 2000s], eds. Anders Burman and Lena Lennerhed (Gothenburg: Daidalos, 2017), 261-303.

31. Jonas Andersson and Pelle Snickars, eds., *Efter The Pirate Bay* (Stockholm: Kung-liga biblioteket, 2010); and Jonas Andersson Schwarz, *Online File Sharing: Innovations in Media Consumption* (London: Routledge, 2013).

32. Somewhat ironically, Anderson received €50,000 for his presentation of the book *Free!* in Malmö in 2009. Madelene Hellström, "Chris Anderson frälste Malmö," [Chris Anderson saved Malmö], *ComputerSweden*, May 2, 2009, https://it24.idg.se/2 .2275/1.210026/chris-anderson-fralste-malmo.

33. Adrian Covert, "Why Did It Take So Long for Spotify to Come to the US?," *Gizmodo*, July 13, 2011, https://gizmodo.com/5821056/why did it-take-so-long-for -spotify-to-come-to-the-us.

34. TradeDoubler AB, "Inbjudan till förvärv av aktier i TradeDoubler AB," [Invitation to acquire shares in TradeDoubler AB], IPO prospectus, October 21, 2005, http://hstse.tradedoubler.com/file/20649/international/ir/TradeDoubler_sw.pdf.

35. TradeDoubler AB, "TradeDoubler Buys Provider of Pay-per-Call and Contextual Advertising Technology," press release, March 27, 2006, http://hstnl.tradedoubler.com/file/945/communicatie/persberichten/PRADVERTIGOenglishFinal.pdf.

36. In some early reports, Felix Hagnö is named as Spotify's third cofounder when he was actually merely an early investor. See, for example, Nils Åkesson, "Så ska grundarna spendera pengarna," [In this way the founders will spend their money], *Dagens Industri*, January 15, 2007, http://www.di.se/artiklar/2007/1/15/sa-ska-grundarna-spendera-pengarna/; and Karolina Palutko Macéus, "De kan tjäna 900 miljoner," [They can earn 900 million], *Dagens Industri*, January 16, 2007.

37. Patricia Hedelius, "Spotifys grundare valde bort Sverige för länge sedan," [The founders of Spotify opted out of Sweden long ago], *Svenska Dagbladet*, April 15, 2016, https://www.svd.se/spotifys-grundare-valde-bort-sverige-for-lange-sedan.

38. Sven Carlsson, "Spotifys vd har ett brevlådebolag på Cypern," [Spotify CEO has a mailbox company on Cyprus], *Dagens Industri*, May 14, 2017, https://digital.di.se/artikel/spotifys-vd-har-ett-brevladebolag-pa-cypern.

39. See entries in the company registration database CY-Check.com, "Spotify Technology Sales Ltd," http://cy-check.com/spotify-technology-sales-ltd/227217.html; and "Spotify Technology Holding Ltd," http://cy-check.com/spotify-technology-holding-ltd/211739.html.

40. Andreas Ehn et al., "Peer-to-Peer Streaming of Media Content," US Patent 8,316,146, filed July 13, 2007, and issued November 20, 2012, https://www.google.com/patents/US8316146.

41. Macéus, "De kan tjäna"; and Åkesson, "Så ska grundarna."

42. Spotify (website), November 27, 2006, https://www.spotify.com, archived at the Wayback Machine, Internet Archive, https://web.archive.org/web/20061127231638/http://www.spotify.com:80/.

43. We know this from personal experience, as one of the authors is also a musician who made recordings that were available in the Spotify beta—only to disappear at the public launch. This has also been reaffirmed by other persons who made similar observations at the time: "Most importantly, I can confirm the pirating part as I was using the Beta, and thought at the time it was a cool thing to do." Magnus Boman, reply to "<nettime> Spotify Threatened Researchers Who Revealed 'Pirate' History," Nettime (mailing list), October 9, 2017, https://nettime.org/Lists-Archives/nettime-l-1710/msg00049.html. Niklas Ivarsson who was then Head of Licensing at Spotify, also stated in an e-mail to one of us authors in November 2008: "All content for the

Beta tests were taken from our own or friends music collections." See also Andersson Schwarz, *Online File Sharing*, 32.

44. Eric Wahlforss, "OMG Spotify!," personal blog, May 9, 2007, http://eric .wahlforss.com/2007/05/09/omg-spotify/ (site discontinued).

45. Eric Wahlforss, "Please Let Me *Not* Own My Music: On Spotify, SoundCloud," personal blog, March 3, 2008, http://eric.wahlforss.com/2008/03/03/please-let-me-not -own-my-music-on-spotify-soundcloud/ (site discontinued); Henric Karlsson, "The swedish model vill erbjuda musik gratis," [The Swedish Model wants to offer music for free], *Göteborgs-Posten*, March 5, 2008, http://www.gp.se/kultur/the-swedish-model -vill-erbjuda-musik-gratis-1.1153611; Adam Svanell, "Reklam ska göra musiken gratis," [Advertising will make the music free], *Svenska Dagbladet*, April 6, 2008, https://www .svd.se/reklam-ska-gora-musiken-gratis; "Årets entreprenörer 2008," [Entrepreneur of the year 2008], *Internetworld*, April 25, 2008, https://internetworld.idg.se/2.1006/1 .157629/arets-entreprenorer-2008; and Andres Lokko, "Internet är allas vår skivsamling," [The internet is our common record collection], *Svenska Dagbladet*, August 15, 2008, https://www.svd.se/internet-ar-allas-var-skivsamling.

46. Spotify, "Spotify skriver licensavtal med sju internationella musikjättar och tillkännager lansering," [Spotify signs licensing deal with seven international record labels and announces launch], press release, *PR Newswire*, October 7, 2008, http://www .prnewswire.co.uk/news-releases/spotify-skriver-licensavtal-med-sju-internationella -musikjattar-och-tillkannager-lansering-152513735.html.

47. Stefan Lundell, "Spotify drar upp volymen på nätet," [Spotify turns up the volume online], *Dagens Industri*, October 18, 2008, https://www.di.se/artiklar/2008 /10/18/spotify-drar-upp-volymen-pa-natet/.

48. Spotify, "Hello Germany. Spotify Here," press release, March 13, 2013, https://press .spotify.com/us/2012/03/13/germany/; and Diego Planas Rego (diegoatspotify), "Hello Italy, Poland and Portugal. Spotify here," *Spotify News* (blog), February 12, 2013, https: //news.spotify.com/us/2013/02/12/hello-italy-poland-portugal/.

49. Andreas Ehn et al., "Peer-to-Peer-strömmning av medieinnehåll," [Peer-to-peer streaming of media content], Swedish Patent SE 0701717–1, filed July 13, 2007, and issued November 10, 2009, http://was.prv.se/spd/patent?p1=2X63xqIWgOR7eM42P9NdVA &p2=MWN663OCkwI&hits=true&tab=1&content=SE+0701717-1.

50. Jörgen Löwenfeldt, "Bredbandsbolaget vill ha ett 'Spotify för film,'" [Bredbands- bolaget wants a Spotify for film], *ComputerSweden*, January 19, 2009, https://it24.idg .se/2.2275/1.206386/bredbandsbolaget-vill-ha-ett-spotify-for-film.

51. See Riksdagens protokoll 2008/09:77 Onsdagen den 25 februari, 8 § [Swedish parliamentary minutes for February 25, 2009], https://www.riksdagen.se/sv/doku ment-lagar/dokument/protokoll/riksdagens-protokoll-20080977-onsdagen-den -25_GW0977, a discussion of the implementation of Directive 2004/48/EC of the

European Parliament and of the Council of 29 April 2004 on the Enforcement of Intellectual Property Rights, 2004 O.J (L 157) 45, http://data.europa.eu/eli/dir/2004/48/oj.

52. Andersson Schwarz, *Online File Sharing*, 138–139.

53. US Embassy in Stockholm to the Office of the US Trade Representative, "Special 301 for Sweden: Post Recommendation," March 2, 2009, unclassified diplomatic cable, archived at Public Library of US Diplomacy, WikiLeaks, https://www.wikileaks.org/plusd/cables/09STOCKHOLM141_a.html.

54. Daniel Mathisen, "Svensk it-veteran bakom mångmiljoninvestering på nätet," [Swedish IT veteran behind multimillion online investment], *Dagens Industri*, July 1, 2009.

55. Johanna Nylander, "Äntligen börjar branschen vakna," *Expressen*, July 2, 2009, https://www.expressen.se/ledare/johanna-nylander-antligen-borjar-branschen-vakna/.

56. Daniel Ek, "Overnight Success Takes a Long Time…," *Spotify News* (blog), October 8, 2009, https://news.spotify.com/us/2009/10/08/overnight-success-takes-a-long-time/.

57. "Media Conglomerates in the Downturn: The Triumph of the Monthly Bill," *Economist*, October 8, 2009, https://www.economist.com/node/14587429.

58. "Can New Digital Services Lure Fans?," *Rolling Stone*, November 26, 2009. We should add that the idea of a shift toward subscriptions was not new in the music industry. Already in 2000, another executive at Universal Music Group had been "very bullish on subscriptions." See, for example, Ashlee Vance, "Music Industry Gets on Copyright Soapbox," *Computerworld*, September 26, 2000, https://www.computerworld.com.au/article/78739/music_industry_gets_copyright_soapbox/.

59. Ek, "Overnight Success."

60. Ek, "Overnight Success."

61. Antony Bruno, "See Spotify Run," *Billboard*, October 17, 2009, 21–22.

62. Ek, "Overnight Success."

63. Bruno, "See Spotify Run."

64. Spotify, "3 UK, Spotify and HTC Hero Join Forces to Make the Internet's Hottest Music Service Truly Mobile," press release, October 19, 2009, https://press.spotify.com/us/2009/10/19/3uk-spotify-and-htc-hero-join-forces-to-make-the-internets-hottest-music-service-truly-mobile/; and Mike Butcher, "Spotify's Deal with 3UK Shows Mobile Networks Are the Next Step," *TechCrunch*, October 19, 2009, https://techcrunch.com/2009/10/19/spotifys-deal-with-3uk-shows-mobile-networks-are-the-next-step/.

65. Rasmus Andersson, "First Ever Spotify Commercial TV Ad," personal blog, October 26, 2009, archived at the Wayback Machine, Internet Archive,

https://web.archive.org/web/20091030071514/http://blog.hunch.se/2009/10/first
-ever-spotify-commercial-tv-ad. Also see Mike Butcher, "Spotify U-Turns on Its 'No
Marketing' Policy with First Ever TV Ad," *TechCrunch*, October 26, 2009, https://
techcrunch.com/2009/10/26/spotify-u-turns-on-its-no-marketing-policy-with-first
-ever-tv-ad/; and spotifydemo, "Spotify TV Ad," YouTube, October 26, 2009, video,
0:30, https://www.youtube.com/watch?v=-H33tFGP0iA.

66. Robert Andrews, "Spotify Needs U.S. Success After Losses Deepened In 2010,"
Gigaom, October 10, 2011, https://gigaom.com/2011/10/10/419-spotify-needs-u-s
-success-after-losses-deepened-in-2010/.

67. Ian Youngs, "Warner Retreats from Free Music Streaming," *BBC News*, February
10, 2010, http://news.bbc.co.uk/2/hi/entertainment/8507885.stm; Mike Butcher,
"Spotify Already Has 30,000 U.S. Users. So Why Hasn't It Launched There Yet?,"
TechCrunch, June 3, 2010, https://techcrunch.com/2010/06/03/spotify-already-has
-30000-u-s-users-so-why-hasnt-it-launched-there-yet/; and Neal Pollack, "Spotify's
Celestial Jukebox," *Wired*, February 2011.

68. This number comes from Crunchbase; it is not confirmed. "Spotify," Crunchbase, accessed March 31, 2018, https://www.crunchbase.com/organization/spotify.
The same figures also appear in Pollack, "Spotify's Celestial Jukebox."

69. Michael Arrington, "Sources: Spotify Takes Investment from Sean Parker at
Founders Fund," *TechCrunch*, February 23, 2010, https://techcrunch.com/2010/02
/23/sources-spotify-takes-investment-from-sean-parker-at-founders-fund/.

70. Many of the patents registered by Facebook engineers mention Spotify. See,
for example, Yofay Kari Lee et al., "Detecting Social Graph Elements for Structured
Search Queries," Patent No. US8782080B2, issued July 15, 2014, https://patents
.google.com/patent/US8782080B2/.

71. Spotify, "Spotify Launches Next Generation Music Platform," press release, April
27, 2010, https://press.spotify.com/us/2010/04/27/spotify-launches-next-generation
-music-platform/; and Mike Butcher, "Major Update from Spotify Introduces New
Social Features," *TechCrunch*, April 27, 2010, https://techcrunch.com/2010/04/27
/major-update-from-spotify-introduces-new-social-features/. See also "Spotify Eyes
US/Japan Expansion," *Music Week*, July 24, 2010, 11.

72. Eamonn Forde, "Sonos and Spotify Become Partners," *Music Week*, September
11, 2010.

73. Steve O'Hear, "Spotify About to Get a Little More Last.fm—New Recommendation Engine," *TechCrunch*, February 3, 2010, https://techcrunch.com/2010/02/03
/spotify-about-to-get-a-little-more-last-fm-new-recommendation-engine/.

74. Pollack, " Spotify's Celestial Jukebox."

75. Glenn Peoples, "Is Spotify Really All That?," *Billboard*, October 29, 2010, https://
www.billboard.com/articles/news/952171/is-spotify-really-all-that.

76. Simon Vozick-Levinson, "Spotify Finally Hits America," *Rolling Stone*, August 4, 2011; and Allie Townsend, "Spot On!," *Time*, August 8, 2011, http://content.time .com/time/magazine/article/0,9171,2084577,00.html. See also Steve O'Hear, "Spotify, the American Dream, and Why Freemium Is a Broken Record," *TechCrunch*, April 14, 2011, https://techcrunch.com/2011/04/14/spotify-the-american-dream -and-why-freemium-is-a-broken-record/; and Mike Butcher, "Source: 'The Labels Put a Gun to Spotify's Head,'" *TechCrunch*, April 14, 2011, https://techcrunch.com/2011 /04/14/source-the-labels-put-a-gun-to-spotifys-head/.

77. John Seabrook, "Revenue Streams: Is Spotify the Music Industry's Friend or Its Foe?," Annals of Music, *New Yorker*, November 24, 2014, https://www.newyorker .com/magazine/2014/11/24/revenue-streams.

78. Micah Singleton, "This Was Sony Music's Contract with Spotify," *Verge*, May 19, 2015, https://www.theverge.com/2015/5/19/8621581/sony-music-spotify-contract.

79. Jefferson Graham, "Where to Get Free (for Now) Tunes," *USA Today*, September 28, 2011.

80. Ben Sisario, "New Service Offers Music in Quantity, Not by Song," *New York Times*, July 13, 2011, https://www.nytimes.com/2011/07/14/technology/spotify -music-streaming-service-comes-to-us.html; Simon Vozick-Levinson, "Spotify Finally Hits America," *Rolling Stone*, August 4, 2011; and Townsend, "Spot On!"

81. Mike Butcher, "Breaking: Spotify Announces Impending US Launch (Really)," *TechCrunch*, July 6, 2011, https://techcrunch.com/2011/07/06/breaking-spotify -announces-impending-us-launch-really/.

82. For a discussion of "platformization," see Anne Helmond, "The Platformization of the Web: Making Web Data Platform Ready," *Social Media + Society* 1, no. 2 (2015), doi:10.1177/2056305115603080.

83. Michael Arrington, "DST About to Lead Huge Spotify Funding," *TechCrunch*, February 21, 2011, https://techcrunch.com/2011/02/20/dst-about-to-lead-huge -spotify-funding/; and "Internet Businesses: Another Digital Gold Rush," *Economist*, May 12, 2011, http://www.economist.com/node/18680048.

84. Mark Zuckerberg, keynote address, F8 2011, San Francisco, CA, September 22, 2011, https://www.youtube.com/watch?v=9r46UeXCzoU. For a transcript of the keynote, see Mark Zuckerberg, "F8 2011 Keynote," Zuckerberg Transcript 40, Zuckerberg Files, University of Wisconsin-Milwaukee Digital Commons, https://dc.uwm .edu/zuckerberg_files_transcripts/40. Also see M. G. Siegler, "Share Buttons? Ha. Facebook Just Schooled the Internet. Again," *TechCrunch*, September 22, 2011, https:// techcrunch.com/2011/09/22/button-down/.

85. Spotify, "Introduce Music to Your Social Life," press release, ca. September 2011, http://mb.cision.com/Public/MigratedWpy/85075/9172844/aff73cd357126ded.pdf.

86. Daniel Ek, "Spotify Introduces Music to Your Social Life," *Spotify News* (blog), September 21, 2011, https://news.spotify.com/se/2011/09/21/spotify-and-facebook/.

87. Lara O'Reilly, "Spotify 'Blazes an Online Music Trail,' Say Rivals," *Marketing Week*, December 7, 2011, https://www.marketingweek.com/2011/12/07/spotify -blazes-an-online-music-trail-say-rivals/; and Josh Constine, "Spotify Fixes Discovery with Apps from Last.fm, Rolling Stone, Songkick, and More," *TechCrunch*, November 30, 2011, https://techcrunch.com/2011/11/30/spotify-platform/.

88. In 2017, Pandora introduced an on-demand variety as a complement to its radio service. The latter, however, remains its core service and is our focus in this section.

89. Josh Constine, "Pandora CTO Reveals Half of the U.S. Pays $0 for Music," *Tech-Crunch*, November 10, 2011, https://techcrunch.com/2011/11/10/pandora-cto/.

90. "Technology Giants at War: Another Game of Thrones," *Economist*, December 1, 2012, https://www.economist.com/news/21567361-google-apple-facebook-and -amazon-are-each-others-throats-all-sorts-ways-another-game.

91. Jordan Crook, "Songza App Review: Pandora and Spotify Better Watch Their Backs," *TechCrunch*, March 28, 2012, https://techcrunch.com/2012/03/28/songza -app-review-pandora-and-spotify-better-watch-their-backs/.

92. "Growth by Curation," *Billboard*, September 17, 2011.

93. Glenn Peoples, "The Next Digital Battleground," *Billboard*, July 28, 2012.

94. Mark Mulligan, "View from the Top: 10 Streaming CEOs on 2012 and 2013," *Music Industry Blog*, December 19, 2012, https://musicindustryblog.wordpress.com /2012/12/19/view-from-the-top-10-streaming-ceos-on-2012-and-2013/.

95. Jeff Bercovici, "Spotify Adds Features, Taking a Page From, Yes, Myspace," *Forbes*, June 12, 2012, 48.

96. Spotify, "Music Discovery on Spotify Gets Personal," press release, December 6, 2012, https://press.spotify.com/us/2012/12/06/music-discovery-on-spotify-gets -personal/.

97. Jason Fry, "Why Twitter Looks Like a Social Network but Feels Like News Media," *NiemanLab*, May 7, 2010, http://www.niemanlab.org/2010/05/why-twitter -looks-like-a-social-network-but-feels-like-news-media/.

98. Spotify, "Music Discovery."

99. Lars Nylin, "Nick Holmstén / Tunigo om livet efter Spotifyköpet," [Nick Holm-stén / Tunigo about his life after the Spotify deal], *Musikindustrin*, August 22, 2013, http://www.musikindustrin.se/2013/08/22/digitalnytt-nick-holmstentunigo-om -livet-efter-spotifykopet/.

100. "Job Opportunities," Spotify, January 8, 2013, https://www.spotify.com/us /jobs/vacancies/, archived at the Wayback Machine, Internet Archive, https://web .archive.org/web/20130108114832/http://www.spotify.com:80/us/jobs/vacancies/.

101. "Music Editor/Playlist Curator," Spotify, April 16, 2014, https://www.spotify .com/us/jobs/view/om1IYfwN/, archived at the Wayback Machine, Internet Archive, https://web.archive.org/web/20140416154742/https://www.spotify.com/us/jobs /view/om1IYfwN/.

102. "Music Editor/Playlist Curator."

103. Will Oremus, "Moments Are Having a Moment," *Slate*, June 22, 2015, http: //www.slate.com/articles/technology/technology/2015/06/_moments_on_insta gram_facebook_spotify_the_making_of_a_silicon_valley_buzzword.html.

104. Josh Constine, "Technology Crossover Ventures Funds All of Spotify's $250M International Growth Round," *TechCrunch*, November 21, 2013, https://techcrunch .com/2013/11/21/technology-crossover-ventures-spotify/.

105. Antonia Molloy, "Spotify Cancels Launch in Russia for the 'Foreseeable Future,'" *Telegraph*, February 2, 2015, http://www.independent.co.uk/news/business /news/spotify-cancels-launch-in-russia-for-the-foreseeable-future-10018693.html.

106. Ernesto van der Sar, "Spotify Starts Shutting Down Its Massive P2P Network," *TorrentFreak*, April 16, 2014, https://torrentfreak.com/spotify-starts-shutting-down -its-massive-p2p-network-140416/.

107. The technical reasoning behind Spotify's peer-to-peer shutdown was soon explained by Gunnar Kreitz, one of Spotify's most senior network engineers and one of five names on its first patent. In addition, he is a postdoctoral researcher in theoretical computer science at Stockholm's KTH Royal Institute of Technology, where he held a presentation on Spotify's peer-to-peer network. He still saw many benefits of using this network, but indicated that it would be better for video distribution, which demands less bandwidth and tends to be fragmented in smaller pieces. And indeed, when Spotify began developing this technology back in 2006, it was with video distribution in mind. See Gunnar Kreitz, "Spotify—Behind the Scenes: A Eulogy to P2P (?)" (PowerPoint presentation, KTH Royal Institute of Technology, Stockholm, Sweden, May 7, 2014), https://www.kth.se/social/upload /536a05d8f2765472d425ac0a/kreitzspotify_kth_kista14.pdf.

108. Spotify, "Spotify: A Perfect Platform for Apps," press release, November 30, 2011, https://press.spotify.com/us/2011/11/30/spotify-a-perfect-platform-for-apps/.

109. Janko Roettgers, "Spotify Kills Its App Platform Three Years after Its Launch," *Gigaom*, November 3, 2014, https://gigaom.com/2014/11/03/spotify-kills-its-app -platform-three-years-after-its-launch/.

110. Darrell Etherington, "Rdio Will Drop the Echo Nest for Music Recommendations Post-Spotify Acquisition," *TechCrunch*, March 12, 2014, https://techcrunch.com/2014/03/12/rdio-will-drop-the-echo-nest-for-music-recommendations-post-spotify-acquisition/.

111. Steve Knopper, "Taylor Swift Abruptly Pulls Entire Catalog from Spotify," *Rolling Stone*, November 3, 2014, https://www.rollingstone.com/music/news/taylor-swift-abruptly-pulls-entire-catalog-from-spotify-20141103; and Taylor Swift, "For Taylor Swift, the Future of Music Is a Love Story," *Wall Street Journal*, July 7, 2014, https://www.wsj.com/articles/for-taylor-swift-the-future-of-music-is-a-love-story-1404763219.

112. Rasmus Fleischer, *Det postdigitala manifestet* [The postdigital manifesto] (Stockholm: Ink bokförlag, 2009); excerpt translated in Rasmus Fleischer, "How Music Takes Place: Excerpts from 'The Post-digital Manifesto,'" *e-flux*, no. 42 (2013), http://www.e-flux.com/journal/42/60255/how-music-takes-place-excerpts-from-the-post-digital-manifesto/.

113. Ingrid Lunden, "Sweden's Telia Sonera Confirms $115M Investment in Spotify, Now Valued at $8.53B," *TechCrunch*, June 10, 2015, https://techcrunch.com/2015/06/10/swedens-telia-sonera-confirms-its-investing-115m-in-spotify/.

114. Keynote, Apple Worldwide Developers Conference 2015, San Francisco, CA, June 8, 2015, http://www.apple.com/apple-events/2015-june-event/; and Stuart Dredge, "Apple Music Interview: 'Algorithms Can't Do It Alone—You Need a Human Touch,'" *Guardian*, June 9, 2015, https://www.theguardian.com/technology/2015/jun/09/apple-music-interview-jimmy-iovine-eddy-cue. For a discussion on curation as commodity, see Rasmus Fleischer, "If the Song has No Price, is it Still a Commodity?," *Culture Unbound*, vol. 9, no. 2 (2017), doi: 10.3384/cu.2000.1525.1792146.

115. Josh Constine, "Spotify Seeks More Personalized Playlists after Discover Weekly Finds 40M Users," *TechCrunch*, May 25, 2016, https://techcrunch.com/2016/05/25/playlists-not-blogs/.

Intervention: Record Label Setup

1. For a preview of Heinz Duthel's astounding book production, see search results for "heinz duthel," Amazon, accessed June 9, 2017, https://www.amazon.com/s/ref=nb_sb_noss?url=search-alias%3Daps&field-keywords=heinz+duthel.

2. Peter Kafka, "Amazon's WikiLeaks Author Explains Why He Yanked His Book—and Why He's Selling It Again," *All Things D*, December 10, 2010, http://allthingsd.com/20101210/amazons-wikileaks-author-explains-why-he-yanked-his-book-and-why-hes-selling-it-again/.

3. For an extended discussion of Heinz Duthel and various forms of bot authorship, see Rasmus Fleischer, *Boken & biblioteket* [The book & the library] (Stockholm: Ink bokförlag, 2011).

4. For a discussion, see Harold Garfinkel, *Studies in Ethnomethodology* (Englewood Cliffs, NJ: Prentice Hall, 1967).

5. David Butz, "Autoethnography as Sensibility," in *The SAGE Handbook of Qualitative Geography*, ed. Dydia DeLyser et al. (London: SAGE, 2010), 138.

6. Celia Lury and Nina Wakeford, "Introduction: A Perpetual Inventory," in *Inventive Methods: The Happening of the Social*, ed. Celia Lury and Nina Wakeford (London: Routledge, 2012), 1–24.

7. YouTube and services such as SoundCloud are, however, important exceptions to this rule, since they allow users to directly upload content.

8. Eric Drott, "The End(s) of Genre," *Journal of Music Theory* 57, no. 1 (2013): 1–45, doi:10.1215/00222909-2017097.

9. Tarleton Gillespie, "The Relevance of Algorithms," in *Media Technologies: Essays on Communication, Materiality, and Society*, ed. Tarleton Gillespie, Pablo J. Boczkowski, and Kirsten A. Foot (Cambridge, MA: MIT Press, 2014), 171.

10. Rovi, "Rovi Corporation Reports Second Quarter 2013 Financial Performance," press release, July 31, 2013, GlobeNewswire, https://globenewswire.com/news-release/2013/07/31/563685/10042754/en/Rovi-Corporation-Reports-Second-Quarter-2013-Financial-Performance.html.

11. Jeremy Wade Morris, "Curation by Code: Infomediaries and the Data Mining of Taste," *European Journal of Cultural Studies* 18, nos. 4–5 (2015): 446–463, doi:10.1177/1367549415577387.

12. In the original experiment, the bots were also programmed to listen to ABBA's hit song "Dancing Queen." For an in-depth discussion on the SpotiBot experiment, see Pelle Snickars and Roger Mähler, "SpotiBot—Turing Testing Spotify," *Digital Humanities Quarterly* 12, no. 2 (2018).

13. Alan M. Turing, "Computing Machinery and Intelligence," *Mind* 59, no. 236 (1950): 433–460, doi:10.1093/mind/LIX.236.433.

14. International Federation of the Phonographic Industry, "IFPI Global Music Report 2017," http://www.ifpi.org/downloads/GMR2017.pdf

15. Paul Resnikoff, "My Band Has 1,000,000 Spotify Streams. Want to See Our Royalties?," *Digital Music News*, May 26, 2016, https://www.digitalmusicnews.com/2016/05/26/band-1-million-spotify-streams-royalties/.

16. Most deviations were caused by wrong behavior by the bot, essentially due to a lack of knowledge of client logic.

Chapter 2: When Do Files Become Music?

1. Spotify Team, "Spotify Paints It Black with New Look for Windows Phone," *Spotify News* (blog), January 19, 2015, https://news.spotify.com/us/2015/01/19/new -look-for-windows-phone/.

2. Lane DeNicola, "EULA, Codec, API: On the Opacity of Digital Culture," in *Moving Data: The iPhone and the Future of Media*, ed. Pelle Snickars and Patrick Vonderau (New York: Columbia University Press, 2011), 265–277.

3. Jeremy Wade Morris, *Selling Digital Music, Formatting Culture* (Berkeley: University of California Press, 2015), 191.

4. Brian Larkin, "The Politics and Poetics of Infrastructure," *Annual Review of Anthropology* 42 (2013): 327–343, doi:10.1146/annurev-anthro-092412-155522; and Anders Blok, Moe Nakazora, and Brit Ross Winthereik, "Infrastructuring Environments," *Science as Culture* 25, no. 1 (2016): 3, doi:10.1080/09505431.2015.1081500.

5. This type of scholarly literature on computational media is naturally heterogeneous and vast—but also driven by a common interest, even if separate media modalities are investigated. Publications that have inspired us include the following: Matthew G. Kirschenbaum, *Mechanisms: New Media and the Forensic Imagination* (Cambridge, MA: MIT Press, 2008); Wendy Hui Kyong Chun, *Programmed Visions: Software and Memory* (Cambridge, MA: MIT Press, 2011); Jonathan Sterne, *MP3: The Meaning of a Format* (Durham, NC: Duke University Press, 2012); Wolfgang Ernst, *Digital Media and the Archive*, ed. Jussi Parikka (Minneapolis: University of Minnesota Press, 2013); Richard Rogers, *Digital Methods* (Cambridge, MA: MIT Press, 2013); and Robert W. Gehl, *Reverse Engineering Social Media: Software, Culture, and Political Economy in New Media Capitalism* (Philadelphia: Temple University Press, 2014).

6. Mirko Tobias Schäfer and Karin van Es, eds., *The Datafied Society: Studying Culture through Data* (Amsterdam: Amsterdam University Press, 2017), 16.

7. Jean-Christophe Plantin et al., "Infrastructure Studies Meet Platform Studies in the Age of Google and Facebook," *New Media & Society* 20, no. 1 (2018): 293–310, doi:10.1177/1461444816661553.

8. For a discussion, see Tarleton Gillespie, "The Politics of 'Platforms,'" *New Media & Society* 12, no. 3 (2010): 347–364, doi:10.1177/1461444809342738; Ganaele Langlois and Greg Elmer, "The Research Politics of Social Media Platforms," *Culture Machine* 14 (2013) https://www.culturemachine.net/index.php/cm/article/view/505/531; and José van Dijck, *The Culture of Connectivity: A Critical History of Social Media* (New York: Oxford University Press, 2013).

9. During the spring of 2016, Spotify's event delivery system was described in detail in three long posts on the *Spotify Labs* blog. See Igor Maravić, "Spotify's Event Delivery—The Road to the Cloud," pts. 1–3, *Spotify Labs* (blog), February 25, 2016,

https://labs.spotify.com/2016/02/25/spotifys-event-delivery-the-road-to-the-cloud
-part-i/; March 3, 2016, https://labs.spotify.com/2016/03/03/spotifys-event-delivery
-the-road-to-the-cloud-part-ii/; and March 10, 2016, https://labs.spotify.com/2016
/03/10/spotifys-event-delivery-the-road-to-the-cloud-part-iii/.

10. Jeremy Wade Morris, "Curation by Code: Infomediaries and the Data Mining of
Taste," *European Journal of Cultural Studies* 18, nos. 4–5 (2015): 446–463, doi:10.1177/
1367549415577387.

11. "The Echo Nest Powers Spotify Radio," *The Echo Next Blog*, December 16, 2011,
http://blog.echonest.com/post/14311681173/spotify-radio-the-echo-nest.

12. Andy Fixmer, "Spotify Said Developing Pandora-Like Online Radio Service,"
Bloomberg, April 26, 2012, https://www.bloomberg.com/news/articles/2012-04-26
/spotify-said-developing-pandora-like-online-radio-service.

13. The Echo Nest, "Spotify Acquires the Echo Nest," press release, March 6, 2014,
http://the.echonest.com/pressreleases/spotify-acquires-echo-nest/.

14. For a further discussion, see Maria Eriksson, "Close Reading Big Data: The Echo
Nest and the Production of (Rotten) Music Metadata," *First Monday* 21, no. 7 (2016),
doi:10.5210/fm.v21i7.6303.

15. Ben Popper, "Tastemaker: How Spotify's Discover Weekly Cracked Human Curation at Internet Scale," *Verge*, September 30, 2015, https://www.theverge.com/2015
/9/30/9416579/spotify-discover-weekly-online-music-curation-interview.

16. Anne Helmond, "The Platformization of the Web: Making Web Data Platform
Ready," *Social Media + Society* 1, no. 2 (2015), doi:10.1177/2056305115603080.

17. Daniel Ek, "Spotify Introduces Music to Your Social Life," *Spotify News* (blog),
September 21, 2011, https://news.spotify.com/se/2011/09/21/spotify-and-facebook/.

18. Vinay Setty et al., "The Hidden Pub/Sub of Spotify," in *Proceedings of the 7th
ACM International Conference on Distributed Event-Based Systems (DEBS '13)* (New
York: ACM, 2013), 231–240, doi:10.1145/2488222.2488273.

19. Courtney Boyd Myers, "The New Spotify Platform Integrates with Apps Like
Songkick, Pitchfork and More," *Next Web*, November 30, 2011, https://thenext
web.com/insider/2011/11/30/the-new-spotify-platform-integrates-with-apps-like
-songkick-pitchfork-and-more.

20. Spotify, "Spotify Apps API (Discontinued)," Spotify Developer, October 29,
2014, https://developer.spotify.com/technologies/apps/.

21. John Paul Titlow, "Why I Shut Off Facebook's Spotify Integration," *ReadWrite*,
November 21, 2011, http://readwrite.com/2011/11/21/why_i_shut_off_facebooks
_spotify_integration/.

22. Diego Planas Rego, "What You Share and How to Control It," *Spotify News* (blog), September 27, 2011, https://news.spotify.com/se/2011/09/27/what-to-share/.

23. Stephen Phillips (@mawsonguy), "Now Playing: Twitter #music," Twitter blog, April 18, 2013, https://blog.twitter.com/2013/now-playing-twitter-music.

24. Nick Summers, "Spotify to Offer In-Dash, Voice-Activated Music Streaming in Volvo Cars with Sensus Connected Touch," *Next Web*, March 6, 2013, https://thenextweb.com/media/2013/03/06/spotify-teams-up-with-volvo-to-offer-voice-activated-music-streaming-in-cars-with-sense-connected-touch/.

25. Spotify Team, "Spotify Partners with Tinder to Swipe Up the Volume," *Spotify News* (blog), September 20, 2016, https://news.spotify.com/us/2016/09/20/spotify-partners-with-tinder-to-swipe-up-the-volume/.

26. Candice Katz, "Updated Terms," *Spotify News* (blog), August 17, 2015, https://news.spotify.com/us/2015/08/17/updated-terms/.

27. Alex Hern and Jennifer Rankin, "Spotify's Chief Executive Apologises after User Backlash over New Privacy Policy," *Guardian*, August 21, 2015, https://www.theguardian.com/technology/2015/aug/21/spotify-faces-user-backlash-over-new-privacy-policy.

28. Henrik Pettersson (@carnalizer), Twitter, August 21, 2015, https://twitter.com/carnalizer/status/634660191754145792; and Markus Persson (@notch), Twitter, August 21, 2015, https://twitter.com/notch/status/634660805573783552.

29. Nathan McAlone, "People Are Quitting Spotify Over Its New Privacy Policy," *Business Insider*, August 21, 2015, http://www.businessinsider.com/people-are-quitting-spotify-over-new-privacy-policy-2015-8?IR=T.

30. Daniel Ek, "SORRY," *Spotify News* (blog), August 21, 2015, https://news.spotify.com/us/2015/08/21/sorry-2/.

31. Rerngvit Yanggratoke et al., "On the Performance of the Spotify Backend," *Journal of Network and Systems Management* 23, no. 1 (2015): 210–237, doi:10.1007/s10922-013-9292-2.

32. "Local Files," Spotify Support, accessed June 9, 2017, https://support.spotify.com/us/using_spotify/playlists/listen-to-local-files/.

33. Ricardo Vice Santos, "Spotify: P2P Music Streaming" (PowerPoint presentation, ISEL Tech 2011, Lisbon, Portugal, May 26, 2011, https://www.slideshare.net/ricardovice/spotify-p2p-music-streaming.

34. Yanggratoke et al., "On the Performance."

35. Ernesto van der Sar, "Spotify Starts Shutting Down Its Massive P2P Network," *TorrentFreak*, April 16, 2014, https://torrentfreak.com/spotify-starts-shutting-down-its-massive-p2p-network-140416/.

36. Nic Cope, "Managing Machines at Spotify," *Spotify Labs* (blog), March 25, 2016, https://labs.spotify.com/2016/03/25/managing-machines-at-spotify/.

37. Spotify Team, "Announcing Spotify Infrastructure's Googley Future," *Spotify News* (blog), February 23, 2016, https://news.spotify.com/us/2016/02/23/announcing-spotify-infrastructures-googley-future/.

38. For a discussion, see Patrick Vonderau, "The Politics of Content Aggregation," *Television & New Media* 16, no. 8 (2015): 717–733, doi:10.1177/1527476414554402.

39. Daniel Johansson, "From Products to Consumption—Changes on the Swedish Music Market as a Result of Streaming Technologies" (working paper, Linnaeus University 2013), http://docplayer.net/343175-From-products-to-consumption-changes-on-the-swedish-music-market-as-a-result-of-streaming-technologies.html.

40. Morris, "Curation by Code."

41. Vonderau, "Politics of Content Aggregation."

42. Patryk Galuszka, "Music Aggregators and Intermediation of the Digital Music Market," *International Journal of Communication* 9 (2015): 254–273, http://hdl.handle.net/11089/7345.

43. See "FAQ," Awal, accessed June 9, 2017, https://www.awal.com/faq/.

44. Galuszka, "Music Aggregators."

45. "Guide," Spotify for Artists, accessed June 9, 2017, https://artists.spotify.com/guide/.

46. "For Artists," Spotify, accessed June 1, 2017, https://support.spotify.com/us/using_spotify/for_artists/i-represent-a-label-or-aggregator-and-would-like-my-content-on-spotify/.

47. As we have described in "Intervention: Record Label Setup," we tried using a number of aggregators for our self-produced sounds/music. TuneCore was one of them, but we did not get access to the Spotify Verified Artist Accounts. This was inconvenient and unfortunate since we wanted to investigate what tools were available for building a "community of followers." As it turned out, however, 250 followers were needed to access TuneCore's Spotify Verified Artist Accounts. We had far fewer.

48. "Get Your Music on TuneCore," TuneCore, accessed June 9, 2017, https://www.tunecore.com/get-your-music-on-spotify.

49. Paullaarhoven, "How Does Spotify Split Royalties of the Same Music Added by Different Music Distributers," Spotify Community (forum), March 8, 2017, https://community.spotify.com/t5/Social-Off-Topic/How-does-spotify-split-royalties-of-the-same-music-added-by/m-p/1604025; and AbridgedPause, "Aggregator Refusing to Remove Music," Spotify Community (forum), February 6, 2017, https://community.spotify.com/t5/Accounts/Aggregator-refusing-to-remove-music/m-p/1574115.

50. Thebigreason, January 4, 2017, comment on Sero_Tone_in, "Best Music Aggre-gation Site for Getting Your Music on Spotify/iTunes?," We Are the Music Makers (forum), Reddit, https://www.reddit.com/r/WeAreTheMusicMakers/comments/5lvf61/best_music_aggregation_site_for_getting_your/; DarkLordAzrael, January 4, 2017, reply to thebigreason; rickenjosh, January 4, 2017, comment on Sero_Tone_In, "Best Music Aggregation"; [deleted account], January 4, 2017, comment on Sero_Tone_In, "Best Music Aggregation"; and Fall_and_fixture, January 4, 2017, reply to [deleted account].

51. Geert Lovink, "Reflections on the MP3 Format: Interview with Jonathan Sterne," *Computational Culture*, no. 4 (2014), http://computationalculture.net/article/reflec-tions-on-the-mp3-format.

52. Stuart Dredge, "Spotify's Daniel Ek: 'We Want Artists to be Able to Afford to Create the Music They Want to Create,'" *Guardian*, December 6, 2012, https://www.theguardian.com/technology/2012/dec/06/spotify-daniel-ek-interview.

53. Apple, "iTunes Music Store Begins Countdown to 100 Million Songs," press release, July 1, 2004, https://www.apple.com/pr/library/2004/07/01iTunes-Music-Store-Begins-Countdown-to-100-Million-Songs.html.

54. Pelle Snickars, "More Music Is Better Music," in *Business Innovation and Disruption in the Music Industry*, ed. Patrik Wikström and Robert DeFillippi (Cheltenham, UK: Edgar Elgar, 2016), 191–210.

55. Forgotify (website), accessed June 9, 2017, http://forgotify.com.

56. Search results for "Spotify radio," Quora, accessed June 9, 2017, https://www.quora.com/search?q=Spotify+radio.

57. Pelle Snickars, "More of the Same—On Spotify Radio," *Culture Unbound* 9, no. 2 (2017): 184–211, doi:10.3384/cu.2000.1525.1792184.

Intervention: How We Tracked Streams

1. The memory cells on an SSD can be written and rewritten a limited number of times. Junk data was being stored on regular hard drives too, but since they don't operate on a finite lifespan as SSDs do, the issue wasn't as pertinent.

2. Dan Goodin, "Spotify Is Writing Massive Amounts of Junk Data to Storage Drives," *Ars Technica*, November 11, 2016, https://arstechnica.com/information-technology/2016/11/for-five-months-spotify-has-badly-abused-users-storage-drives/.

3. Chris Hampton, "Spotify Is Killing Your Computer's Storage with Junk Data," *Chart Attack*, November 17, 2016, http://www.chartattack.com/news/2016/11/17/spotify-killing-computers-storage-junk-data/.

4. See Goodin, "Spotify Is Writing."

5. "Spotify Patches 'Data Gobbling' Glitch," *BBC News*, November 11, 2016, http://www.bbc.com/news/technology-37950627.

6. Aaron Brown, "Spotify Could Be Damaging Your Computer behind Your Back, and This Is Why," *Express*, November 15, 2016, https://www.express.co.uk/life-style/science-technology/732176/Spotify-Bug-App-SSD-Lifespan.

7. For worried readers: Spotify later released a software update that cured the bug that had caused the trash issue. By then, however, the software malfunction had already been running for months.

8. "About Wireshark," Wireshark, accessed January 16, 2018, https://www.wireshark.org/#aboutWS.

9. Richard Rogers, *Digital Methods* (Cambridge, MA: MIT Press, 2013).

10. John L. Locke, *Eavesdropping: An Intimate History* (Oxford: Oxford University Press, 2010), 16.

11. Wendy Hui Kyong Chun, *Control and Freedom: Power and Paranoia in the Age of Fiber Optics* (Cambridge, MA: MIT Press, 2006), 3.

12. Ali Sarrafi, "How 'Data' Drives Spotify" (PowerPoint presentation, Stockholm School of Entrepreneurship, Stockholm, Sweden, August 10, 2016), https://www.slideshare.net/alisarrafi3/how-data-drives-spotify.

13. Igor Maravić, "Spotify's Event Delivery—The Road to the Cloud," pt. 1, *Spotify Labs* (blog), February 25, 2016, https://labs.spotify.com/2016/02/25/spotifys-event-delivery-the-road-to-the-cloud-part-i/.

14. See Rerngvit Yanggratoke et al., "On the Performance of the Spotify Backend," *Journal of Network and Systems Management* 23, no. 1 (2015): 210–37, doi:10.1007/s10922-013-9292-2; and Nick Cope, "Managing Machines at Spotify," *Spotify Labs* (blog), March 25, 2016, https://labs.spotify.com/2016/03/25/managing-machines-at-spotify/.

15. See Cope, "Managing Machines"; and Guillaume Leygues, "Spotify Chooses Google Cloud Platform to Power Data Infrastructure," Google Cloud Platform blog, February 23, 2016, https://cloudplatform.googleblog.com/2016/02/Spotify-chooses-Google-Cloud-Platform-to-power-data-infrastructure.html.

16. Dbarrosop, "SDN Internet Router," pt. 2, *Spotify Labs* (blog), January 27, 2016, https://labs.spotify.com/2016/01/27/sdn-internet-router-part-2/.

17. In order to facilitate this, Spotify also relies on over 175 different services at the back end, which manage things such as user analytics and marketing. For an overview, see "Spotify," Siftery, accessed January 16, 2018, https://siftery.com/company/spotify.

18. The songs were part of a playlist that already existed on the older premium account. We shared the playlist with the newly registered account via email. In detail, the songs that were played were: "Esse Olhar Que Era Só Teu" by Dead Combo (5:54), "Planet Caravan" by Black Sabbath (4:27), "Demon Host" by Timber Timbre (3:39), "The Healer" by Erykah Badu (3:59), and "SAT" by Boban i Marko Marković Orkestar (4:23). The music was played as it appeared in the playlist, with the exception of a few songs that were manually skipped between Timber Timbre's "Demon Host" and Erykah Badu's "The Healer".

19. When a computer sends and receives information (or packets) across a network, different actors use different ports. If you think of your computer as a destination to which many doors lead, then ports would make up the different doors through which data traffic can be routed. We found out that Spotify uses ports 80, 443 and 4070 by observing network traffic in Wireshark. We cannot rule out that Spotify might have sent data through other ports as well, but as far as we could tell, these three seemed to be the main ones.

20. Federica Frabetti, "'Does It Work?': The Unforeseeable Consequences of Quasi-failing Technology," *Culture Machine* 11 (2010): 108, http://www.culturemachine .net/index.php/cm/article/view/388/409.

21. Frabetti, "'Does It Work?'"

22. Nicole Starosielski, "Fixed Flow: Undersea Cables as Media Infrastructures," in *Signal Traffic: Critical Studies of Media Infrastructures*, ed. Lisa Parks and Nicole Starosielski (Springfield: University of Illinois Press, 2015), 54.

23. Following the Snowden revelations regarding PRISM, a National Security Agency (NSA) surveillance program, Level 3 was singled out as one of the major actors that might have enabled the NSA to wiretap Google's and Yahoo's communications. See Nicole Perlroth and John Markoff, "N.S.A. May Have Hit Internet Companies at a Weak Spot," *New York Times*, November 25, 2013, http://www.nytimes.com/2013 /11/26/technology/a-peephole-for-the-nsa.html.

24. Level 3, "Corporate Fact Sheet," March 2016, http://news.level3.com/download /2016_Level+3+Communications_FastFactsupdate_5-19-16_vF.pdf.

25. Level 3, "Corporate Fact Sheet."

26. See Level 3, "Netflix Signs Multi-year Deal with Level 3 for Streaming Services," press release, November 11, 2010, http://news.level3.com/index.php?s=23600 &item=65041; Level 3, "Level 3 Powers Pandora," press release, November 1, 2006, http://news.level3.com/news-archive?item=65154; Level 3, "Level 3 Enhances Groove-shark's Music Streaming Capabilities," press release, October 14, 2010, http://news .level3.com/news-archive?item=65035; and Level 3, "U.S. Department of Defense Finalizes Selection of Level 3 for 10-Year, Multimillion Dollar Task Order," press release, May 7, 2012, http://news.level3.com/news-archive?item=128074.

27. See AppNexus, "AppNexus Announces Technology Partnership with Spotify," press release, July 20, 2016, https://www.appnexus.com/en/company/news-and -events/press-releases/news-2016-0720; Rubicon Project, "Spotify Taps Rubicon Project to Automate Audio Inventory," press release, July 20, 2016, http://rubiconproject .com/press-releases/spotify-taps-rubicon-project-to-automate-audio-inventory/; and "Partner Info: Spotify," MediaMatch, accessed January 16, 2018, https://open .mediamath.com/partners/spotify.

28. For more information about Ogg Vorbis, see "Vorbis," Xiph.Org Foundation, accessed January 16, 2018, https://www.xiph.org/vorbis/.

29. For more information about the TrIPE protocol, see "Service Name and Transport Protocol Port Number Registry," Internet Assigned Numbers Authority, accessed January 16, 2018, https://www.iana.org/assignments/service-names-port-numbers /service-names-port-numbers.xhtml?amp=&page=78; and Mark Wooding, "TrIPE: Trivial IP Encryption," personal website, updated April 19, 2010, https://git.distorted .org.uk/~mdw/tripe/blob/refs/heads/master:/README.

30. Noa Resare, "Making Open Source a Priority at Spotify," presentation abstract, LinuxCon North America, Chicago, Illinois, August 20–22, 2014, https://lccona14 .sched.com/event/1ouHhHB/making-open-source-a-priority-at-spotify-noa-resare -spotify.

31. The most up-to-date list of these open-source projects can be found by clicking "Help > Third-party Software" in the top menu of any Spotify client. Spotify has also given back to the open source community by publishing a number of different repositories on Github.

32. Stephen Graham and Simon Marvin, *Splintering Urbanism: Networked Infrastructures, Technological Mobilities and the Urban Condition* (London: Routledge, 2001).

33. Emy Tseng and Kyle Eischen, "The Geography of Cyberspace," *M/C Journal* 6, no. 4 (2003), http://www.journal.media-culture.org.au/0308/03-geography.php.

34. For an extended discussion, see Jennifer Holt, "Regulating Connected Viewing: Media Pipelines and Cloud Policy," in *Connected Viewing: Selling, Streaming & Sharing Media in the Digital Era*, ed. Jennifer Holt & Kevin Sanson (London: Routledge, 2014), 19–39.

35. Tiziana Terranova, *Network Culture: Politics for the Information Age* (Ann Arbor, MI: Pluto Press, 2004), 65.

36. Terranova, *Network Culture*, 68.

37. Brian Larkin, "The Politics and Poetics of Infrastructure," *Annual Review of Anthropology* 42 (2013): 329, doi:10.1146/annurev-anthro-092412-155522.

Chapter 3: How Does Spotify Package Music?

1. Candice Katz, "Introducing a Better Way to Discover Music," *Spotify News* (blog), December 6, 2012, https://news.spotify.com/us/2012/12/06/discover/.

2. Spotify, "Want the Right Playlist? Just Browse," press release, August 5, 2013, https://press.spotify.com/us/2013/08/05/want-the-right-playlist-just-browse/.

3. Nick Montfort, "Continuous Paper: The Early Materiality and Workings of Electronic Literature" (paper, Modern Language Association Convention, Philadelphia, PA, December 27–30, 2004), http://nickm.com/writing/essays/continuous_paper_mla.html; and Matthew G. Kirschenbaum, *Mechanisms: New Media and the Forensic Imagination* (Cambridge, MA: MIT Press, 2008).

4. Johanna Drucker, *Graphesis: Visual Forms of Knowledge Production* (Cambridge, MA: Harvard University Press, 2014), 157.

5. This line of thinking is loosely inspired by discussions on the performativity of software and algorithms, such as Ezekiel Dixon-Román, "Algo-Ritmo: More-than-Human Performative Acts and the Racializing Assemblages of Algorithmic Architectures," Cultural Studies ↔ Critical Methodologies 16, no. 5 (2016): 482–490, doi:10.1177/1532708616655769; Rob Kitchin, "Thinking Critically about and Researching Algorithms," *Information, Communication & Society* 20, no. 1 (2017): 14–29, doi:10.1080/1369118X.2016.1154087; and Adrian Mackenzie and Theo Vurdubakis, "Codes and Codings in Crisis: Signification, Performativity and Excess," *Theory, Culture & Society* 28, no. 6 (2011): 3–23, doi:10.1177/0263276411424761.

6. A set of approximately four thousand playlists was studied in spring 2017, using accounts registered in ten different territories (Australia, Hong Kong, Japan, Mexico, Norway, Singapore, Spain, Sweden, Switzerland, and the United States). This data set contains many duplicates and has been used mainly as a backdrop for contextualization, while close reading has been performed of the 224 playlists specifically found in the Mood category as seen from a Swedish and a US user account. The results have also been checked against our previously analyzed collection of 542 Featured Playlists from 2015. For more on the latter, see Maria Eriksson and Anna Johansson, "'Keep Smiling!': Time, Functionality and Intimacy in Spotify's Featured Playlists," *Cultural Analysis* 16, no. 1 (2017): 67–82, https://www.ocf.berkeley.edu/~culturalanalysis/volume16/pdf/ErikssonJohansson.pdf.

7. See, for example, Jeremy Wade Morris, *Selling Digital Music, Formatting Culture* (Berkeley: University of California Press, 2015).

8. Morris, *Selling Digital Music*; Rob Drew, "Mixed Blessings: The Commercial Mix and the Future of Music Aggregation," *Popular Music and Society* 28, no. 4 (2005): 533–551, doi:10.1080/03007760500159088; Jörgen Skågeby, "Slow and Fast Music Media: Comparing Values of Cassettes and Playlists," *Transformations*, no. 20 (2011),

http://www.transformationsjournal.org/wp-content/uploads/2016/12/Skageby _Trans20.pdf; and Patrik Wikström and Robert Burnett, "Same Songs, Different Wrapping: The Rise of the Compilation Album," *Popular Music and Society* 32, no. 4 (2009): 507–522, doi:10.1080/03007760802327599.

9. Morris, *Selling Digital Music*, 162.

10. However, as Patrik Åker notes, the album format is still also central to Spotify, although the meaning of this cultural form has been somewhat transformed in the process of remediation. See Patrik Åker, "Spotify as the Soundtrack to Your Life: Encountering Music in the Customized Archive," in *Streaming Music: Practices, Media, Cultures*, ed. Sofia Johansson, Ann Werner, Patrik Åker, and Gregory Goldenzwaig (London: Routledge, 2017), 81-104.

11. In many respects, these two alleged solutions to the problem of overabundance correspond to what Emília Barna calls "the tyranny of the hit" and "the tyranny of choice," respectively. See Emília Barna, "'The Perfect Guide in a Crowded Musical Landscape': Online Music Platforms and Curatorship," *First Monday* 22, no. 4 (2017), doi:10.5210/fm.v22i4.6914.

12. Rasmus Fleischer, "Towards a Postdigital Sensibility: How to Get Moved by Too Much Music," *Culture Unbound* 7, no. 2 (2015): 259–260, doi:10.3384/cu.2000. 1525.1572255.

13. See Katz, "Introducing a Better Way"; and Spotify, "Want the Right Playlist?" For a discussion and examples of changes to the Spotify interface over the years, see Åker, "Spotify as the Soundtrack." Spotify's turn toward a recommendation-based interface is paralleled in the development of other major music streaming services, although, as Morris and Powers have discussed, they target slightly different user segments and thus provide different forms of user control and curatorship. See Jeremy Wade Morris and Devon Powers, "Control, Curation and Musical Experience in Streaming Music Services," *Creative Industries Journal* 8, no. 2 (2015): 106–122, doi :10.1080/17510694.2015.1090222. At the time of writing, for example, Apple Music prompts users to select favorite genres and artists upon registration, which will then provide the basis for the time-sensitive recommendations provided "for you," and they also emphasize their human-curated playlists. Tidal can be said to target a niche market by delivering exclusive content and high-quality sound through an interface remarkably similar to Spotify's. Google Play Music offers, among other things, a geolocation feature that recommends music depending on where you are—provided that you allow it to access your geo-data.

14. Richard, "Introducing Great New Ways to Discover Music," *Community Blog*, Spotify Community, December 6, 2012, https://community.spotify.com/t5/Com munity-Blog/Introducing-great-new-ways-to-discover-music/bc-p/362202.

15. Drew, "Mixed Blessings."

16. Wikström and Burnett, "Same Songs, Different Wrapping."

17. It should be noted that ads are displayed in different formats, such as audio, video, and various forms of image overlays. See "Formats," Spotify for Brands, accessed January 20, 2018, https://spotifyforbrands.com/en-US/formats/.

18. "Get a List of Featured Playlists," Spotify Developer, accessed January 20, 2018, https://developer.spotify.com/web-api/get-list-featured-playlists/; and Daniel Ek, "Say Hello to the Most Entertaining Spotify Ever," *Spotify News* (blog), May 20, 2015, https://news.spotify.com/us/2015/05/20/say-hello-to-the-most-entertaining-spotify-ever/.

19. Cf. Reggie Ugwu, "Inside the Playlist Factory," *BuzzFeed*, July 12, 2016, https://www.buzzfeed.com/reggieugwu/the-unsung-heroes-of-the-music-streaming-boom; and Kali Wilder, "Meet the Spotify Curator that Keeps the R&B Playlists Jammin'," *Black Enterprise*, December 5, 2016, http://www.blackenterprise.com/meet-spotify-curator-rb-soul-playlists/.

20. According to a snapshot analysis from 2015, about 89 percent of curated lists found through Spotify Browse were created by Spotify's in-house curators. See Chris Price, "Who Owns the Editorial Voice on Spotify?," *New Slang Media* (blog), March 26, 2015, http://www.newslangmedia.com/major-label-curation-brands-who-owns-the-editorial-voice-on-spotify/. This fits roughly with the overall patterns noted in our data.

21. See "Audiences," Spotify for Brands, accessed January 20, 2018, http://spotify-forbrands.com/en-US/audiences/; and Spotify, "Spotify Launches Playlist Targeting for Brands," press release, April 16, 2015, https://press.spotify.com/us/2015/04/16/spotify-launches-playlist-targeting-for-brands/.

22. Barna, "Perfect Guide."

23. Frequently mentioned success stories include those of artists Lorde and Hozier, both of whom are said to have made their breakthroughs by being included on popular playlists. See, for example, Mark Hogan, "How Playlists Are Curating the Future of Music," *Pitchfork*, July 16, 2015, https://pitchfork.com/features/article/9686-up-next-how-playlists-are-curating-the-future-of-music. Cf. "Discovery on Spotify: What It Means for Artists," Spotify for Artists, accessed January 20, 2018, https://artists.spotify.com/blog/discovery-on-spotify-what-it-means-for-artists; and Will Page, Jomar Perez, and Chris Tynan, "Anatomy of a Hit: How Mr Probz Came To America," *Spotify Insights* (blog), September 30, 2014, https://insights.spotify.com/us/2014/09/30/anatomy-of-a-hit-how-mr-probz-came-to-america/.

24. See, for example, Glenn Peoples, "How 'Playola' Is Infiltrating Streaming Services: Pay for Play Is 'Definitely Happening,'" *Billboard*, August 19, 2015, https://www.billboard.com/articles/business/6670475/playola-promotion-streaming-services; "Getting Your Songs on Spotify Playlists," CD Baby, accessed January 20, 2018, https://members.cdbaby.com/campaigns/request-spotify-playlist-guide.aspx; and NecroSonic, "How Do You Get in Touch with Playlist Owners as an Artist?," Spotify Community

(forum), June 9, 2014, https://community.spotify.com/t5/Content-Questions/How-do
-you-get-in-touch-with-playlist-owners-as-an-artist/td-p/817235.

25. "FAQ," Spotify for Artists, accessed January 20, 2018, https://artists.spotify.com
/faq.

26. "Running," Spotify, accessed January 20, 2018, https://www.spotify.com/us
/running/ (service retired and page discontinued on February 26, 2018).

27. "Lifestyle Features: Running," Spotify, accessed January 20, 2018, https://sup-
port.spotify.com/us/using_spotify/lifestyle_features/running/ (service retired and
page discontinued on February 26, 2018).

28. Morris and Powers, "Control, Curation and Musical Experience," 107.

29. The present chapter elaborates on some of the arguments from this publication,
albeit with a broader focus and drawing on a different set of empirical data. See
Eriksson and Johansson, "'Keep Smiling!'"

30. Esther Weltevrede, Anne Helmond, and Carolin Gerlitz, "The Politics of Real-
Time: A Device Perspective on Social Media Platforms and Search Engines," *Theory,
Culture & Society* 31, no. 6 (2014): 125–150, doi:10.1177/0263276414537318.

31. Eriksson and Johansson, "'Keep Smiling!'"

32. The comparison between Genres & Moods in different geographical contexts
included eighteen countries: Australia, Brazil, Canada, Denmark, France, Germany,
Hong Kong, Ireland, Italy, Japan, Mexico, Norway, Singapore, Spain, Sweden, Switzerland, the Netherlands, the United Kingdom, and the United States. A number of broad
music genres were displayed in all countries: Pop, Electronic/Dance, Hip Hop, Rock,
R&B, Jazz, Indie, Metal, Country, Folk & Americana, Soul, Classical, Blues, Reggae,
Latino, Punk, and Funk. However, at the time of comparison, each genre's ranking
on the page differed between national contexts.

33. "Targeting," Spotify for Brands, accessed June 9, 2017, https://spotifyforbrands
.com/sv-SE/targeting/.

34. Eriksson and Johansson, "'Keep Smiling!'"; and Tia DeNora, *Music in Everyday
Life* (Cambridge: Cambridge University Press, 2000).

35. Anahid Kassabian, *Ubiquitous Listening: Affect, Attention, and Distributed Subjectivity* (Los Angeles: University of California Press, 2013). For a discussion on the
significance of situational approaches in crowd-generated music categories on You-
Tube, see Massimo Airoldi, Davide Beraldo, and Alessandro Gandini, "Follow the
Algorithm: An Exploratory Investigation of Music on YouTube," *Poetics* 57 (2016):
1–13, doi:10.1016/j.poetic.2016.05.001. From a business perspective, Spotify's take
on the matter has been described as pioneering. See Thiago R. Pinto, "Our Changing
Relationship with Music and Its New Practical Function," *Music x Tech x Future*

(blog), Medium, August 18, 2016, https://medium.com/music-x-tech-x-future/our
-changing-relationship-with-music-and-its-new-practical-function-32bd0e56eac.

36. Lauren Keating, "Spotify Launches New Personal DJ Feature that Spins Mood-
Based Party Playlists," *Tech Times*, December 16, 2015, http://www.techtimes.com
/articles/116976/20151216/spotify-launches-new-personal-dj-feature-spins-mood
-based-party.htm.

37. "Headspace," Spotify, accessed January 20, 2018, https://www.spotify.com/se
/headspace/.

38. Eriksson and Johansson, "'Keep Smiling!'"

39. Morris and Powers, "Control, Curation and Musical Experience."

40. Paul Allen Anderson, "Neo-Muzak and the Business of Mood," *Critical Inquiry*
41, no. 4 (2015): 838, doi:10.1086/681787. The user perspective has been discussed
in James Lynden, "Experiencing Mood on Spotify," *Music x Tech x Future* (blog),
Medium, January 21, 2017, https://medium.com/music-x-tech-x-future/experienc
ing-mood-on-spotify-5c58eeb9fa5a. According to Lynden, "mood is a vital aspect
of participants' behaviour on Spotify, and it seems that participants listen to music
through the platform to manage or at least react to their moods. Yet the role of
mood is normally implicit and unconscious in the participants' listening. The mood
playlists represent an alternative listening pathway where moods are satisfied explicitly and consciously, happening in a more limited range of circumstances."

41. Sam Binkley, "Happiness, Positive Psychology and the Program of Neoliberal
Governmentality," *Subjectivity* 4, no. 4 (2011): 391, doi:10.1057/sub.2011.16. Cf.
Lauren Berlant, *Cruel Optimism* (Durham, NC: Duke University Press, 2011); and
Barbara Ehrenreich, *Smile or Die: How Positive Thinking Fooled America and the World*
(London: Granta, 2009).

42. Similarly, building on an autoethnography of mobile music streaming, Ann
Werner argues that such technologies produce a forward orientation in space and
achievement that turns public space into "happy space." However, Werner notes
how mobile music technologies sometimes fail, and while such failures induce
anger, they can also be seen as moments for reflecting on one's orientation. Ann
Werner, "Moving Forward: A Feminist Analysis of Mobile Music Streaming," *Culture
Unbound* 7, no. 7 (2015): 197–212, doi:10.3384/cu.2000.1525.1572197.

43. Christina Scharff, "The Psychic Life of Neoliberalism: Mapping the Contours of
Entrepreneurial Subjectivity," *Theory, Culture & Society* 33, no. 6 (2016): 107–122,
doi:10.1177/0263276415590164.

44. Lev Manovich, "Designing and Living Instagram Photography: Themes,
Feeds, Sequences, Branding, Faces, Bodies," in *Instagram and Contemporary Image*

(self-published, 2016), http://manovich.net/content/04-projects/097-designing-and -living-instagram-photography/instagram_book_part_4.pdf.

45. David Machin, "Building the World's Visual Language: The Increasing Global Importance of Image Banks in Corporate Media," *Visual Communication* 3, no. 3 (2004): 316–336, doi:10.1177/1470357204045785.

46. Maria Eriksson and Anna Johansson, "Tracking Gendered Streams," *Culture Unbound* 9, no. 2 (2017): 163–183, doi:10.3384/cu.2000.1525.1792163. By "recom- mended artists," we refer here to the specific Discover category Top Recommenda- tions for You.

47. Cf. Scharff, "Psychic Life of Neoliberalism," 110.

48. Rosalind Gill, "Unspeakable Inequalities: Post Feminism, Entrepreneurial Sub- jectivity, and the Repudiation of Sexism among Cultural Workers," *Social Politics* 21, no. 4 (2014): 509–528, doi:10.1093/sp/jxu016.

49. Melia Robinson, "Spotify's New Refugee-Themed Playlist Is Being Criticized by Some People for Being in Bad Taste," *Business Insider*, January 30, 2017, http://www .businessinsider.com/spotify-the-refugee-playlist-2017-1.

50. Countrystar, "Spotify Needs to Stop Being Political," Spotify Community (forum), February 12, 2017, https://community.spotify.com/t5/Social-Off-Topic/Spotify-needs -to-stop-being-political/td-p/1579532; pawelpap, "[Browse][Other] Don't Support Political Causes in Browse," Spotify Community (forum), July 10, 2016, https://com munity.spotify.com/t5/Live-Ideas/Browse-Other-Don-t-Support-Political-Causes-in -Browse/idi-p/1390911; and -WOKE-, "Offended," Spotify Community (forum), July 10, 2016, https://community.spotify.com/t5/forums/v3_1/forumtopicpage/board-id /spotifyaccountrelated/thread-id/212515.

51. Spotify Team, "Spotify, Mic and Headcount.Org Partner to Launch 'Clarify,' an Original Audio and Video Series to Encourage Young People to Vote," *Spotify News* (blog), September 13, 2016, https://news.spotify.com/us/2016/09/13/spotify-mic -and-headcount-org-partner-to-launch-clarify-an-original-audio-and-video-series-to -encourage-young-people-to-vote/.

52. Rosalind Gill, "Post-postfeminism? New Feminist Visibilities in Postfeminist Times," *Feminist Media Studies* 16, no. 4 (2016): 611, doi:10.1080/14680777.2016. 1193293.

53. "FAQ: Stats," Spotify for Artists, accessed June 9, 2017, https://artists.spotify .com/faq/stats.

54. Nick Seaver, "Algorithmic Recommendations and Synaptic Functions," *Limn*, no. 2 (2012), https://limn.it/articles/algorithmic-recommendations-and-synaptic -functions/.

55. See, for example, David Beer, *Popular Culture and New Media: The Politics of Circulation* (New York: Palgrave Macmillan, 2013); Tarleton Gillespie, "The Relevance of Algorithms," in *Media Technologies: Essays on Communication, Materiality, and Society*, ed. Tarleton Gillespie, Pablo J. Boczkowski, and Kirsten A. Foot (Cambridge, MA: MIT Press, 2014), 167–194; Kitchin, "Thinking Critically"; and Ted Striphas, "Algorithmic Culture," *European Journal of Cultural Studies* 18, nos. 4–5 (2015): 395–412, doi:10.1177/1367549415577392.

56. John Cheney-Lippold, *We Are Data: Algorithms and the Making of Our Digital Selves* (New York: New York University Press, 2017).

57. Cheney-Lippold, *We Are Data*.

58. Alex Heath, "Spotify Has a Secret 'Taste Profile' on Everyone, and They Showed Me Mine," *Business Insider*, September 14, 2015, http://www.businessinsider.com /how-spotify-taste-profiles-work-2015-9; and Walt Hickey, "Spotify Knows Me Better than I Know Myself," *FiveThirtyEight*, September 16, 2014, https://fivethirtyeight .com/features/spotify-knows-me-better-than-i-know-myself/.

59. Stuart Dredge, "Spotify Has Six Years of My Music Data, but Does It Understand My Tastes?," *Guardian*, January 6, 2015, https://www.theguardian.com/technology /2015/jan/06/spotify-music-streaming-taste-profile. Cf. Josh Constine, "Inside The Spotify-Echo Nest Skunkworks," *TechCrunch*, October 19, 2014, https://techcrunch .com/2014/10/19/the-sonic-mad-scientists/.

60. Ben Popper, "Tastemaker: How Spotify's Discover Weekly Cracked Human Curation at Internet Scale," *Verge*, September 30, 2015, https://www.theverge.com/2015 /9/30/9416579/spotify-discover-weekly-online-music-curation-interview.

61. bartjehoel, "'Reset Taste Profile/History' Option," Spotify Community (forum), February 1, 2016, https://community.spotify.com/t5/Live-Ideas/All-Platforms-Other -quot-Reset-Taste-Profile-History-quot-Option/idi-p/1283748; and nikon84, "Access to Your Spotify Taste Profile," Spotify Community (forum), December 22, 2015, https://community.spotify.com/t5/Live-Ideas/Music-Access-to-your-Spotify-taste -profile/idi-p/1260929.

62. Paul Lamere, "Gender Specific Listening," *Music Machinery* (blog), February 10, 2014, https://musicmachinery.com/2014/02/10/gender-specific-listening; and Paul Lamere, "Exploring Age-Specific Preferences in Listening," *Music Machinery* (blog), February 13, 2014, https://musicmachinery.com/2014/02/13/age-specific-listening.

63. Lamere, "Gender Specific Listening."

64. Ajay Kalia, "'Music Was Better Back Then': When Do We Stop Keeping Up with Popular Music?," *Skynet & Ebert* (blog), April 22, 2015, https://skynetandebert .com/2015/04/22/music-was-better-back-then-when-do-we-stop-keeping-up-with -popular-music/.

65. Lisa Nakamura, *Cybertypes: Race, Ethnicity, and Identity on the Internet* (New York: Routledge, 2002).

66. Rena Bivens, "The Gender Binary Will Not Be Deprogrammed: Ten Years of Coding Gender on Facebook," *New Media & Society* 19, no. 6 (2017): 880–898, doi:10.1177/1461444815621527.

67. justFuR, "Make a Gender Neutral Option for Profile Sign Up," Spotify Community (forum), July 24, 2013, https://community.spotify.com/t5/Implemented -Ideas/Make-a-gender-neutral-option-for-profile-sign-up/idi-p/482938; and tobias-talia, "Are Non-Binary People Not Welcome to Use Spotify?," Spotify Community (forum), July 20, 2015, https://community.spotify.com/t5/Accounts/Are-non-binary -people-not-welcome-to-use-Spotify/td-p/1173171.

68. Cf. Bivens, "Gender Binary"; and Rena Bivens and Oliver L. Haimson, "Baking Gender into Social Media Design: How Platforms Shape Categories for Users and Advertisers," *Social Media + Society* 2, no. 4 (2016), doi:10.1177/2056305116672486.

69. The case study on gender did not indicate any notable differences in recommendations to male and female users. For more details, see Eriksson and Johansson, "Tracking Gendered Streams."

70. minuszero, "Discover (Top Recommendations for You) Not Updating," Spotify Community (forum), May 16, 2015, https://community.spotify.com/t5/Accounts /Discover-Top-Recommendations-For-You-not-updating/td-p/1133802.

71. That is, artists that were recommended to both bots of the same age but not to any other bots.

72. For comparison, the Latin and country groups had fewer diverse recommendations than the Spotify Rewind group, with fewer unique artist recommendations. Among Latin listeners, the youngest bots (thirteen-year-olds) received the highest number of unique artist recommendations, but the difference was not as remarkable as among Spotify Rewind listeners.

73. A closer look at the artists recommended to bots of different ages does not provide any immediate clues. Well-known as well as lesser-known artists associated with different genres and active through different time periods were recommended to all users. For instance, one of our thirteen-year-old bots was recommended music by the well-known but fairly dated Cab Calloway and Glenn Miller Orchestra, while the ninety-three-year-olds received recommendations for reggae and dub poetry by Linton Kwesi Johnson and recommendations for artists that are also very popular today, such as Leonard Cohen.

74. Eriksson and Johansson, "Tracking Gendered Streams."

75. Tom Wiggins, "The 7 Secrets of Spotify's Discover Weekly," *Stuff*, November 17, 2015, https://www.stuff.tv/features/7-secrets-spotifys-discover-weekly.

76. Cheney-Lippold, *We Are Data*, 87.

77. Göran Bolin and Jonas Andersson Schwarz, "Heuristics of the Algorithm: Big Data, User Interpretation and Institutional Translation," *Big Data & Society* 2, no. 2 (2015), doi:10.1177/2053951715608406.

78. Eriksson and Johansson, "'Keep Smiling!'"

79. Spotify, "Introducing Discover Weekly: Your Ultimate Personalised Playlist," press release, July 20, 2015, https://press.spotify.com/li/2015/07/20/introducing-discover -weekly-your-ultimate-personalised-playlist/.

80. Cheney-Lippold, *We Are Data*.

Intervention: Too Much Data

1. Notes from project meeting, April 26, 2016.

2. David M. Berry, "The Computational Turn: Thinking about the Digital Humanities," *Culture Machine* 12 (2011), http://www.culturemachine.net/index.php/cm /article/view/440/470.

3. Similar issues have been raised in debates about big data in the humanities and social sciences. See, for example, danah boyd and Kate Crawford, "Critical Questions for Big Data," *Information, Communication & Society* 15, no. 5 (2012): 662–679, doi:10.1080/1369118X.2012.678878; Axel Bruns, "Faster than the Speed of Print: Reconciling 'Big Data' Social Media Analysis and Academic Scholarship," *First Monday* 18, no. 10 (2013), doi:10.5210/fm.v18i10.4879; and Rob Kitchin, "Big Data, New Epistemologies and Paradigm Shifts," *Big Data & Society* 1, no. 1 (2014), doi:10.1177/2053951714528481.

4. For a discussion of the results from this study, see Maria Eriksson and Anna Johansson, "Tracking Gendered Streams," *Culture Unbound* 9, no. 2 (2017): 163–183, doi:10.3384/cu.2000.1525.1792163.

5. Paul Lamere, "Gender Specific Listening," *Music Machinery* (blog), February 10, 2014, https://musicmachinery.com/2014/02/10/gender-specific-listening; and Paul Lamere, "Exploring Age-Specific Preferences in Listening," *Music Machinery* (blog), February 13, 2014, https://musicmachinery.com/2014/02/13/age-specific-listening.

6. See Christian Sandvig et al., "Auditing Algorithms: Adding Accountability to Automated Authority," accessed January 17, 2018, http://auditingalgorithms.science/.

7. Notably, the actual captured content makes up only a small part of this number; the main part consisted of time stamps, bot IDs, session numbers, input data, etc.

8. Notes from project meeting, April 22, 2016.

9. Eriksson and Johansson, "Tracking Gendered Streams."

10. Anna Johansson and Anna Sofia Lundgren, "Fantasies of Scientificity: Ethnographic Identity and the Use of QDA Software," in *Research Methods for Reading Digital Data in the Digital Humanities*, ed. Gabriele Griffin and Matt Hayler (Edinburgh: Edinburgh University Press, 2016), 149.

11. Jason Glynos, "Ideological Fantasy at Work," *Journal of Political Ideologies* 13, no. 3 (2008): 283, doi:10.1080/13569310802376961.

12. Johansson and Lundgren, "Fantasies of Scientificity," 156–157. Cf. Mike Fortun, Kim Fortun, and George E. Marcus, "Computers in/and Anthropology: The Poetics and Politics of Digitization," in *The Routledge Companion to Digital Ethnography*, ed. Larissa Hjorth et al. (New York: Routledge, 2017), 11–20; and Nick Seaver, "Computers and Sociocultural Anthropology," *Savage Minds: Notes and Queries in Anthropology* (blog), May 19, 2014, https://savageminds.org/2014/05/19/computers-and-sociocultural -anthropology/. However, it should be noted that many ethnographers have also developed digital approaches that fruitfully combine the methodological benefits of ethnography with the use of digital tools and methods. See, for example, Anne Beaulieu, "Vectors for Fieldwork: Computational Thinking and New Modes of Ethnography," in *The Routledge Companion to Digital Ethnography*, ed. Larissa Hjorth et al. (London: Routledge, 2017); Georgina Born and Christopher Haworth, "Mixing It: Digital Ethnography and Online Research Methods—A Tale of Two Global Digital Music Genres," in *The Routledge Companion to Digital Ethnography*, ed. Larissa Hjorth et al. (New York: Routledge, 2017), 70–86; and Wendy F. Hsu, "Digital Ethnography toward Augmented Empiricism: A New Methodological Framework," *Journal of Digital Humanities* 3, no. 1 (2014), http://journalofdigitalhumanities.org/3-1/digital -ethnography-toward-augmented-empiricism-by-wendy-hsu/.

13. A similar issue has been discussed in specific relation to big data, which, according to boyd and Crawford, "risks re-inscribing established divisions in the long running debates about scientific method and the legitimacy of social science and humanistic inquiry." See boyd and Crawford, "Critical Questions," 667.

14. Glynos, "Ideological Fantasy at Work."

15. Johansson and Lundgren, "Fantasies of Scientificity," 160.

Chapter 4: What Is the Value of Free?

1. Quotes and observations were collected by Patrick Vonderau at the Spotify press event, New York, New York, May 20, 2015. Thanks to Tim Klimeš (AVE Gesellschaft für Fernsehproduktion) for allowing Vonderou to attend this event.

2. Vonderau, Spotify press event.

3. Sahil Patel, "Spotify Plans More Original Video Series," *Digiday*, August 22, 2016, https://digiday.com/media/spotify-wants-original-video-series-less-syndicated-fare/.

4. For an overview, see Patrik Aspers, Nigel Dodd, and Ellinor Anderberg, introduction to *Re-imagining Economic Sociology*, ed. Patrik Aspers and Nigel Dodd (Oxford: Oxford University Press, 2015), 1–33.

5. James Curran, Natalie Fenton, and Des Freedman, *Misunderstanding the Internet* (London: Routledge, 2012), 69.

6. Yochai Benkler, *The Wealth of Networks: How Social Production Transforms Markets and Freedom* (New Haven, CT: Yale University Press, 2006), 13, 37.

7. Patrik Wikström, *The Music Industry: Music in the Cloud* (Cambridge: Polity Press, 2009), 12.

8. "Information wants to be free" is only the first half of Stewart Brand's well-known aphorism, first uttered at the Hackers Conference in Marin County, California, in 1984. See Cory Doctorow, "Saying Information Wants to Be Free Does More Harm than Good," *Guardian*, May 18, 2010, https://www.theguardian.com/technology/2010/may/18/information-wants-to-be-free.

9. Fred Turner, *From Counterculture to Cyberculture: Stewart Brand, the Whole Earth Network, and the Rise of Digital Utopianism* (Chicago: University of Chicago Press, 2010), 254.

10. András Kelen, *The Gratis Economy: Privately Provided Public Goods* (Budapest: Central European University Press, 2001), 5.

11. Wenjuan Ma and Steven S. Wildman, "Online Advertising Economics," in *Handbook on the Economics of the Internet*, ed. Johannes M. Bauer and Michael Latzer (Cheltenham, UK: Edward Elgar, 2016), 426–442.

12. Joseph Turow, *The Daily You: How the New Advertising Industry Is Defining Your Identity and Your Worth* (New Haven, CT: Yale University Press, 2011), 42.

13. Arnold Picot and Dominik K. Heger, "Does the Internet Need a New Competition Policy? A Global Problem from a German Point of View," in *E-Merging Media: Communication and the Media Economy of the Future*, ed. Axel Zerdick et al. (Berlin: Springer, 2005), 339–356.

14. Joëlle Farchy, "The Internet: Culture for Free," in *A Handbook of Cultural Economics*, ed. Ruth Towse, 2nd ed. (Cheltenham, UK: Edward Elgar, 2011), 245–253.

15. Jean-Charles Rochet and Jean Tirole, "Platform Competition in Two-Sided Markets," *Journal of the European Economic Association* 1, no. 4 (2003): 990–1029, doi:10.1162/154247603322493212. See also Bernhard Rieder and Guillaume Sire, "Conflicts of Interest and Incentives to Bias: A Microeconomic Critique of Google's Tangled Position on the Web," *New Media & Society* 16, no. 2 (2014): 195–211, doi:10.1177/1461444813481195.

16. Ray Fisman and Tim Sullivan, *The Inner Lives of Markets: How People Shape Them—and They Shape Us* (London: John Murray, 2016), 110.

17. Peter Decherney, *Hollywood's Copyright Wars: From Edison to the Internet* (New York: Columbia University Press, 2013).

18. Ruth Towse and Christian Handke, eds., *Handbook on the Digital Creative Economy* (Cheltenham, UK: Edward Elgar, 2013); Ruth Towse, "Economics of Music Publishing: Copyright and the Market," *Journal of Cultural Economics* 41, no. 4 (2017): 403–420, doi:10.1007/s10824-016-9268-7; and Patrik Wikström and Robert DeFillippi, eds., *Business Innovation and Disruption in the Music Industry* (Cheltenham, UK: Edward Elgar, 2016).

19. Chris Anderson, *Free: The Future of a Radical Price* (London: Random House, 2009), 114.

20. Lee Marshall, "'Let's Keep Music Special. F—k Spotify': On-Demand Streaming and the Controversy over Artist Royalties," *Creative Industries Journal* 8, no. 2 (2015): 177–189, doi:10.1080/17510694.2015.1096618.

21. A search for "advertising" on the Spotify Community forum (https://community.spotify.com) retrieves a substantial number of complaints.

22. Matthias Verbergt, "Spotify Revenue Rose in 2015 but Losses Grew on Expansion Investment," *Wall Street Journal*, May 23, 2016, https://www.wsj.com/articles/spotify-revenue-rises-in-2015-but-losses-grow-on-expansion-investment-1464024455.

23. Tim Ingham, "Spotify Revenues Topped $2BN Last Year as Losses Hit $194M," *Music Business Worldwide*, May 23, 2016, https://www.musicbusinessworldwide.com/spotify-revenues-topped-2bn-last-year-as-losses-hit-194m/.

24. Tim J. Anderson, *Popular Music in a Digital Music Economy: Problems and Practices for an Emerging Service Industry* (New York: Routledge, 2011), 134.

25. Stuart Dredge, "Spotify Financial Results Show Struggle to Make Streaming Music Profitable," *Guardian*, May 11, 2015, https://www.theguardian.com/technology/2015/may/11/spotify-financial-results-streaming-music-profitable.

26. The idea that market models, or economics more generally, "perform" rather than just depict the economy is borrowed from Michel Callon. For an introduction, see Donald MacKenzie, Fabian Muniesa, and Lucia Siu, eds., *Do Economists Make Markets? On the Performativity of Economics* (Princeton, NJ: Princeton University Press, 2007).

27. See, for instance, Nick Srnicek, *Platform Capitalism* (Cambridge: Polity Press, 2017); and Michael Curtin and Kevin Sanson, eds., *Precarious Creativity: Global Media, Local Labor* (Berkeley: University of California Press, 2016).

28. For a discussion, see Patryk Galuszka, "Music Aggregators and Intermediation of the Digital Music Market," *International Journal of Communication* 9 (2015): 254–273, http://hdl.handle.net/11089/7345; and Patrick Waelbroeck, "Digital Music," in *Handbook on the Digital Creative Economy*, ed. Ruth Towse and Christian Handke (Cheltenham, UK: Edward Elgar, 2013), 389–399.

29. See Jonathan Sterne, *MP3: The Meaning of a Format* (Durham, NC: Duke University Press, 2012); and Jeremy Wade Morris, *Selling Digital Music, Formatting Culture* (Berkeley: University of California Press, 2015).

30. This overlooks, among other things, the relevance of pricing even in Marx's account of commodification. Platform economists Rochet and Tirole have developed their approach in relation to pricing issues. See Rochet and Tirole, "Platform Competition."

31. Morris, *Selling Digital Music*, 10.

32. Patrik Aspers, *Markets* (Cambridge: Polity Press, 2011), 4.

33. Aspers, *Markets*, 9.

34. Aspers, *Markets*, 83–84.

35. A good overview is provided by Rieder and Sire, "Conflicts of Interest."

36. Aspers, *Markets*, 9.

37. See Rieder and Sire, "Conflicts of Interest," 200.

38. Lee McGuigan and Vincent Manzerolle, eds., *The Audience Commodity in a Digital Age: Revisiting a Critical Theory of Commercial Media* (New York: Peter Lang, 2014).

39. Harrison C. White, *Markets from Networks: Socioeconomic Models of Production* (Princeton, NJ: Princeton University Press, 2002), 1.

40. Aspers, *Markets*, 33.

41. Melissa Gregg, "Inside the Data Spectacle," *Television & New Media* 16, no. 1 (2015): 37–51, doi:10.1177/1527476414547774.

42. Anna Lowenhaupt Tsing, *Friction: An Ethnography of Global Connection* (Princeton, NJ: Princeton University Press, 2005), 57.

43. Tsing, *Friction*, 58.

44. Jill Bederoff, "One of Spotify's Owners Says It's NOT Unlikely that Facebook Buys the Company," *Business Insider Nordic*, September 16, 2016, http://nordic.businessinsider.com/gp-bullhound-facebook-might-buy-spotify-before-the-ipo-2016-9/.

45. Beverley Skeggs and Simon Yuill, "Capital Experimentation with Person/a Formation: How Facebook's Monetization Refigures the Relationship between Property, Personhood and Protest," *Information, Communication & Society* 19, no. 3 (2016): 384, doi:10.1080/1369118X.2015.1111403.

46. Josh Constine, "Spotify Raises $1 Billion in Debt with Devilish Terms to Fight Apple Music," *TechCrunch*, March 29, 2016, https://techcrunch.com/2016/03/29/stream-with-the-devil/.

47. Max Haiven, *Cultures of Financialization: Fictitious Capital in Popular Culture and Everyday Life* (New York: Palgrave Macmillan, 2014), 12.

48. Mary Poovey, "On 'The Limits of Financialization,'" *Dialogues in Human Geography* 5, no. 2 (2015): 221, doi:10.1177/2043820615588159.

49. Anders Blok, Moe Nakazora, and Brit Ross Winthereik, "Infrastructuring Environments," *Science as Culture* 25, no. 1 (2016): 1–22, doi:10.1080/09505431.2015.1081 500.

50. Michael Wolff, *Television Is the New Television: The Unexpected Triumph of Old Media in the Digital Age* (New York: Portfolio/Penguin, 2015), 34.

51. Tom Goodwin, "The Battle Is for the Customer Interface," *TechCrunch*, March 3, 2015, https://techcrunch.com/2015/03/03/in-the-age-of-disintermediation-the -battle-is-all-for-the-customer-interface/.

52. Johan Lindquist, "Brokers and Brokerage, Anthropology of," in *International Encyclopedia of the Social & Behavioral Sciences*, ed. James D. Wright, 2nd ed. (Amsterdam: Elsevier, 2017), 2:870–874.

53. Ramon Lobato and Julian Thomas, *The Informal Media Economy* (Cambridge: Polity Press, 2015), 67.

54. Bruno Latour, *Reassembling the Social: An Introduction to Actor-Network-Theory* (Oxford: Oxford University Press, 2005), 39.

55. Spotify was initially known for its peer-to-peer network, a technology associated with piracy software. Programmer Ludvig Strigeus, who developed uTorrent (still a commonly used file-sharing client, later worked at Spotify. Daniel Ek was also briefly CEO at uTorrent.

56. *AB* stands for the Swedish word *aktiebolag*, or "shareholder company." Information around all Swedish companies (such as Spotify) can be found at Bolagsverket: Swedish Companies Registration Office (website), accessed June 9, 2017, http://www .bolagsverket.se/en/.

57. Philip Napoli and Robyn Caplan, "Why Media Companies Insist They're Not Media Companies, Why They're Wrong, and Why It Matters," *First Monday* 22, no. 5 (2017), doi:10.5210/fm.v22i15.7051.

58. See Statistiska centralbyrån, "SNI Swedish Standard Industrial Classification 2007," May 30, 2008, http://www.sni2007.scb.se/_pdf/080530kortversionsnisorterad2007eng .pdf.

59. Joern Block and Philipp Sandner, "What Is the Effect of the Financial Crisis on Venture Capital Financing? Empirical Evidence from US Internet Start-Ups," *Venture Capital* 11, no. 4 (2009): 295–309, doi:10.1080/13691060903184803.

60. GP Bullhound, *European Unicorns 2016: Survival of the Fittest* (GP Bullhound, 2016), http://www.gpbullhound.com/wp-content/uploads/2016/06/GP-Bullhound -Research-European-Unicorns-2016-Survival-of-the-fittest.pdf.

61. Here, we are referring to the general lack of regulation when it comes to digital companies, as compared to the existing policies for media companies.

62. Iain Hardie and Donald MacKenzie, "The Material Sociology of Arbitrage," in *The Oxford Handbook of the Sociology of Finance*, ed. Karen Knorr Cetina and Alex Preda (Oxford: Oxford University Press, 2012), 187–202.

63. Daniel Beunza and David Stark, "Tools of the Trade: The Socio-technology of Arbitrage in a Wall Street Trading Room," *Industrial and Corporate Change* 13, no. 2 (2004): 369–400, doi:10.1093/icc/dth015.

64. Morris, *Selling Digital Music*, 167.

65. Paul Allen Anderson, "Neo-Muzak and the Business of Mood," *Critical Inquiry* 41, no. 4 (2015): 811, doi:10.1086/681787.

66. Lee Marshall, "'Let's Keep Music Special.'"

67. UK Association of Online Publishers, *Digital Landscape Report 2016*, accessed June 9, 2017, https://www.ukaop.org/digital-landscape-report.

68. Joseph Turow, *The Daily You: How the New Advertising Industry Is Defining Your Identity and Your Worth* (New Haven, CT: Yale University Press, 2011), 82.

69. See Interactive Advertising Bureau, *IAB Internet Advertising Revenue Report: 2016 Full Year Results* (IAB, April 2017), https://www.iab.com/wp-content/uploads/2016 /04/IAB_Internet_Advertising_Revenue_Report_FY_2016.pdf.

70. Eric Blattberg, "Why Agencies Are Bullish on Spotify," *Digiday*, March 2, 2015, https://digiday.com/marketing/agencies-bullish-spotify/.

71. For key insights into Spotify's ad infrastructure, see Kinshuk Mishra, "Architec- tural Overhaul: Ad Serving @ Spotify Scale" (PowerPoint, QCon, London, UK, March 7, 2017), https://www.slideshare.net/kinshukm1/qcon-london-2017-architecture -overhaul-ad-serving-spotify-scale.

72. The experiment is documented in full in Roger Mähler and Patrick Vonderau, "Do Bots Have Human Friends? Experimental Methods for Studying Ad Tech Infra- structures," *Culture Unbound* 9, no. 2 (2017): 212–221, http://www.cultureunbound .ep.liu.se/v9/a14/cu17v9a14.pdf.

73. A similar tool has been developed by the Digital Methods Initiative (Amster- dam), called TrackerTracker.

74. Jana Jakovljevic (head of programmatic advertising at Spotify, New York), inter- view by Patrick Vonderau, September 23, 2016.

75. However, Ghostery does not specify what information is exchanged between the nodes in this network; their organizational or transactional relations have to be interpreted. Any mapping also remains partial at best, given that Ghostery does not list all relevant nodes, and because of the region-dependent, technical division of labor at work in programmatic advertising.

76. Benjamin Dick, "Understanding the Programmatic Value Chain," News, Internet Advertising Bureau, March 24, 2016, https://www.iab.com/news/managing -programmatic-investments/.

77. Jakovljevic, interview.

78. Brian Morrissey, "The Programmatic Manifesto," *Digiday*, June 27, 2016, https:// digiday.com/marketing/programmatic-manifesto/.

79. The most comprehensive account of this dynamic so far is Katharina Hölck, "Beyond the Single Platform: An Assessment of the Functioning and Regulatory Challenges of Multi-layered Platform Systems in the Media and Communication Sector" (PhD diss., Vrije Universiteit Brussel, 2016), https://ssrn.com /abstract=2992487.

80. Tsing, *Friction*, 57.

Intervention: Introducing Songblocker

1. transmediale is a Berlin-based festival and year-round project that draws out new connections between art, culture, and technology. For more information, see transmediale 2017 (website), accessed January 16, 2018, https://2017.transmediale.de/.

2. Songblocker, "Songblocker—More than Just a Blocker," YouTube, February 13, 2017, video, 1:01, https://www.youtube.com/watch?v=BviZnSYNPL0.

3. See Songblocker, "Songblocker Launch at transmediale (Berlin, 2017)," YouTube, February 20, 2017, video, 13:40, https://www.youtube.com/watch?v=4mAfl2L4a48.

4. See Songblocker (@songblocker), Twitter profile, accessed January 16, 2018, https: //twitter.com/songblocker.

5. See Songblocker, "Songblocker—More than Just a Blocker."

6. For more information about Songblocker, visit Songblocker (website), accessed January 16, 2018, https://www.songblocker.com/.

7. Songblocker (website).

8. Celia Lury and Nina Wakeford, eds., *Inventive Methods: The Happening of the Social* (London: Routledge, 2012).

9. The journalist Lily Kelting interviewed Rasmus Fleischer on NPR Berlin. See Lily Kelting, "transmediale—A Convergence of Technology and Art," February 7, 2017,

in *Life in Berlin*, NPR Berlin, https://player.fm/series/life-in-berlin/life-in-berlin-transmediale-a-convergence-of-technology-and-art.

10. Alex Hern, "From Nasty to Nice: How Adblockers Are Trying to Pivot," *Guardian*, April 12, 2017, https://www.theguardian.com/media/2017/apr/12/adblockers-trying-pivot-nasty-nice.

11. Martin Bryant, "Adblockers Are Immoral and Mobile Networks Should Know Better," *Next Web*, May 17, 2015, https://thenextweb.com/insider/2015/05/17/adblockers-are-immoral-and-mobile-networks-should-know-better/.

12. Bryant, "Adblockers Are Immoral."

13. Adam Piltch, "Why Using an Ad Blocker Is Stealing (Op-Ed)," *Tom's Guide*, May 22, 2015, https://www.tomsguide.com/us/ad-blocking-is-stealing,news-20962.html.

14. Nilay Patel, "Welcome to Hell: Apple vs. Google vs. Facebook and the Slow Death of the Web," *Verge*, September 17, 2015, https://www.theverge.com/2015/9/17/9338963/welcome-to-hell-apple-vs-google-vs-facebook-and-the-slow-death-of-the-web.

15. Marco Arment, "Just Doesn't Feel Good," personal blog, September 18, 2015, https://marco.org/2015/09/18/just-doesnt-feel-good.

16. For a discussion, see Bo Brinkman, "Ethics and Pervasive Augmented Reality: Some Challenges and Approaches," in *Emerging Pervasive Information and Communication Technologies (PICT): Ethical Challenges, Opportunities and Safeguards*, ed. Kenneth D. Pimple (London: Springer, 2014), 149–175.

17. Brinkman, "Ethics and Pervasive Augmented Reality," 173.

18. However, it should be noted that PageFair is an anti-ad-blocking company that naturally has (at least some) interest in upholding ad blocking as a severe threat to the publishing industries. See PageFair, *The State of the Blocked Web: 2017 Global Adblock Report* (PageFair, February 2017), https://pagefair.com/downloads/2017/01/PageFair-2017-Adblock-Report.pdf.

19. Jack Marshall, "The Rise of the Anti-Ad Blockers," *Wall Street Journal*, June 13, 2016, https://www.wsj.com/articles/the-rise-of-the-anti-ad-blockers-1465805039.

20. See Admiral (website), accessed January 16, 2018, https://getadmiral.com/; and Sourcepoint (website), accessed January 16, 2018, https://www.sourcepoint.com/.

21. Patel, "Welcome to Hell."

22. Alex Hern, "Adblock Plus Opens Up about How 'Acceptable Ads' Work," *Guardian*, February 25, 2016, https://www.theguardian.com/technology/2016/feb/25/adblock-plus-opens-up-acceptable-ads-work.

23. To access Songblocker's source code for Windows or Mac, click the appropriate "Licenses and credits" link at "Download Now," Songblocker, accessed January 16, 2018, https://www.songblocker.com/download-now.

24. J. D. Dewsbury, "Performative, Non-representational, and Affect-Based Research: Seven Injunctions," in *The SAGE Handbook of Qualitative Geography*, ed. Dydia DeLyser et al. (London: SAGE, 2010), 333.

25. Mike Michael, "Anecdote," in *Inventive Methods: The Happening of the Social*, ed. Celia Lury and Nina Wakeford (London: Routledge, 2012), 26.

Conclusion

1. See, for instance, sociologist Violaine Roussel's *Representing Talent: Hollywood Agents and the Making of Movies* (Chicago: University of Chicago Press, 2017). Also see the research conducted by the Media Industries Project, University of California, Santa Barbara, especially Michael Curtin, Jennifer Holt, and Kevin Sanson, eds., *Distribution Revolution: Conversations about the Digital Future of Film and Television* (Oakland: University of California Press, 2014); and Michael Curtin and Kevin Sanson, eds., *Precarious Creativity: Global Media, Local Labor* (Berkeley: University of California Press, 2016).

2. Spotify USA, Terms and Conditions of Use § 4. Rights We Grant You, effective July 6, 2017, https://www.spotify.com/us/legal/end-user-agreement/.

3. Spotify USA, Terms and Conditions of Use § 7. Rights You Grant Us.

4. Spotify USA, Terms and Conditions of Use § 8. User Guidelines.

5. "You will not collect users' content or information, or otherwise access Facebook, using automated means (such as harvesting bots, robots, spiders, or scrapers) without our prior permission." Facebook, Statement of Rights and Responsibilities § 3. Safety, last revised January 30, 2015, https://www.facebook.com/terms.php.

6. Twitter, Terms of Service (US version), effective October 2, 2017, https://twitter.com/en/tos.

7. "Clouds & Concerts: Trends in Music Culture," University of Oslo, Department of Musicology, accessed January 18, 2018, http://www.hf.uio.no/imv/english/research/projects/cloudsandconcerts/.

8. In an interview with Sweden's main public television broadcaster SVT, Pelle Snickars described the difficulty of gaining access to Spotify and the idea of creative workarounds that included studying Spotify "from the inside." Matilda Svensson Glaser, "De ska studera Spotify inifrån," [They will study Spotify from within], *SVT Nyheter*, November 1, 2013, https://www.svt.se/kultur/musik/de-ska-studera-spotify-inifran.

9. Björn Wallenberg, "Han skriver en bok om Spotify," [He is writing a book about Spotify], *Dagens Industri*, May 7, 2017, https://digital.di.se/artikel/han-skriver-en-bok-om-spotify-det-var-fran-borjan-en-pirattjanst; Andy, "Spotify's Beta Used 'Pirate'

MP3 Files, Some from Pirate Bay," *TorrentFreak*, May 9, 2017, https://torrentfreak .com/spotifys-beta-used-pirate-mp3-files-some-from-pirate-bay-170509/; and Paul Resnikoff, "Spotify Illegally Streamed MP3s before Getting Proper Licenses, Investigator Claims," *Digital Music News*, May 9, 2017, https://www.digitalmusicnews.com /2017/05/09/spotify-illegal-mp3s-investigator/.

10. Resnikoff, "Spotify Illegally Streamed."

11. Benjamin Helldén-Hegelund (legal counsel, Spotify) to Kerstin Sahlin (secretary general, Artistic Research/Humanities and the Social Sciences, Swedish Research Council), undated. The letter was forwarded to the project's administering university, which in turn contacted the research team.

12. The project received the highest grades with respect to methodology. Only 5 to 7 percent of project applications were funded.

13. Noortje Marres, *Digital Sociology: The Reinvention of Social Research* (Cambridge: Polity Press, 2017), 182.

14. Motahhare Eslami et al., "'Be Careful; Things Can Be Worse than They Appear'— Understanding Biased Algorithms and Users' Behavior around Them in Rating Platforms," in *Proceedings of the Eleventh International Conference on Web and Social Media* (Palo Alto, CA: AAAI Press, 2017), 62–71, https://aaai.org/ocs/index.php/ICWSM /ICWSM17/paper/view/15697.

15. Amit Datta, Michael Carl Tschantz, and Anupam Datta, "Automated Experiments on Ad Privacy Settings: A Tale of Opacity, Choice, and Discrimination," *Proceedings on Privacy Enhancing Technologies*, no. 1 (2015): 92–112, doi:10.1515/popets-2015-0007; Le Chen, Alan Mislove, and Christo Wilson, "Peeking beneath the Hood of Uber," in *Proceedings of the 2015 Internet Measurement Conference* (New York: ACM, 2015), 495–508, doi:10.1145/2815675.2815681; and Benjamin Edelman, Michael Luca, and Dan Svirsky, "Racial Discrimination in the Sharing Economy: Evidence from a Field Experiment," *American Economic Journal: Applied Economics* 9, no. 2 (2017): 1–22, doi:10.1257/app.20160213.

16. Christian Sandvig et al., "When the Algorithm Itself Is a Racist: Diagnosing Ethical Harm in the Basic Components of Software," *International Journal of Communication* 10 (2016): 4972–4990, http://ijoc.org/index.php/ijoc/article/view/6182.

17. Christian Sandvig, "Heading to the Courthouse for Sandvig v. Sessions," *Social Media Collective* (blog), posted October 19, 2017, https://socialmediacollective.org /2017/10/19/heading-to-the-courthouse-for-sandvig-v-sessions/. Also see "Sandvig v. Sessions—Challenge to CFAA Prohibition on Uncovering Racial Discrimination Online," ACLU, updated September 12, 2017, https://www.aclu.org/cases/sandvig -v-sessions-challenge-cfaa-prohibition-uncovering-racial-discrimination-online; and E. Tammy Kim, "How an Old Hacking Law Hampers the Fight against Online Discrimination," Currency, *New Yorker*, October 1, 2016, https://www.newyorker

.com/business/currency/how-an-old-hacking-law-hampers-the-fight-against-online
-discrimination.

18. Yannis Bakos, Florencia Marotta-Wurgler, and David R. Trossen, "Does Anyone Read the Fine Print? Consumer Attention to Standard-Form Contracts," *Journal of Legal Studies* 43, no. 1 (2014): 1–35, doi:10.1086/674424.

19. See the contributions to Michael Zimmer and Katharina Kinder-Kurlanda, eds., *Internet Research Ethics for the Social Age: New Challenges, Cases, and Contexts* (New York: Peter Lang, 2017).

20. Charles Ess, "Foreword: Ground Internet Research Ethics 3.0: A View from (the) AoIR," in Zimmer and Kinder-Kurlanda, *Internet Research Ethics*, xii.

21. SIGCHI Research Ethics, "Do Researchers Need to Follow TOS?," Medium, November 30, 2017, https://medium.com/sigchi-ethics-committee/do-researchers -need-to-follow-tos-f3bde1950d3c.

22. Gerwin van Schie, Irene Westra, and Mirko Tobias Schäfer, "Get Your Hands Dirty: Emerging Data Practices as Challenge for Research Integrity," in *The Datafied Society: Studying Culture through Data*, ed. Mirko Tobias Schäfer and Karin van Ess (Amsterdam: Amsterdam University Press, 2017), 183–200. Mirko Tobias Schäfer and his team also have developed the "Data Ethics Decision Aid (DEDA)," Utrecht Data School, accessed January 18, 2018, https://dataschool.nl/research/deda/?lang=en.

23. Wixen Music Publishing Inc. v. Spotify USA Inc., No. 2:17CV09288 (C.D. Calif.).

24. Much in line with Facebook's strategy of asking for forgiveness rather than per- mission, Spotify CEO Daniel Ek said "Sorry" in a blog post after these changes had been made public. Daniel Ek, "SORRY," *Spotify News* (blog), August 21, 2015, https:// news.spotify.com/int/2015/08/21/sorry-2/.

25. Charlie Rose, "Daniel Ek CEO of Spotify | Charlie Rose," YouTube, May 22, 2014, video, 2:26, https://www.youtube.com/watch?v=D55XlVKjzPw.

26. Stuart Kirsch, *Mining Capitalism: The Relationship between Corporations and Their Critics* (Oakland: University of California Press, 2014), 3.

27. David Calvey, *Covert Research: The Art, Politics and Ethics of Undercover Fieldwork* (London: SAGE, 2017), 460.

28. Nick Seaver, "Studying Up: The Ethnography of Technologists," *Ethnography Mat- ters*, March 10, 2014, https://ethnographymatters.net/blog/2014/03/10/studying-up/.

29. Barbara Czarniawska, *Shadowing, and Other Techniques for Doing Fieldwork in Modern Societies* (Malmö, Sweden: Liber, 2007).

30. Thanks to Mati Kaalep, Estonian Ministry of Culture, who pointed this issue out to us.

Intervention: Work at Spotify!

1. Dave Zatz, "Spotify to Launch Hardware, Cites Alexa and Snapchat," *Zatz Not Funny!*, April 24, 2017, https://zatznotfunny.com/2017-04/spotify-wearable/.

2. Jacob Kastrenakes, "Spotify Is Working on Its Own Music Hardware," *Verge*, April 24, 2017, https://www.theverge.com/2017/4/24/15407210/spotify-hardware-plans -revealed.

3. For instance, consider Amazon's and Google's recent developments of "smart speakers" for the home, as discussed in Jon Porter and Nick Pino, "Amazon Echo vs Apple HomePad vs Google Home: The Battle of the Smart Speakers," *TechRadar*, October 5, 2017, http://www.techradar.com/news/amazon-echo-vs-homepod-vs -google-home-the-battle-of-the-smart-speakers.

4. See Wanted Analytics (website), accessed June 9, 2017, https://www.wantedanalytics .com.

5. Some scholarly literature has used similar approaches. See, for example, Yu Cheng et al., "JobMiner: A Real-Time System for Mining Job-Related Patterns from Social Media," in *Proceedings of the 19th ACM SIGKDD International Conference on Knowledge Discovery and Data Mining*, ed. Rayid Ghani (New York: ACM, 2013), 1450–1453.

6. The Spotify job postings were automatically scraped and stored on a dedicated server run by Humlab at Umeå University. The scraping tool was configured to collect all new (or updated) job listings that appeared at https://www.spotify.com /se/jobs/opportunities/, at a rate of once per day. Since the scraping was done on a daily basis, we can rule out the possibility that any postings from the website could be missing from our data. (If the scraping failed, the ad would have been col- lected the next day.) All quotes in this chapter concerning different job positions at Spotify are taken from our downloaded dataset, which can be accessed upon request. Finally, we have not explored the extent to which more than one person was sought for a given position.

7. Daniel Ek (@eldsjal), Twitter, January 9, 2017, https://twitter.com/eldsjal/status /818501713665650688.

8. Natalia Brzezinski (@nataliabrzezinski), "Tonight President Obama invited all of the Ambassadors he personally chose to an intimate reception at the White House," Instagram photo, January 4, 2017, https://www.instagram.com/p/BO3FVbfD-eC/.

9. On several occasions, Obama released public, handpicked, and highly popular summer playlists on Spotify. For example, see Obama White House, "The Presi- dents 2016 Summer Playlist: Day," created August 11, 2016, Spotify, https:// open.spotify.com/user/obamawhitehouse/playlist/1rHf2piPQEc18Bs6ZFyLEw ?si=9bklycTxS2a2m-0zXoi0Hw.

10. For a discussion of the job description, see "Spotify Offers Barack Obama a Job as 'President of Playlists,'" *BBC News*, January 10, 2017, http://www.bbc.com/news /world-us-canada-38566623.

11. Universum Global, *Sweden's Most Attractive Employers—Trends and Rankings* (Universum Global, 2017), accessed June 9, 2017, https://universumglobal.com/rankings /sweden/student/2016/.

12. For different perspectives on the issue, see Christian Fuchs, *Digital Labour and Karl Marx* (London: Routledge, 2014); and Ned Rossiter, *Software, Infrastructure, Labor: A Media Theory of Logistical Nightmares* (London: Routledge, 2016).

13. See, for example, Anne-Laure Fayard and John Van Maanen, "Making Culture Visible: Reflections on Corporate Ethnography," *Journal of Organizational Ethnography* 4, no. 1 (2015): 4–27, doi:10.1108/JOE-12-2014-0040.

14. "Backstage," Spotify Jobs, accessed June 9, 2017, https://www.spotifyjobs.com /backstage/.

15. Subrat Patnaik, "Spotify Is Adding 1000 New Jobs and Moving Its US Headquarters to the World Trade Center," *Business Insider*, February 16, 2017, http://www .businessinsider.com/r-spotify-to-relocate-us-headquarters-to-4-world-trade-center -2017-2.

16. Ching-Wei Chen and Vidhya Murali, "Machine Learning & Big Data for Music Discovery" (PowerPoint, Galvanize, New York, New York, March 9, 2017), https:// www.slideshare.net/cweichen/machine-learning-and-big-data-for-music-discovery -at-spotify?qid=b7ca7727-0a01-4441-9107-14410ccf0e7d.

17. Spotify, "Niland Team Joins Spotify," press release, May 17, 2017, https://press .spotify.com/bo/2017/05/17/niland-team-joins-spotify/.

Bibliography

Airoldi, Massimo, Davide Beraldo, and Alessandro Gandini. "Follow the Algorithm: An Exploratory Investigation of Music on YouTube." *Poetics* 57 (2016): 1–13. doi:10.1016/j.poetic.2016.05.001.

Åker, Patrik. "Spotify as the Soundtrack to Your Life: Encountering Music in the Customized Archive." In *Streaming Music: Practices, Media, Cultures*, edited by Sofia Johansson, Ann Werner, Patrik Åker, and Gregory Goldenzwaig, 81–104. London: Routledge, 2017.

Anderson, Chris. *Free: The Future of a Radical Price*. London: Random House, 2009.

Anderson, Paul Allen. "Neo-Muzak and the Business of Mood." *Critical Inquiry* 41, no. 4 (2015): 811–840. doi:10.1086/681787.

Anderson, Tim J. *Popular Music in a Digital Music Economy: Problems and Practices for an Emerging Service Industry*. New York: Routledge, 2011.

Andersson, Jonas, and Pelle Snickars, eds. *Efter the Pirate Bay*. [After the Pirate Bay.] Stockholm: Kungliga biblioteket, 2010.

Andersson Schwarz, Jonas. *Online File Sharing: Innovations in Media Consumption*. London: Routledge, 2013.

Andersson Schwarz, Jonas, and Johan Hammarlund. "Kontextförlust och kontextkollaps: Metodproblem vid innehållsanalys av sociala medier." [Contextual loss and collapse: Methodological problems in content analysis of social media.] *Nordicom-Information* 38, no. 3 (2016): 41–55.

Ankerson, Megan Sapnar. "Historicizing Web Design: Software, Style, and the Look of the Web." In *Convergence Media History*, edited by Janet Staiger and Sabine Hake, 192–203. New York: Routledge, 2009.

Appadurai, Arjun, ed. *The Social Life of Things: Commodities in Cultural Perspective*. Cambridge: Cambridge University Press, 1986.

Aspers, Patrik. *Markets*. Cambridge: Polity Press, 2011.

Aspers, Patrik, Nigel Dodd, and Ellinor Anderberg. Introduction to *Re-imagining Economic Sociology*, edited by Patrik Aspers and Nigel Dodd, 1–33. Oxford: Oxford University Press, 2015.

Auer, Dirk, and Nicolas Petit. "Two-Sided Markets and the Challenge of Turning Economic Theory into Antitrust Policy." *Antitrust Bulletin* 60, no. 4 (2015): 426–461. doi:10.1177/0003603X15607155.

Bakos, Yannis, Florencia Marotta-Wurgler, and David R. Trossen. "Does Anyone Read the Fine Print? Consumer Attention to Standard-Form Contracts." *Journal of Legal Studies* 43 (1) (2014): 1–35. doi:10.1086/674424.

Barbrook, Richard. *Imaginary Futures: From Thinking Machines to the Global Village.* London: Pluto Press, 2007.

Barna, Emília. "'The Perfect Guide in a Crowded Musical Landscape': Online Music Platforms and Curatorship." *First Monday* 22, no. 4 (2017). doi:10.5210/fm.v22 i14.6914.

Beaulieu, Anne. "Vectors for Fieldwork: Computational Thinking and New Modes of Ethnography." In *The Routledge Companion to Digital Ethnography*, edited by Larissa Hjorth, Heather Horst, Anne Galloway, and Genevieve Bell, 30–39. London: Routledge, 2017.

Beckert, Jens. "Imagined Futures: Fictional Expectations in the Economy." *Theory and Society* 42 (3) (2013): 219–240. doi:10.1007/s11186-013-9191-2.

Beer, David. *Popular Culture and New Media: The Politics of Circulation.* New York: Palgrave Macmillan, 2013.

Benkler, Yochai. *The Wealth of Networks: How Social Production Transforms Markets and Freedom.* New Haven, CT: Yale University Press, 2006.

Berlant, Lauren. *Cruel Optimism.* Durham, NC: Duke University Press, 2011.

Berry, David M. "The Computational Turn: Thinking about the Digital Humanities." *Culture Machine* 12 (2011). http://www.culturemachine.net/index.php/cm/article /view/440/470.

Beunza, Daniel, and David Stark. "Tools of the Trade: The Socio-technology of Arbitrage in a Wall Street Trading Room." *Industrial and Corporate Change* 13, no. 2 (2004): 369–400. doi:10.1093/icc/dth015.

Bhandari, Esha, and Rachel Goodman. "Data Journalism and the Computer Fraud and Abuse Act: Tips for Moving Forward in an Uncertain Landscape." Paper presented at the Computation+Journalism Symposium 2017, Northwestern University, Evanston, IL, October 13–14, 2017. https://northwestern.box.com/s/mnyympjp2 a7iqau9o73v4f9mrt1satoc.

Binkley, Sam. "Happiness, Positive Psychology and the Program of Neoliberal Governmentality." *Subjectivity* 4, no. 4 (2011): 371–394. doi:10.1057/sub.2011.16.

Birkinbine, Benjamin J., Rodrigo Gómez, and Janet Wasko, eds. *Global Media Giants*. London: Routledge, 2017.

Bivens, Rena. "The Gender Binary Will Not Be Deprogrammed: Ten Years of Coding Gender on Facebook." *New Media & Society* 19, no. 6 (2017): 880–898. doi:10.1177/1461444815621527.

Bivens, Rena, and Oliver L. Haimson. "Baking Gender into Social Media Design: How Platforms Shape Categories for Users and Advertisers." *Social Media + Society* 2, no. 4 (2016). doi:10.1177/2056305116672486.

Block, Joern, and Philipp Sandner. "What Is the Effect of the Financial Crisis on Venture Capital Financing? Empirical Evidence from US Internet Start-Ups." *Venture Capital* 11, no. 4 (2009): 295–309. doi:10.1080/13691060903184803.

Blok, Anders, Moe Nakazora, and Brit Ross Winthereik. "Infrastructuring Environments." *Science as Culture* 25, no. 1 (2016): 1–22. doi:10.1080/09505431.2015.1081500.

Bogost, Ian, and Nick Montfort. "Platform Studies: Frequently Questioned Answers." Paper presented at the Digital Arts and Culture Conference, Irvine, California, December 12–15, 2009. http://pdf.textfiles.com/academics/bogost_montfort_dac_2009.pdf.

Bolin, Göran, and Jonas Andersson Schwarz. "Heuristics of the Algorithm: Big Data, User Interpretation and Institutional Translation." *Big Data & Society*, 2, no. 2 (2015). doi:10.1177/2053951715608406.

Born, Georgina, and Christopher Haworth. "Mixing It: Digital Ethnography and Online Research Methods—A Tale of Two Global Digital Music Genres." In *The Routledge Companion to Digital Ethnography*, edited by Larissa Hjorth, Heather Horst, Anne Galloway, and Genevieve Bell, 70–86. New York: Routledge, 2017.

boyd, danah, and Kate Crawford. "Critical Questions for Big Data." *Information, Communication & Society* 15, no. 5 (2012): 662–679. doi:10.1080/1369118X.2012.678878.

Bratton, Benjamin H. *The Stack: On Software and Sovereignty*. Cambridge, MA: MIT Press, 2015.

Brinkman, Bo. "Ethics and Pervasive Augmented Reality: Some Challenges and Approaches." In *Emerging Pervasive Information and Communication Technologies (PICT): Ethical Challenges, Opportunities and Safeguards*, edited by Kenneth D. Pimple, 149–175. London: Springer, 2014.

Broersma, Marcel, and Todd Graham. "Social Media as Beat: Tweets as a News Source during the 2010 British and Dutch Elections." *Journalism Practice* 6 (3) (2012): 403–419. doi:10.1080/17512786.2012.663626.

Bruns, Axel. "Faster than the Speed of Print: Reconciling 'Big Data' Social Media Analysis and Academic Scholarship." *First Monday* 18, no. 10 (2013). doi:10.5210/fm.v18i10.4879.

Brynjolfsson, Erik, Felix Eggers, and Avinash Gannamaneni. "Using Massive Online Choice Experiments to Measure Changes in Well-Being." NBER Working Paper No. 24514. National Bureau of Economic Research, April 2018. http://www.nber.org/papers/w24514

Bucher, Tania. "About a Bot: Hoax, Fake, Performance Art." *M/C Journal* 17, no. 3 (2014). http://journal.media-culture.org.au/index.php/mcjournal/article/view/814.

Burgess, Jean. "From 'Broadcast Yourself' to 'Follow Your Interests': Making Over Social Media." *International Journal of Cultural Studies* 18, no. 3 (2015): 281–285. doi:10.1177/1367877913513684.

Butz, David. Autoethnography as Sensibility. In *The SAGE Handbook of Qualitative Geography*, ed. Dydia DeLyser, Steve Herbert, Stuart Aitken, Mike Crang and Linda McDowell. 138–155. London: SAGE, 2010.

Caldwell, John Thornton. *Production Culture: Industrial Reflexivity and Critical Practice in Film and Television*. Durham, NC: Duke University Press, 2008.

Callon, Michel. "An Essay on Framing and Overflowing: Economic Externalities Revisited by Sociology." In "The Laws of Markets," edited by Michel Callon. Supplement, *Sociological Review* 46, no. S1 (1998): 244–269. doi:10.1111/j.1467-954X.1998.tb03477.x.

Callon, Michel, and Bruno Latour. Unscrewing the Big Leviathan: How Actors Macro-structure Reality and How Sociologists Help Them to Do So. In *Advances in Social Theory and Methodology: Toward an Integration of Micro- and Macro-sociologies*, ed. Karen Knorr-Cetina and Aaron V. Cicourel. 277–303. Boston: Routledge & Kegan Paul, 1981.

Calvey, David. *Covert Research: The Art, Politics and Ethics of Undercover Fieldwork*. London: SAGE, 2017.

Cerwonka, Allaine, and Liisa H. Malkki. *Improvising Theory: Process and Temporality in Ethnographic Fieldwork*. Chicago: University of Chicago Press, 2007.

Chen, Ching-Wei, and Vidhya Murali. "Machine Learning & Big Data for Music Discovery." PowerPoint presentation at Galvanize, New York, New York, March 9, 2017. https://www.slideshare.net/cweichen/machine-learning-and-big-data-for-music-discovery-at-spotify?qid=b7ca7727-0a01-4441-9107-14410ccf0e7d.

Chen, Le, Alan Mislove, and Christo Wilson. "Peeking beneath the Hood of Uber." In *Proceedings of the 2015 Internet Measurement Conference*, 495–508. New York: ACM, 2015. doi:10.1145/2815675.2815681.

Cheney-Lippold, John. *We Are Data: Algorithms and the Making of Our Digital Selves.* New York: New York University Press, 2017.

Cheng, Yu, Yusheng Xie, Zhengzhang Chen, Ankit Agrawal, Alok Choudhary, and Songtao Guo. "JobMiner: A Real-Time System for Mining Job-Related Patterns from Social Media." In *Proceedings of the 19th ACM SIGKDD International Conference on Knowledge Discovery and Data Mining,* edited by Rayid Ghani, Ted E. Senator, Paul Bradley, Rajesh Parekh, and Jingrui He, 1450–1453. New York: ACM, 2013.

Chun, Wendy Hui Kyong. *Control and Freedom: Power and Paranoia in the Age of Fiber Optics.* Cambridge, MA: MIT Press, 2006.

Chun, Wendy Hui Kyong. *Programmed Visions: Software and Memory.* Cambridge, MA: MIT Press, 2011.

Curran, James, Natalie Fenton, and Des Freedman. *Misunderstanding the Internet.* London: Routledge, 2012.

Curtin, Michael, Jennifer Holt, and Kevin Sanson, eds. *Distribution Revolution: Conversations about the Digital Future of Film and Television.* Oakland: University of California Press, 2014.

Curtin, Michael, and Kevin Sanson, eds. *Precarious Creativity: Global Media, Local Labor.* Berkeley: University of California Press, 2016.

Czarniawska, Barbara. *Cyberfactories: How News Agencies Produce News.* Cheltenham, UK: Edward Elgar, 2011.

Czarniawska, Barbara. "On Time, Space, and Action Nets." *Organization* 11, no. 6 (2004): 773–791. doi:10.1177/1350508404047251.

Czarniawska, Barbara. *Shadowing, and Other Techniques for Doing Fieldwork in Modern Societies.* Malmö, Sweden: Liber, 2007.

Datta, Amit, Michael Carl Tschantz, and Anupam Datta. "Automated Experiments on Ad Privacy Settings: A Tale of Opacity, Choice, and Discrimination." *Proceedings on Privacy Enhancing Technologies,* no. 1 (2015): 92–112. doi:10.1515/popets-2015-0007.

Davidsson, Pamela, and Olle Findahl. *Svenskarna och internet 2017: Undersökning om svenskarnas internetvanor* [Swedes and the Internet 2017: Report on Swedish Internet Habits], edited by Marianne Ahlgren, v. 1.1 (Stockholm: Internetstiftelsen i Sverige, 2017). https://www.iis.se/docs/Svenskarna_och_internet_2017.pdf.

Decherney, Peter. *Hollywood's Copyright Wars: From Edison to the Internet.* New York: Columbia University Press, 2013.

DeNicola, Lane. "EULA, Codec, API: On the Opacity of Digital Culture." In *Moving Data: The iPhone and the Future of Media,* edited by Pelle Snickars and Patrick Vonderau, 265–277. New York: Columbia University Press, 2012.

DeNora, Tia. *Music in Everyday Life*. Cambridge: Cambridge University Press, 2000.

Deuten, J. Jasper, and Arie Rip. "Narrative Infrastructure in Product Creation Processes." *Organization* 7 (1) (2000): 69–93. doi:10.1177/135050840071005.

Dewsbury, J. D. "Performative, Non-representational, and Affect-Based Research: Seven Injunctions." In *The SAGE Handbook of Qualitative Geography*, edited by Dydia DeLyser, Steve Herbert, Stuart Aitken, Mike Crang, and Linda McDowell, 321–334. London: Sage, 2010.

Dixon-Román, Ezekiel. "Algo-Ritmo: More-than-Human Performative Acts and the Racializing Assemblages of Algorithmic Architectures." *Cultural Studies ↔ Critical Methodologies* 16, no. 5 (2016): 482–490. doi:10.1177/1532708616655769.

Draper, Nora. "Fail Fast: The Value of Studying Unsuccessful Technology Companies." *Media Industries Journal* 4, no. 1 (2017). doi:10.3998/mij.15031809.0004.101.

Drew, Rob. "Mixed Blessings: The Commercial Mix and the Future of Music Aggregation." *Popular Music and Society* 28, no. 4 (2005): 533–551. doi:10.1080/03007760500159088.

Drott, Eric. "The End(s) of Genre." *Journal of Music Therapy* 57 (1) (2013): 1–45. doi:10.1215/00222909-2017097.

Drucker, Johanna. *Graphesis: Visual Forms of Knowledge Production*. Cambridge, MA: Harvard University Press, 2014.

Duffy, Brooke Erin. *(Not) Getting Paid to Do What You Love: Gender, Social Media, and Aspirational Work*. New Haven, CT: Yale University Press, 2017.

Edelman, Benjamin, Michael Luca, and Dan Svirsky. "Racial Discrimination in the Sharing Economy: Evidence from a Field Experiment." *American Economic Journal. Applied Economics* 9 (2) (2017): 1–22. doi:10.1257/app.20160213.

Ehn, Andreas, Magnus Hult, Fredrik Niemelä, Ludvig Strigeus, and Gunnar Kreitz. "Peer-to-Peer Streaming of Media Content." US Patent 8,316,146, filed July 13, 2007, and issued November 20, 2012. https://www.google.com/patents/US8316146.

Ehn, Andreas, Magnus Hult, Fredrik Niemelä, Ludvig Strigeus, and Gunnar Kreitz. "Peer-to-Peer-strömmning av medieinnehåll." [Peer-to-peer streaming of media content], Swedish Patent SE 0701717-1, filed July 13, 2007, and issued November 10, 2009. http://was.prv.se/spd/patent?p1=2X63xqIWgOR7eM42P9NdVA&p2=MWN 663OCkwI&hits=true&tab=1&content=SE+0701717-1.

Ehrenreich, Barbara. *Smile or Die: How Positive Thinking Fooled America and the World*. London: Granta, 2009.

Elberse, Anita. *Blockbusters: Why Big Hits—and Big Risks—Are the Future of the Entertainment Business*. London: Faber & Faber, 2014.

Eriksson, Maria. "Close Reading Big Data: The Echo Nest and the Production of (Rotten) Music Metadata." *First Monday* 21, no. 7 (2016). doi:10.5210/fm.v21i7.6303.

Eriksson, Maria, and Anna Johansson. "'Keep Smiling!': Time, Functionality and Intimacy in Spotify's Featured Playlists." *Cultural Analysis* 16, no. 1 (2017): 67–82.

Eriksson, Maria, and Anna Johansson. "Tracking Gendered Streams." *Culture Unbound* 9 (2) (2017): 163–183. doi:10.3384/cu.2000.1525.1792163.

Ernst, Wolfgang. *Digital Media and the Archive*. Edited and with an introduction by Jussi Parikka. Minneapolis: University of Minnesota Press, 2013.

Eslami, Motahhare, Kristen Vaccaro, Karrie Karahalios, and Kevin Hamilton. "'Be Careful; Things Can Be Worse than They Appear'—Understanding Biased Algorithms and Users' Behavior around Them in Rating Platforms." In *Proceedings of the Eleventh International Conference on Web and Social Media*, 62–71. Palo Alto, CA: AAAI Press, 2017. https://aaai.org/ocs/index.php/ICWSM/ICWSM17/paper/view/15697.

Ess, Charles. Foreword: Ground Internet Research Ethics 3.0: A View from (the) AoIR. In *Internet Research Ethics for the Social Age: New Challenges, Cases, and Contexts*, ed. Michael Zimmer and Katharina Kinder-Kurlanda. ix–xv. New York: Peter Lang, 2017.

Evans, David S., and Richard Schmalensee. "The Industrial Organization of Markets with Two-Sided Platforms." *Competition Policy International* 3 (1) (2007): 151–179.

Farchy, Joëlle. "The Internet: Culture for Free." In *A Handbook of Cultural Economics*, edited by Ruth Towse, 245–253. 2nd ed. Cheltenham, UK: Edward Elgar, 2011.

Fayard, Anne-Laure, and John Van Maanen. "Making Culture Visible: Reflections on Corporate Ethnography." *Journal of Organizational Ethnography* 4, no. 1 (2015): 4–27. doi:10.1108/JOE-12-2014-0040.

Fisman, Ray, and Tim Sullivan. *The Inner Lives of Markets: How People Shape Them—and They Shape Us*. London: John Murray, 2016.

Fleischer, Rasmus. *Boken & biblioteket* [The book & the library]. Stockholm: Ink bokförlag, 2011.

Fleischer, Rasmus. *Det postdigitala manifestet* [The postdigital manifesto]. Stockholm: Ink bokförlag, 2009.

Fleischer, Rasmus. "Från lagringskultur till streamingkultur: Om att skriva samtidens näthistoria" [From storage culture to streaming culture: Writing the story of contemporary times]. In *Återkopplingar* [Feedback], edited by Marie Cronqvist, Patrik Lundell, and Pelle Snickars, 219–234. Mediehistoriskt arkiv 28. Lund, Sweden: Lunds universitet, 2014.

Fleischer, Rasmus. "How Music Takes Place: Excerpts from 'The Post-digital Manifesto.'" *e-flux*, no. 42 (2013). http://www.e-flux.com/journal/42/60255/how-music-takes-place-excerpts-from-the-post-digital-manifesto/.

Fleischer, Rasmus. "If the Song Has No Price, Is It Still a Commodity? Rethinking the Commodification of Digital Music." *Culture Unbound* 9, no. 2 (2017): 146–162. doi:10.3384/cu.2000.1525.1792146.

Fleischer, Rasmus. "Protecting the Musicians and/or the Record Industry? On the History of 'Neighbouring Rights' and the Role of Fascist Italy." *Queen Mary Journal of Intellectual Property* 5, no. 3 (2015): 327–343. doi:10.4337/qmjip.2015.03.05.

Fleischer, Rasmus. "Swedish Music Export: The Making of a Miracle." In *Made in Sweden: Studies in Popular Music,* edited by Alf Björnberg and Thomas Bossius, 153–162. New York: Routledge, 2017.

Fleischer, Rasmus. "Towards a Postdigital Sensibility: How to Get Moved by Too Much Music." *Culture Unbound* 7, no. 2 (2015): 255–269. doi:10.3384/cu.2000.1525.1572255.

Fleischer, Rasmus. "Nätutopier och nätdystopier: Om 2000-talets sökande efter internets väsen." [Net utopia and dystopia: Searching for the soul of the internet during the early 2000s.] In *Samtider: Perspektiv på 2000-talets idéhistoria* [The Present: Perspectives on the History of Ideas during the Early 2000s], edited by Anders Burman and Lena Lennerhed, 261–303. Gothenburg, Sweden: Daidalos, 2017.

Fleischer, Rasmus, and Christopher Kullenberg. "The Political Significance of Spotify in Sweden—Analysing the #backaspotify Campaign Using Twitter Data." *Culture Unbound* 11 (1) (2018).

Fortun, Mike, Kim Fortun, and George E. Marcus. "Computers in/and Anthropology: The Poetics and Politics of Digitization." In *The Routledge Companion to Digital Ethnography,* edited by Larissa Hjorth, Heather Horst, Anne Galloway, and Genevieve Bell, 11–20. New York: Routledge, 2017.

Frabetti, Federica. "'Does It Work?': The Unforeseeable Consequences of Quasi-failing Technology." *Culture Machine* 11 (2010): 107–135. http://www.culturemachine.net/index.php/cm/article/view/388/409.

Fuchs, Christian. *Digital Labour and Karl Marx.* London: Routledge, 2014.

Galuszka, Patryk. "Music Aggregators and Intermediation of the Digital Music Market." *International Journal of Communication* 9 (2015): 254–273. http://hdl.handle.net/11089/7345

Garfinkel, Harold. *Studies in Ethnomethodology.* Englewood Cliffs, NJ: Prentice Hall, 1967.

Gawer, Annabelle. "Bridging Differing Perspectives on Technological Platforms: Toward an Integrative Framework." *Research Policy* 43, no. 7 (2014): 1239–1249. doi:10.1016/j.respol.2014.03.006.

Gehl, Robert W. *Reverse Engineering Social Media: Software, Culture, and Political Economy in New Media Capitalism.* Philadelphia: Temple University Press, 2014.

Gerlitz, Carolin, and Anne Helmond. "The Like Economy: Social Buttons and the Data-Intensive Web." *New Media & Society* 15, no. 8 (2013): 1348–1365. doi: 10.1177/1461444812472322.

Gill, Rosalind. "Post-postfeminism? New Feminist Visibilities in Postfeminist Times." *Feminist Media Studies* 16 (4) (2016): 610–630. doi:10.1080/14680777.2016.1193293.

Gill, Rosalind. "Unspeakable Inequalities: Post Feminism, Entrepreneurial Subjectivity, and the Repudiation of Sexism among Cultural Workers." *Social Politics* 21, no. 4 (2014): 509–528. doi:10.1093/sp/jxu016.

Gillespie, Tarleton. "Platforms Intervene." *Social Media + Society* 1, no. 1 (2015). doi:10.1177/2056305115580479.

Gillespie, Tarleton. "The Politics of 'Platforms.'" *New Media & Society* 12, no. 3 (2010): 347–364. doi:10.1177/1461444809342738.

Gillespie, Tarleton. "The Relevance of Algorithms." In *Media Technologies: Essays on Communication, Materiality, and Society*, edited by Tarleton Gillespie, Pablo J. Boczkowski, and Kirsten A. Foot, 167–194. Cambridge, MA: MIT Press, 2014.

Glynos, Jason. "Ideological Fantasy at Work." *Journal of Political Ideologies* 13, no. 3 (2008): 275–296. doi:10.1080/13569310802376961.

Graham, Stephen, and Simon Marvin. *Splintering Urbanism: Networked Infrastructures, Technological Mobilities and the Urban Condition*. London: Routledge, 2001.

Greenberg, David M., Michal Kosinski, David J. Stillwell, Brian L. Monteiro, Daniel J. Levitin, and Peter J. Rentfrow. "The Song Is You: Preferences for Musical Attribute Dimensions Reflect Personality." *Social Psychology and Personality Science* 7, no. 6 (2016): 597–605. doi:10.1177/1948550616641473.

Gregg, Melissa. "Inside the Data Spectacle." *Television & New Media* 16, no. 1 (2015): 37–51. doi:10.1177/1527476414547774.

Gusterson, Hugh. "Studying Up Revisited." *PoLAR: Political and Anthropological Review* 20 (1) (1997): 114–119. doi:10.1525/pol.1997.20.1.114.

Haiven, Max. *Cultures of Financialization: Fictitious Capital in Popular Culture and Everyday Life*. New York: Palgrave Macmillan, 2014.

Hardie, Iain, and Donald MacKenzie. "The Material Sociology of Arbitrage." In *The Oxford Handbook of the Sociology of Finance*, edited by Karen Knorr Cetina and Alex Preda, 187–202. Oxford: Oxford University Press, 2012.

Helmond, Anne. "The Platformization of the Web: Making Web Data Platform Ready." *Social Media + Society* 1, no. 2 (2015). doi:10.1177/2056305115603080.

Holt, Jennifer. "Regulating Connected Viewing: Media Pipelines and Cloud Policy." In *Connected Viewing: Selling, Streaming & Sharing Media in the Digital Era*, edited by Jennifer Holt and Kevin Sanson, 19–39. London: Routledge, 2014.

Holt, J., and A. Perren, eds. *Media Industries: History, Theory, and Method*. Malden, MA: Blackwell, 2009.

Hsu, Wendy F. "Digital Ethnography toward Augmented Empiricism: A New Methodological Framework." *Journal of Digital Humanities* 3, no. 1 (2014). http://journalof digitalhumanities.org/3-1/digital-ethnography-toward-augmented-empiricism-by -wendy-hsu/.

Jensen, Klaus Bruhn. New Media, Old Methods—Internet Methodologies and the Online/Offline Divide. In *The Handbook of Internet Studies*, ed. Mia Consalvo and Charles Ess. 43–68. Chichester, UK: Wiley-Blackwell, 2011.

Johansson, Anna, and Anna Sofia Lundgren. Fantasies of Scientificity: Ethnographic Identity and the Use of QDA Software. In *Research Methods for Reading Digital Data in the Digital Humanities*, ed. Gabriele Griffin and Matt Hayler. 148–164. Edinburgh: Edinburgh University Press, 2016.

Johansson, Daniel. "From Products to Consumption—Changes on the Swedish Music Market as a Result of Streaming Technologies." Working paper, Linnaeus University, 2013. http://docplayer.net/343175-From-products-to-consumption-changes -on-the-swedish-music-market-as-a-result-of-streaming-technologies.html.

Kassabian, Anahid. *Ubiquitous Listening: Affect, Attention, and Distributed Subjectivity*. Los Angeles: University of California Press, 2013.

Kelen, András. *The Gratis Economy: Privately Provided Public Goods*. Budapest: Central European University Press, 2001.

Kelty, Christopher M. "Against Networks." *Spheres: Journal for Digital Cultures*, no. 1 (2014). http://spheres-journal.org/against-networks/. Excerpted from an unpublished manuscript written in 2005 and revised in 2007, which is available at https://kelty .org/or/papers/unpublishable/Kelty.AgainstNetworks.2007.pdf.

Kirsch, Stuart. *Mining Capitalism: The Relationship between Corporations and Their Critics*. Oakland: University of California Press, 2014.

Kirschenbaum, Matthew G. *Mechanisms: New Media and the Forensic Imagination*. Cambridge, MA: MIT Press, 2008.

Kitchin, Rob. "Big Data, New Epistemologies and Paradigm Shifts." *Big Data & Society* 1, no. 1 (2014). doi:10.1177/2053951714528481.

Kitchin, Rob. "Thinking Critically about and Researching Algorithms." *Information, Communication & Society* 20, no. 1 (2017): 14–29. doi:10.1080/1369118X.2016.1154087.

Kreitz, Gunnar. "Spotify—Behind the Scenes: A Eulogy to P2P (?)." PowerPoint presentation at the KTH Royal Institute of Technology, Stockholm, Sweden, May 7, 2014. https://www.kth.se/social/upload/536a05d8f2765472d425ac0a/kreitzspotify _kth_kista14.pdf.

Kunda, Gideon. *Engineering Culture: Control and Commitment in a High-Tech Corporation*. Rev. ed. Philadelphia: Temple University Press, 2006.

Langlois, Ganaele, and Greg Elmer. "The Research Politics of Social Media Platforms." *Culture Machine* 14 (2013). https://www.culturemachine.net/index.php/cm/article/view/505/531.

Larkin, Brian. "The Politics and Poetics of Infrastructure." *Annual Review of Anthropology* 42 (2013): 327–343. doi:10.1146/annurev-anthro-092412-155522.

Latour, Bruno. *Reassembling the Social: An Introduction to Actor-Network-Theory*. Oxford: Oxford University Press, 2005.

Latour, Bruno, Pablo Jensen, Tommaso Venturini, Sébastian Grauwin, and Dominique Boullier. "'The Whole Is Always Smaller than Its Parts'—A Digital Test of Gabriel Tardes' Monads." *British Journal of Sociology* 63 (4) (2012): 590–615. doi:10.1111/j.1468-4446.2012.01428.x.

Lindquist, Johan. "Brokers and Brokerage, Anthropology of." In *International Encyclopedia of the Social & Behavioral Sciences*, edited by James D. Wright, 2:870–874. 2nd ed. Amsterdam: Elsevier, 2017.

Lobato, Ramon, and Julian Thomas. *The Informal Media Economy*. Cambridge: Polity Press, 2015.

Locke, John L. *Eavesdropping: An Intimate History*. Oxford: Oxford University Press, 2010.

Lorenz, Chris, and Berber Bevernage, eds. *Breaking Up Time: Negotiating the Borders between Present, Past and Future*. Göttingen, Germany: Vandenhoeck & Ruprecht, 2013.

Lotz, Amanda D., and Timothy Havens. *Understanding Media Industries*. 2nd ed. Oxford: Oxford University Press, 2016.

Lovink, Geert. "Reflections on the MP3 Format: Interview with Jonathan Sterne." *Computational Culture*, no. 4 (2014). http://computationalculture.net/article/reflections-on-the-mp3-format.

Lury, Celia, and Nina Wakeford. Introduction: A Perpetual Inventory. In *Inventive Methods: The Happening of the Social*, ed. Celia Lury and Nina Wakeford. 1–24. London: Routledge, 2012.

Lury, Celia, and Nina Wakeford, eds. *Inventive Methods: The Happening of the Social*. London: Routledge, 2012.

Ma, Wenjuan, and Steven S. Wildman. "Online Advertising Economics." In *Handbook on the Economics of the Internet*, edited by Johannes M. Bauer and Michael Latzer, 426–442. Cheltenham, UK: Edward Elgar, 2016.

Machin, David. "Building the World's Visual Language: The Increasing Global Importance of Image Banks in Corporate Media." *Visual Communication* 3, no. 3 (2004): 316–336. doi:10.1177/1470357204045785.

Mackenzie, Adrian, Richard Mills, Stuart Sharples, Matthew Fuller, and Andrew Goffey. Digital Sociology in the Field of Devices. In *Routledge International Handbook of the Sociology of Art and Culture*, ed. Laurie Hanquinet and Mike Savage. 367–382. London: Routledge, 2016.

Mackenzie, Adrian, and Theo Vurdubakis. "Codes and Codings in Crisis: Signification, Performativity and Excess." *Theory, Culture & Society* 28, no. 6 (2011): 3–23. doi:10.1177/0263276411424761.

MacKenzie, Donald, Fabian Muniesa, and Lucia Siu, eds. *Do Economists Make Markets? On the Performativity of Economics*. Princeton, NJ: Princeton University Press, 2007.

Mähler, Roger, and Patrick Vonderau. "Do Bots Have Human Friends? Experimental Methods for Studying Ad Tech Infrastructures." *Culture Unbound* 9 (2) (2017): 212–221. http://www.cultureunbound.ep.liu.se/v9/a14/cu17v9a14.pdf.

Malinowski, Bronisław. *Argonauts of the Western Pacific: An Account of Native Enterprise and Adventure in the Archipelagos of Melanesian New Guinea*. London: Routledge & Kegan Paul, 1922.

Manovich, Lev. "Designing and Living Instagram Photography: Themes, Feeds, Sequences, Branding, Faces, Bodies." In *Instagram and Contemporary Image*. Self-published, 2016. http://manovich.net/content/04-projects/097-designing-and-living-instagram-photography/instagram_book_part_4.pdf.

Marres, Noortje. *Digital Sociology: The Reinvention of Social Research*. Cambridge: Polity Press, 2017.

Marshall, Lee. "'Let's Keep Music Special. F—k Spotify': On-Demand Streaming and the Controversy over Artist Royalties." *Creative Industries Journal* 8, no. 2 (2015): 177–189. doi:10.1080/17510694.2015.1096618.

McGuigan, L., and V. Manzerolle, eds. *The Audience Commodity in a Digital Age: Revisiting a Critical Theory of Commercial Media*. New York: Peter Lang, 2014.

Michael, Mike. "Anecdote." In *Inventive Methods: The Happening of the Social*, edited by Celia Lury and Nina Wakeford, 25–35. London: Routledge, 2012.

Mishra, Kinshuk. "Architectural Overhaul: Ad Serving @ Spotify Scale." PowerPoint presentation at the QCon, London, UK, March 7, 2017. https://www.slideshare.net/kinshukm1/qcon-london-2017-architecture-overhaul-ad-serving-spotify-scale.

Montfort, Nick. "Continuous Paper: The Early Materiality and Workings of Electronic Literature." Paper presented at the Modern Language Association Convention,

Philadelphia, PA, December 27–30, 2004. http://nickm.com/writing/essays/continu ous_paper_mla.html.

Morris, Jeremy Wade. "Curation by Code: Infomediaries and the Data Mining of Taste." *European Journal of Cultural Studies* 18 (4–5) (2015): 446–463. doi:10.1177 /1367549415577387.

Morris, Jeremy Wade. *Selling Digital Music, Formatting Culture*. Berkeley: University of California Press, 2015.

Morris, Jeremy Wade, and Devon Powers. "Control, Curation and Musical Experience in Streaming Music Services." *Creative Industries Journal* 8, no. 2 (2015): 106–122. doi:10.1080/17510694.2015.1090222.

Nader, Laura. "Up the Anthropologist—Perspectives Gained from Studying Up." In *Reinventing Anthropology*, edited by Dell Hymes, 284–311. New York: Vintage Books, 1974.

Nahon, Karine. "Toward a View of Platforms as Ecosystems." Paper presented at "Digital Imaginaries," the 16th Association of Internet Researchers Conference, Phoenix, AZ, October 21–24, 2015.

Nakamura, Lisa. *Cybertypes: Race, Ethnicity, and Identity on the Internet*. New York: Routledge, 2002.

Napoli, Philip, and Robyn Caplan. "Why Media Companies Insist They're Not Media Companies, Why They're Wrong, and Why It Matters." *First Monday* 22, no. 5 (2017). doi:10.5210/fm.v22i15.7051.

Picot, Arnold, and Dominik K. Heger. "Does the Internet Need a New Competition Policy? A Global Problem from a German Point of View." In *E-Merging Media: Communication and the Media Economy of the Future*, edited by Axel Zerdick, Arnold Picot, Klaus Schrape, Jean-Claude Burgelman, Roger Silverstone, Valerie Feldmann, Christian Wernick, and Carolin Wolff, 339–356. Berlin: Springer, 2005.

Plantin, Jean-Christophe, Carl Lagoze, Paul N. Edwards, and Christian Sandvig. "Infrastructure Studies Meet Platform Studies in the Age of Google and Facebook." *New Media & Society* 20, no. 1 (2018): 293–310. doi:10.1177/1461444816661553.

Poovey, Mary. "On 'The Limits to Financialization.'" *Dialogues in Human Geography* 5, no. 2 (2015): 220–224. doi:10.1177/2043820615588159.

Rieder, Bernhard, and Guillaume Sire. "Conflicts of Interest and Incentives to Bias: A Microeconomic Critique of Google's Tangled Position on the Web." *New Media & Society* 16, no. 2 (2014): 195–211. doi:10.1177/1461444813481195.

Rochet, Jean-Charles, and Jean Tirole. "Platform Competition in Two-Sided Markets." *Journal of the European Economic Association* 1, no. 4 (2003): 990–1029. doi:10.1162/ 154247603322493212.

Rogers, Richard. *Digital Methods*. Cambridge, MA: MIT Press, 2013.

Rossiter, Ned. *Software, Infrastructure, Labor: A Media Theory of Logistical Nightmares*. London: Routledge, 2016.

Roussel, Violaine. *Representing Talent: Hollywood Agents and the Making of Movies*. Chicago: University of Chicago Press, 2017.

Ruef, Annette, and Jochen Markard. "What Happens after a Hype? How Changing Expectations Affected Innovation Activities in the Case of Stationary Fuel Cells." *Technology Analysis and Strategic Management* 22 (3) (2010): 317–338. doi:10. 1080/09537321003647354.

Ruppert, Evelyn, John Law, and Mike Savage. "Reassembling Social Science Methods: The Challenge of Digital Devices." *Theory, Culture & Society* 30, no. 4 (2013): 22–46. doi:10.1177/0263276413484941.

Salganik, Matthew J. *Bit by Bit: Social Research in the Digital Age*. Princeton, NJ: Princeton University Press, 2018.

Sandvig, Christian, and Eszter Hargittai. How to Think about Digital Research. In *Digital Research Confidential: The Secrets of Studying Behavior Online*, ed. Eszter Hargittai and Christian Sandvig. 1–28. Cambridge, MA: MIT Press, 2015.

Sandvig, Christian, Kevin Hamilton, Karrie Karahalios, and Cedric Langbort. "When the Algorithm Itself Is a Racist: Diagnosing Ethical Harm in the Basic Components of Software." *International Journal of Communication* 10 (2016): 4972–4990. http:// ijoc.org/index.php/ijoc/article/view/6182.

Santos, Ricardo Vice. "Spotify: P2P Music Streaming." PowerPoint presentation at ISEL Tech 2011, Lisbon, Portugal, May 26, 2011. https://www.slideshare.net/ricardo vice/spotify-p2p-music-streaming.

Sarrafi, Ali. "How 'Data' Drives Spotify." PowerPoint presentation at the Stockholm School of Entrepreneurship, Stockholm, Sweden, August 10, 2016. https://www .slideshare.net/alisarrafi3/how-data-drives-spotify.

Schäfer, Mirko Tobias, and Karin van Es, eds. *The Datafied Society: Studying Culture through Data*. Amsterdam: Amsterdam University Press, 2017.

Scharff, Christina. "The Psychic Life of Neoliberalism: Mapping the Contours of Entrepreneurial Subjectivity." *Theory, Culture & Society* 33, no. 6 (2016): 107–122. doi:10.1177/0263276415590164.

Seaver, Nick. "Algorithmic Recommendations and Synaptic Functions." *Limn*, no. 2 (2012), https://limn.it/articles/algorithmic-recommendations-and-synaptic-functions/.

Seaver, Nick. "Computers and Sociocultural Anthropology." *Savage Minds: Notes and Queries in Anthropology* (blog), May 19, 2014. https://savageminds.org/2014/05/19 /computers-and-sociocultural-anthropology/.

Seaver, Nick. "Studying Up: The Ethnography of Technologists." *Ethnography Matters*, March 10, 2014. https://ethnographymatters.net/blog/2014/03/10/studying-up/.

Setty, Vinay, Gunnar Kreitz, Roman Vitenberg, Maarten van Steen, Guido Urdaneta, and Staffan Gimåker. "The Hidden Pub/Sub of Spotify." In *Proceedings of the 7th ACM International Conference on Distributed Event-Based Systems (DEBS '13)*, 231–240. New York: ACM, 2013. doi:10.1145/2488222.2488273.

Skågeby, Jörgen. "Slow and Fast Music Media: Comparing Values of Cassettes and Playlists." *Transformations*, no. 20 (2011). http://www.transformationsjournal.org/wp-content/uploads/2016/12/Skageby_Trans20.pdf.

Skeggs, Beverley, and Simon Yuill. "Capital Experimentation with Person/a Formation: How Facebook's Monetization Refigures the Relationship between Property, Personhood and Protest." *Information, Communication & Society* 19, no. 3 (2016): 380–396. doi:10.1080/1369118X.2015.1111403.

Smith, Michael D., and Rahul Telang. *Streaming, Sharing, Stealing: Big Data and the Future of Entertainment*. Cambridge, MA: MIT Press, 2016.

Snickars, Pelle. "More Music Is Better Music." In *Business Innovation and Disruption in the Music Industry*, edited by Patrik Wikström and Robert DeFillippi, 191–210. Cheltenham, UK: Edward Elgar, 2016.

Snickars, Pelle. "More of the Same—On Spotify Radio." *Culture Unbound* 9, no. 2 (2017): 184–211. doi:10.3384/cu.2000.1525.1792184.

Snickars, Pelle, and Roger Mähler. "SpotiBot—Turing Testing Spotify." *Digital Humanities Quarterly* 12, no. 2 (2018).

Srnicek, Nick. *Platform Capitalism*. Cambridge: Polity Press, 2017.

Starosielski, Nicole. "Fixed Flow: Undersea Cables as Media Infrastructures." In *Signal Traffic: Critical Studies of Media Infrastructures*, edited by Lisa Parks and Nicole Starosielski, 53–70. Springfield: University of Illinois Press, 2015.

Sterne, Jonathan. *MP3: The Meaning of a Format*. Durham, NC: Duke University Press, 2012.

Striphas, Ted. "Algorithmic Culture." *European Journal of Cultural Studies* 18, nos. 4–5 (2015): 395–412. doi:10.1177/1367549415577392.

Terranova, Tiziana. *Network Culture: Politics for the Information Age*. Ann Arbor, MI: Pluto Press, 2004.

Terranova, Tiziana. "New Economy, Financialization and Social Production in the Web 2.0." In *Crisis in the Global Economy: Financial Markets, Social Struggles, and New Political Scenarios*, edited by Andrea Fumagalli and Sandro Mezzadra, 153–170. Los Angeles: Semiotext(e), 2010.

Towse, Ruth. "Economics of Music Publishing: Copyright and the Market." *Journal of Cultural Economics* 41, no. 4 (2016): 403–420. doi:10.1007/s10824-016-9268-7.

Towse, Ruth, and Christian Handke, eds. *Handbook on the Digital Creative Economy.* Cheltenham, UK: Edward Elgar, 2013.

Tseng, Emy, and Kyle Eischen. "The Geography of Cyberspace." *M/C Journal* 6, no. 4 (2003). http://www.journal.media-culture.org.au/0308/03-geography.php.

Tsing, Anna Lowenhaupt. *Friction: An Ethnography of Global Connection.* Princeton, NJ: Princeton University Press, 2005.

Turing, Alan M. "Computing Machinery and Intelligence." *Mind* 59, no. 236 (1950): 433–460. doi:10.1093/mind/LIX.236.433.

Turner, Fred. *From Counterculture to Cyberculture: Stewart Brand, the Whole Earth Network, and the Rise of Digital Utopianism.* Chicago: University of Chicago Press, 2010.

Turow, Joseph. *The Daily You: How the New Advertising Industry Is Defining Your Identity and Your Worth.* New Haven, CT: Yale University Press, 2011.

Uricchio, William. Historicizing Media in Transition. In *Rethinking Media Change: The Aesthetics of Transition*, ed. David Thorburn and Henry Jenkins. 23–38. Cambridge, MA: MIT Press, 2004.

Van Dijck, José. *The Culture of Connectivity: A Critical History of Social Media.* New York: Oxford University Press, 2013.

Van Schie, Gerwin, Irene Westra, and Mirko Tobias Schäfer. Get Your Hands Dirty: Emerging Data Practices as Challenge for Research Integrity. In *The Datafied Society: Studying Culture through Data*, ed. Mirko Tobias Schäfer and Karin van Es. 183–200. Amsterdam: Amsterdam University Press, 2017.

Vonderau, Patrick. "'Where Ideas Are Free': Scientific Knowledge in the Algorithm Economy." *Media Fields Journal*, no. 10 (2015). http://mediafieldsjournal.squarespace.com/where-ideas-are-free/.

Vonderau, Patrick. "The Politics of Content Aggregation." *Television & New Media* 16, no. 8 (2015): 717–733. doi:10.1177/1527476414554402.

Vonderau, Patrick. "The Video Bubble: Multichannel Networks and the Transformation of YouTube." *Convergence* 22, no. 4 (2016): 361–375. doi:10.1177/1354856516641882.

Vonderau, Patrick. "The Spotify Effect: Digital Distribution and Financial Growth." *Television & New Media.* Published ahead of print, November 21, 2017. doi:10.1177/1527476417741200.

Vonderau, Patrick. "Technology and Language, or, How to Apply Media Industries Research?" In *Applied Media Studies*, edited by Kirsten Ostherr. New York: Routledge, 2018 (in press).

Vonderau, Patrick. "Access and Mistrust in Media Industries Research." In *Making Media: Production, Practices and Professions*, edited by Mark Deuze and Mirjam Prenger. Amsterdam: Amsterdam University Press, 2018 (in press).

Waelbroeck, Patrick. "Digital Music." In *Handbook on the Digital Creative Economy*, edited by Ruth Towse and Christian Handke, 389–399. Cheltenham, UK: Edward Elgar, 2013.

Weltevrede, Esther, Anne Helmond, and Carolin Gerlitz. "The Politics of Real-Time: A Device Perspective on Social Media Platforms and Search Engines." *Theory, Culture & Society* 31, no. 6 (2014): 125–150. doi:10.1177/0263276414537318.

Werner, Ann. "Moving Forward: A Feminist Analysis of Mobile Music Streaming." *Culture Unbound* 7, no. 2 (2015): 197–212. doi:10.3384/cu.2000.1525.1572197.

White, Harrison C. *Markets from Networks: Socioeconomic Models of Production*. Princeton, NJ: Princeton University Press, 2002.

Wikström, Patrik. *The Music Industry: Music in the Cloud*. Cambridge: Polity Press, 2009.

Wikström, Patrik, and Robert Burnett. "Same Songs, Different Wrapping: The Rise of the Compilation Album." *Popular Music and Society* 32, no. 4 (2009): 507–522. doi:10.1080/03007760802327599.

Wikström, Patrik, and Robert DeFillippi, eds. *Business Innovation and Disruption in the Music Industry*. Cheltenham, UK: Edward Elgar, 2016.

Wolff, Michael. *Television Is the New Television: The Unexpected Triumph of Old Media in the Digital Age*. New York: Portfolio/Penguin, 2015.

Wyatt, Sally. "Danger! Metaphors at Work in Economics, Geophysiology, and the Internet." *Science, Technology & Human Values* 29 (2) (2004): 242–261. doi:10.1177/0162243903261947.

Yanggratoke, Rerngvit, Gunnar Kreitz, Mikael Goldmann, Rolf Stadler, and Viktoria Fodor. "On the Performance of the Spotify Backend." *Journal of Network and Systems Management* 23, no. 1 (2015): 210–237. doi:10.1007/s10922-013-9292-2.

Zimmer, M., and K. Kinder-Kurlanda, eds. *Internet Research Ethics for the Social Age: New Challenges, Cases, and Contexts*. New York: Peter Lang, 2017.

Zittrain, Jonathan. *The Future of the Internet and How to Stop It*. New Haven, CT: Yale University Press, 2008.

Zittrain, Jonathan L. "The Generative Internet." *Harvard Law Review* 119, no. 7 (2006): 1974–2040. doi:10.1145/1435417.1435426.

Index